KEIZER KAREL

DE KONINCK

AFFLIGEM TRIPLE

PATER LIEVEN BLOND

WITTEKERKE

PASSENDALE

GEUZE BOON

WESTMALLE TRIPEL

DUVEL

LA GAULOISE

TONGERLO DUBBEL

D1289456

Michael Jackson's
Great Beers
of.
Belgium
Monthly Gourmet Selections

Cheers!

-Michael Jackson

ABOUT THE AUTHOR

Michael Jackson is the world's leading consumer-writer on beer, and is known by readers in many countries for his love of Belgian brews. He received the Mercurius Award from Crown Prince Philippe of Belgium in 1994. The award was made with particular reference to the television series The Beer Hunter and The Great Beers of Belgium, of which this is the fourth, extensively revised and updated, edition. In 2001, A GREAT BEERS OF BELGIUM club was established on the internet. This is a beer-of-the-month club, making available, initially in the United States, brews that have not previously been exported.

Jackson is an Officer of Honor in the Chevalerie de Fourquet. In 1997, he was made a member of the Belgian Confederation of Brewers. This was the first time the honor had been extended to someone who was not a brewer.

Colour, head formation, aroma, flavour...the author at his daily work.

For his writing on beer, Jackson has been honoured in Italy, France, Germany, Finland, Great Britain and the United States. He has won The André Simon Award; the Glenfiddich Trophy; Glenfiddich

Awards for books, journalism and television; the Gold Tankard of the British Guild of Beer Writers; awards for CD-roms, "Columnist of the Year" and historical writing, from the North American Guild of Beer Writers; and is a James Beard nominee. In the United States, he was the first recipient of the Achievement Award of the Institute of Fermentation Studies.

Jackson is a Consultant Editor to Beer Passion magazine, and has contributed to Journal du Brasseur , Bière, Pint , What's Brewing, All About Beer, and magazines on drinks and food in many countries. He has written for Playboy, GQ and The Washington Post, and in Britain is a regular contributor to The Independent and The Observer. A library of his writings can be found at www.beerhunter.com

He has conducted tastings at the Belgian Embassy in Tokyo and the Belgian Consulate in New York, and lectured at Cornell University, the Museum of Archaeology and Anthropology (University of Pennsylvania), the Culinary Institute of America, the Smithsonian Institution, the National Geographic Society and the Cambridge Union. He is Patron of the Oxford University Beer Appreciation Society .

Michael Jackson's
GREAT BEERS OF BELGIUM

Fourth fully revised and expanded edition.
Original title: Michael Jackson's Great beers of Belgium
Photography: Joris Luyten, Marc Joye, Ben Vinken, Michael Jackson
Linguistic supervision: Belga Translations, Brussels
Layout: Arcobel E-Media, Antwerp (www.e-media.arcobel.com)
Printed by: Stige S.p.a, Torino
June 2001, all rights reserved

First published in Belgium MMC
ISBN 90-5373-011-7

Published by: Media Marketing Communications SA (MMC)
St. Lucaslaan 34 / 2180 Antwerpen
tel 03/645 72 47 / fax 03/645 72 53
info@beerpassion.com
www.beerpassion.com

Cover photograph: Glasses by Ritzenhoff

Michael Jackson's
Great Beers of Belgium

PREFACE

In London and New York, San Francisco and Tokyo, the „Style" pages of newspapers and magazines have a new obsession: Belgian fashion designers...Belgian restaurants...Belgian chocolate...Belgian beer. I am pleased to say that it started with beer (and would even like to think I had a hand in rolling the barrel). Now the very designation "Belgian" has gained a momentum of its own.
Do most Belgians realise this? Perhaps not. They are too busy cooking, eating, or having a beer. It did not bother them unduly when the rest of the world scarcely had time to say hello.

Remember that movie?: "If it's Tuesday, it must be Belgium". Now, it must be Belgium whatever day it is. It is not so much that Belgium has changed; more that it has belatedly been noticed.
When those fashion designers were at art school, they knew they were in the country of Magritte, Rubens and Bruegel. The love of good food and drink? Belgians say they are "Burgundian" as though that were yesterday.

People are seldom nationalistically Belgian, perhaps because it is two nations, plus other odd bits. As a state of mind though, Belgium may be more durable than it thinks.   A Belgian brewing company is second biggest in the world - at least until someone else makes larger acquisitions. Hoegaarden and Leffe are becoming international names. Chimay already is. A restaurant in Philadelphia presents a dinner that begins with beer from Achel, and features every Trappist brewery. Even more remarkably, it presents another dinner with more than a dozen draught Lambics, mainly from Cantillon.

The best news in this fourth edition is of a wholly new Lambic brewery, at Drie Fonteinen, in Beersel. Another among several breweries new to this edition is Paeleman, in Wetteren. I asked André Paeleman why he had been so determined to brew. "Because I am a Belgian" he responded, unprompted. Once again, there are born-again breweries in this new edition. Why did Marc Beirens re-start Duysters, in Diest? "It,s in my genes" was his way of looking at it. My contention that Belgian brewers are the most idiosyncratic was seized by Antoine Bosteels: "I want to be the definitively idiosyncratic Belgian brewer," he announced over lunch.
A lot of lunching happens in this book, and a lot of beer is consumed. The book looks smarter than ever, and contains much new material. It is a guide in its own idiosyncratic way. I hope it helps people to understand beer. Or Belgians. Or both...

Michael Jackson

Michael Jackson, London 2001

TABLE OF CONTENTS

Beer Passion

The regard reserved for fine wine in most countries is in Belgium accorded also to great beer. Its serving is sometimes a seduction. A chemise of tissue paper may be gently removed to reveal the bottle, perhaps bearing the promise Grand Cru or Grande Réserve. Or a basket cradling the bottle may be brought to the table. It may be a Champagne bottle, but it contains beer. Its wired cork undone, a foaming brew emerges into a flûte, Burgundy sampler, goblet or snifter. A glass of beer should look appetising, and the Belgians know it. They do not rush about their drink, any more than they do about their food. Both are worth savouring. People who genuinely appreciate fine wines, as opposed simply to embracing the snobbism, can hardly be blind to the complex aromas and flavors of great beer. No country is wholly innocent of snobbism, but true appreciation of fine wines is widespread in Belgium; so is the understanding of beer as a part of its gastronomic culture.

WHAT IS SPECIAL ABOUT BELGIAN BEER?

No country has given birth to so many different styles of beer (though several have far more breweries). Belgium has about 120 breweries, making around 500 beers in ten or a dozen major styles and at least 50 or 60 sub-categories). No country has beers that are quite so complex in character as the finest in Belgium.

No country has so many individualistic, idiosyncratic, beers. Some are so unlike conventional beers as to shock the unwary consumer. The most winey-tasting beers are made in Belgium, but so are brews with sour, sweet, fruity, spicy, chocolatey, nutty, and flowery aromas and flavors. In turning barley into malt, no country coaxes so many aromas and flavors from the grain. The use of pale and dark candy sugars is an art specific to Belgian brewing. Nowhere has the tradition of using herbs, spices and fruits, in addition to hops, survived so well. Nowhere are brewers so adventurous in their training of yeasts, or in the use of wooden vessels for fermentation or maturation.

In no other country are the native beers so food-friendly. This is especially true of the more acidic styles. Nor does any country have such a sophisticated beer cuisine (extending far beyond mussels, beef stews, and other dishes that are commonly associated with beer).

In what way are Belgian beers individualistic or idiosyncratic? The winey-tasting, spontaneously-fermenting, Lambic beers of the Zenne (in French, Senne) Valley and Payottenland to the West of the city of Brussels represent a tradition unique to Belgium. Lambic is the oldest style of beer to be brewed in the Western world.

The tart, acidic, "sour" beers of Flanders, often gaining their character from huge wooden tuns, are also a tradition unique to Belgium. In the production of top-fermenting brews and wheat beers, Belgium is one of the world leaders.

No country has as many beers, in which a second or even third fermentation is induced in the bottle either by a dosage of yeast or a blending of young and mature brews. (It is these yeasty brews that are stored horizontally, and sometimes brought from the cellar in basket, so that the sediment is not disturbed.

Austria, Germany and Belgium are the only countries to have kept alive the practice of monastic brewing. Only Belgium has breweries owned by Trappists. (In The Netherlands, a Trappist abbey accommodates a brewery, but no longer owns it). Beyond all of these specialities, some beers have so many distinctive features as simply to defy categorisation.

Food-friendly: Palm Ale cosies up to wild pheasant with Belgian endive.
The dish was prepared with "Double Palm", at the brewery's Diepensteyn Castle.

WHY IN BELGIUM?

Just as wine is made in warm countries that grow fruits (especially grapes), so beer is produced in the cooler nations that grow grains (notably barley). Beer was made by the earliest civilisations, and spread west from Mesopotamia. The ancient Greeks and Romans made wine, which spread to France and Iberia. To the immediate north, possibly Celtic tribes brewed beer in what is now the Czech Republic, Germany, Belgium, Britain and Ireland. Note which country is in the middle of this beer-belt.

King of Beer: King Albert of the Belgians visits Interbrew. Left: Chief Executive Hugo Powell, right Chairman Paul Baron De Keersmaeker.

By the time the Romans came west, beer was already being brewed by the hard, stubborn, tribes they called the Belgae. There are in Belgium brewery ruins from the 3rd and 4th centuries AD. The Belgae were the forbears of the Wallonians, or Walloons (the word is related to "Welsh"), and possibly also to the Flemings.

These two peoples (the Walloons speaking French, while the Flemings prefer a version of Dutch) are largely contained between the forested, rolling hills of the Ardennes and the flatlands around

the delta of the river Schelde, with a central position in the European seaboard. The forests gave rise to charcoal, and the development of craft-based industries, often beginning in hermitages or monasteries. The sea made Flanders a powerful trading nation in the 15th century. The monasteries, the craft tradition, and the early growth of prosperous towns (Ypres and Bruges are especially fine examples) fostered a brewing industry with a cuisine bourgeoise to match. The historic influences survive today, as Ruth Van Waerebeek observes in her book Everybody Eats Well in Belgium.

The Walloons and the Flemings, along with two cantons of German-speakers make up the modern Kingdom of Belgium, which was established in 1831. The capital, Brussels, is officially bilingual. The city being Europe's "federal capital", English and many other languages are heard on its streets an in its cafés.

Belgium is perhaps united more by its love of beer and food than any other force. A particular historical influence was Burgundy, now a region of France known to the world for its Pinot Noir wines and a hearty cuisine starring Charollais beef and Dijon mustard. In the Middle Ages, Burgundy's extensive territories included the lands that are now Belgium. In other periods, these lands have been ruled by Spain, France and The Netherlands. Parts of Northern France still regard themselves as being Flemish, and the Belgian provinces of Brabant and Limburg have namesakes in the southern part of The Netherlands. There is also a town of Limburg in Germany. There are also two Luxembourgs: the independent Grand Duchy, and an adjoining province of Belgium.

Even today, the term "Burgundian" is used in Belgium to indicate a man who enjoys his food and drink, in both quantity and quality. "Burgundian" is a usefully approving word, which I would like to draft into English to replace "gourmand". At the height of Burgundian power, the abbey of Cluny was the intellectual capital of Europe, and the Benedictines exercised widespread influence for centuries.

Benedictine abbeys at Hoegaarden and Affligem were in the first three or four centuries of the last millennium influential in Belgian brewing tradition. The extravagance of life at Cluny also prompted a reaction: the establishment of the more ascetic Cistercian Order of Cîteaux (also in Burgundy) and later the yet-stricter abbey of La Trappe, in Normandy, France. This abbey, which still operates, begat the Trappist monasteries of Belgium and The Netherlands.

The soubriquet "The Burgundies of Belgium" is still used to describe the beers of Wallonia and Flanders. Even within France, grapes begin to yield to barley in the Champagne region, and the border with Belgium becomes a meeting point of more than the two nations. It is also a rendezvous of wine and beer; the French and Flemish languages; two cultures, one Latin in origin, the other Germanic.

Benedictine influence:
at the abbey of Affligem

Perhaps French wine has influenced Belgian beer. Certainly the French and Belgian kitchens have elements in common, whether the cuisine is bourgeoise or haute.

Like French children being offered wine with meals, young Belgians have traditionally enjoyed low-alcohol table beers. This is changing in the era of Coca-Cola, and children are developing sweet tastes that do not augur well for a hoppy future.

NORTH SEA

ANTWE

Ettelgem ●   ● Brugge   ● Antwer

● Ichtegem   ● Ertvelde   Belsele ●

                    EAST FLANDERS   ● Waarlo

Essen-Diksmuide   ● Lochristi

                              ● Laarne   ● Breendonk

Kortemark ● Dentergem ●   Melle ●   Buggenhout ●   ● Me

WEST FLANDERS   ● Roeselare   ● Wetteren   ● Steenhuff

Ingelmunster ●   ● Opwijk

Westvleteren Wevelgem ● ● Harelbeke ● Gavere

● Boezinge   ● Bavikhove   ● Herzele   Kobbegem ●

            ● St Elooiswinkel Zottegem ● St Lievens-Esse   ● Zellik

● Poperinge   ● Vichte ● Oudenaarde   Ninove ●   ● Brussels

              ● Bellegem   ● Gooik ● Vlezenbeek

                                                              ● Beersel

                    Ezelle ●   ● Galmaarden   ● Lembeek

                                                  ● Quenast   B

                          Silly ●

                    ● Pipaix

                    ● Tourpes

            ● Rongy-Brunehaut

                              HAINAUT

                    ● Peruwelz   ● Le Roeulx

                          ● Blaugies   Jumet ●

                    ● Montignies-sur-Roc   ● Binche

                                    Gozée ●

            FRANCE   ● P

                                                  ● Silenrie

                                                  ● Marie

                                    Chimay
                                      ●

                                  Momignies

The breweries...and the provinces

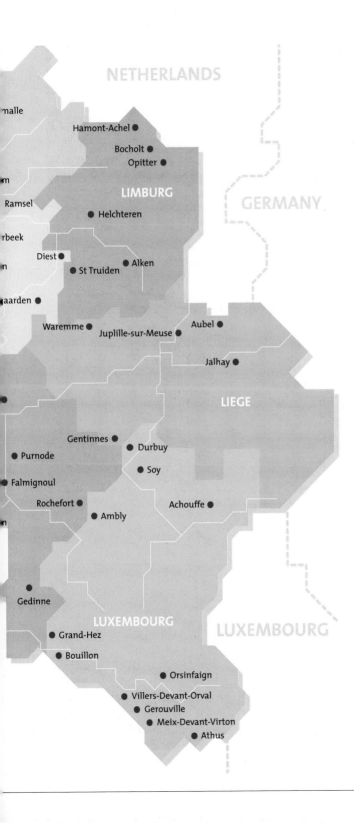

malle

Hamont-Achel ●

Bocholt ●

Opitter ●

LIMBURG

m

Ramsel

● Helchteren

rbeek

Diest ●

St Truiden ● Alken ●

n

aarden ●

Waremme ●

Juplille-sur-Meuse ● Aubel ●

Jalhay ●

LIEGE

Gentinnes ●

Durbuy ●

● Purnode

Soy ●

● Falmignoul

Rochefort ● Achouffe ●

n

Ambly ●

●
Gedinne

LUXEMBOURG

● Grand-Hez

● Bouillon

● Orsinfaign

● Villers-Devant-Orval

● Gerouville

● Meix-Devant-Virton

● Athus

NETHERLANDS

GERMANY

LUXEMBOURG

France's famous Michelin guide grants fewer stars per head in its home country than it does in Belgium. Does the winey Michelin realise that some of its starred restaurants in Belgium serve and cook with, beer? External influences, whether governments,invaders or allies have been welcomed for any positive contributions they had to offer, especially of food or drink, but not for attempts to impose order. Belgians will not be told what to do. Whether in the Ardennes or the Schelde delta, every valley, often every town or village, has its own accent of French or Flemish, its own dishes, and its own ways of making beer. Once, the other great brewing nations were like this: each town with its own style of beer. It was only with the development of steam power that breweries grew big enough to sell their products beyond the shadow of their chimneys, and national styles emerged; only with the development of widespread literacy that the wisdoms - and follies - of uniformity could be learned.

Sole with a fish mousse of cod, subtly garned with green leek...Grisette Blonde accompanies this delicious meal at Restaurant Devos, in Mons.

THE SAINTS OF BEER AND BELGIUM'S SPECIAL PRESENCE

Even in Czechoslovakia, during Communist times, I have seen a crucifix on the wall of a brewhouse. Such symbols in a brewery can surprise visitors from Protestant countries, but in Roman Catholic regions of the beer world, crucifixes and figures of saints are universal. Their watchful presence emphasises the agricultural nature of brewing. If God provides no rain, there will be no water with which to brew. If he supplies no sun, there will be no grain or hops. Too much of either will ruin the crop.

Introduction of a new member of the Knights of the mashing fork: Alain Delaet (Huyghe) says his word of thanks.

A score of saints are in various ways associated with brewing. Among them, a handful are regarded as patron saints of brewing in particular regions. The Czech brewers' saint is the canonised King Wenceslas of Bohemia; the Germans have St Florian; the

French opt for St Arnold (or Arnoud and various others spellings), of Metz. As some of the most interesting breweries in France are near the Belgian border, there is some confusion between the two countries' saints of beer and the many legends surrounding them. The Belgian brewers' patron is another St Arnold, of Soissons. He is the best-known of the world's beer saints, and the one most visibly honored in his own country. Arnold was born in 1040, at Tiegem (in what is now the heartland of West Flanders "red" beer); was a monk at the abbey of St Médard, at Soissons (near the Champagne town of Rheims); and later a bishop. Arnold founded the abbey of Oudenburg, between Ostend and Bruges. At a time of plague, Arnold is said to have immersed his crucifix in a brew-kettle, thus

Robed to pay homage...Knights of the mashing fork, on Brussels, Grand, Place. encouraging the populace to drink beer, rather than water. Suddenly, the plague ended. The water had probably been communicating the infection, while beer - being boiled during production - remains a much safer drink. Another story has Arnold miraculously producing beer after the destruction of an abbey brewery.

The abbey of Oudenburg was itself largely destroyed during the French Revolution and its role was inherited by the abbey of Steenbrugge, in Bruges. This abbey lends its name to beers produced today by the Gouden Boom ("Golden Tree") brewery in Bruges.

St Arnold's Day is August 18, and this is sometimes marked by some small ritual in the brewery. More publicly, Belgium's brewers pay homage each September at a church service in Brussels. The service has in recent years become part of a "Weekend of Beer". From the church a procession of brewers, colourfully robed as Knights of the Mashing Fork (Chevalerie du Fourquet), march through the streets to the Grande Place. The style of the procession varies, but they have over the years been accompanied by horses-and-drays, old brewery trucks, bands, and stilt-walkers. (The latter skill is prized in the sometimes-waterlogged flatlands).

In 1997, I was honoured to be asked to ride at the head of the parade, in a horse-and-carriage, with renowned brewer Modeste Van den Bogaert, of De Koninck. I was astonished at the good-natured greetings from pedestrians and motorists whose way was blocked by the procession, which took over an hour. In Paris, London or New York, there would have been shaking fists or honking horns.

In the square, there is more music, and entertainment. In 1997, the highspot was provided by a tightrope walker. He paraded at a height of 40 yards, from the gable of the 1707 Brewers' Guild House to a pylon in the centre of the square. In the midst of his walk, he used a pulley to raise a glass of beer, with which he refreshed himself. Afterwards, the brewers retired to the magnificent City Hall (dating in part from the 1400s). Watched over by the tapestry panels in the hall's Gothic Chamber, they initiated new Officers of the Mashing Fork (Chevalerie de Fourquet). The tapestries celebrate trades, prominently including weaving and brewing.

In 2000, the theme chosen was the benefits to health of moderate drinking. I was amused to see a tall pennant, erected by the Belgian Confederation of Brewers. Rising above the crowd, it announced, in Flemish, French and English: "A pint or two a day keeps the doctor away." I especially liked the added, open-ended, qualifier: "or two". It is hard to imagine such a truthful slogan being permitted in my own country, the United Kingdom. Or the United States.

THE KING OF BEER: A BELGIAN

Belgian brewing likes to proclaim itself with hearty pageantry. Much of this centres on a character whose name is sometimes spelled Cambrinus but more often rendered with a "G". He is the legendary King of Beer. While the Romans usually called beer cerevisia (from the same root as cereal), they also used the word camum, which may be of Celtic origin. The term cam, which may relate to "comb", was also used in Northern France and Belgium to identify the yoke that supported a brew-kettle over a fire in a farmhouse brewery. Did these words lead to the Northern French cambier, meaning a brewer? And perhaps to the town name Cambrai, in French Flanders?

The blessed barrel leads the procession from the church and through the city.

Therein lies one of several theories about the origin of the name. The more common spelling suggests a more widely-accepted belief. Gambrinus is usually considered to be a corruption of the 13th-century "Jan Primus", or Duke Jean I, the Burgundian ruler of Brabant, Louvain and Antwerp: regions and cities of what is today Belgium.

Jean was a warrior and a bon viveur. He issued licences to brew and serve beer, and introduced a law against its adulteration. It is said that, during a single feast, Gambrinus could drink 144 mugs of beer; perhaps the feast lasted as long as some Belgian lunches I have enjoyed. Gambrinus is also credited with having invented the toast, though it surely dates beyond him, to superstitions intended to ward off evil spirits. Figures of Gambrinus often show him astride a barrel, raising a foaming glass in a toast.

The "Jan Primus" theory is supported by the acceptance of Gambrinus as King of Beer in "rival" brewing traditions. I have seen evidence of this from Portugal to Finland, but it is especially evident in the Czech Republic, and in breweries of German origin, whether in Europe or the Americas.

As with many issues in brewing history, this may be a matter of family. The world has had many breweries called Gambrinus, the best known of which is in Pilsen, in the Czech Republic. When I asked a Czech why this name had been chosen, it was pointed out to me that the line continued with King Jan of Bohemia, who was in turn father of the German Emperor Charles IV.

CHAPTER II

Water

The land that gave the world "Spa".

Devotees of spring water know that the word "spa" originates from the name of a town in the Belgian Ardennes. The springs there were known to Pliny and rediscovered in the Middle Ages, and the word "spa" was introduced to the English language by two British doctors in the 1700s. The term has been suffixed to many towns, but there is only one called simply Spa, with a capital "s", and that is the original, in Belgium.

From his house the brewer at Rodenbach could keep an eye on the water supply.

The town of Spa still offers baths where the cure can be taken, pavilions and fountains (as well as the traditional casino), and a spectacularly deep valley setting, with skiing in a snowy winter. Having restored their health, visitors can indulge themselves in a gentle cup of bouillon (named after another town in the region) and perhaps a snack of local trout or oak-smoked Ardennes ham. Spa has at least 25 springs. Several bring forth water that is rich in iron and carbonic acid, and this has over the years been taken, both as a bath and a drink, by people suffering from anaemia, gout and rheumatism. Other springs in the town pour water that is unusually pure. The mineral water that has been for 100 years sold commercially in bottles with the label Spa has a far lower level of dissolved solids that any of its principal competitors.

Several Belgian breweries use spring water from the Ardennes, the rolling hills and forests that rise to the east of the river Meuse. There is another famous source at Chaudfontaine, near Liège, and its waters are also available commercially bottled.

The production of beer requires water in mashing and brewing, and loses much in evaporation, in spent grain and handling. A great deal of water is also used in washing equipment, bottles, kegs and the brewhouse itself. When breweries grew to an industrial scale, the volume of water accessible to them became an issue. They needed huge quantities of it, reliably available, summer as well as winter, and free from spoilage. The first industrial breweries were sited with this in mind, but not necessarily with a view to a particular mineral composition in the water. It subsequently emerged that the character of the water helped determine the style of beer.

A brewer wanting to make lager beers resembling those produced in Budweis, Pilsen or Munich requires soft water like that found in those cities. The characteristic firmness of a pale ale is best achieved with hard water, high in calcium sulphate, like that available in Burton, England. A brewer producing a porter or stout might look for water rich in calcium chloride or calcium carbonate, like those of London or Dublin.

Today, brewers can remove or add the appropriate natural salts to produce the character of water they seek. A brewer with his own spring or well tends to enjoy talking about it. Such an asset makes him feel good. The deeper and cooler and faster running it is, the more secure he feels in his supply. It is the first step toward the purity and consistency of his beer. It will not in itself ensure a wonderful beer, but it is a valuable beginning.

CHAPTER III

Grain

*There is more to beer than pale barley malts.
Belgium's ashtonishing assortment
emphasises subtlety of color, fullnes
of flavor and aroma.*

Civilisation may have begun with beer. On
the basis of that theory, it might be argued
that the Belgians have their priorities right.
In pursuing their enthusiasm for beer, they
are simply seeking to be a civilised people.
The suggestion is that, when humans stopped being hunters and gatherers, and settled in organised societies in order to grow
grain, their purpose was not to bake bread,
but to brew beer. Research in this field has
been based on excavations stretching from
Ancient Egypt to what is now Israel, Syria,
Iraq and Turkey.

Wild barley was being gathered at least 33,000 years ago, in what is now northern Israel and Syria, according to recent studies. It was apparently roasted, and may have been used to make beer, though no one knows. It is now thought that barley and wheat may have been planted in the same area as early as 13,000 years ago. These conclusions are based on examination of flint tools. The segment of Iraq that formed Mesopotamia, with its region of Babylonia and its district of Sumer, provides the earliest evidence of beer being consumed, as depicted in a decorative seal of 6,000 years ago. A series of Sumerian tablets 5,000 years old, which has been described as the world's oldest recipe, explains the making of beer from barley.

GRAPES AND GRAIN

Grapes take plenty of water from the soil, and turn it into juice. They can simply be crushed to release this juice, which is rich in fermentable sugar. Grains do not take up so much water. They must be steeped, sprouted and infused in water before they will give up their fermentable sugars. Were the ancients making porridges, gruels or bread-doughs when the wild yeasts of the atmosphere turned their grains to beer? Or was a barley bread, probably hard and unappetising, stored as a form of "instant beer"?

Malted grains, delivered in sacks, make heavy work for the small brewer. Bulk silos are used by bigger brewers.

The thought that beer may have preceded bread could have been inspired by an expression common to the brewing monasteries of Austria and Germany and Belgium. In the strictest regimes, the monks were always allowed to drink beer during Lent, and called it "liquid bread". The academic theory had its origins in a German-language paper published in the 1920s, and excavations in Iraq in the 1930s, and was further developed by Professor Solomon Katz, of the University of Philadelphia, in the late 1980s. In the 1990s, at Georgetown University, Washington, D.C., the Jesuit scholar Father Ronald Murphy proposed to me that "bread" and "brewed" were originally the same word. He also suggested that the name "barley" derived from its being the "beer-like" grain. Some etymological dictionaries take the same view.

Father Murphy also has St Vaast, a country priest living near Rheims in the fifth or sixth century, driving the Devils from infected, gushing, beer by chanting alu, a very old Indo-European word implying release and ecstasy, but also relating to taboos. Alu survives in alus (Lithuanian and Latvian), õlu (Estonian), olut (Finnish), öl (Swedish), øl (Norwegian and Danish) and ale English. The Baltic and Scandinavian variants all mean simply "beer". The English used only "ale" until they adapted "beer" from the Flemish bier. "Ale" originally meant beer without hops. Today, it means beer made with a top-fermenting yeast. St Vaast, meanwhile, is remembered in the names of two small towns or villages in northern France and one between Mons and Charleroi, in Belgium.

Beer may have preceded wine, but snobbism soon developed. During the early Roman Empire, Tacitus noted of the Germanic peoples: "Their beverage they prepare from barley or wheat, a brew which slightly resembles an inferior quality of wine." By then, it seems, the warmer countries were concentrating on the grape and the cooler ones on the grain (though some made mead, from honey; or cider, from apples).

Perhaps the snobbism derives from the fact that wine was the drink of the governing classes, and beer of the colonies, when the Romans held sway over Europe, when the Normans conquered England, and in the various periods when the Burgundians and the Napoleonic French ruled Belgium. Perhaps the Romance tongues have imparted a greater sensuousness to their native drinks than the Germanic languages have to theirs. Perhaps the warm south, and the fleshy grape, are themselves more sensuous than the cool north and the less yielding grain.

BARLEY, WHEAT, RYE, OATS

Barley is the grain that can most easily be turned into beer, and it is one of the least satisfactory in the baking of bread. Wheat and rye are more suited to the baker. It is thus that barley has always been the principal grain in brewing, though wheat is an ingredient in several classic styles of beer, and is especially widely used in Bavaria and Belgium. Rye is occasionally used. Oats are used in some Belgian beers, and very occasionally in the English-speaking world. Barley imparts a firm, clean sweetness; wheat has a tart, quenching quality in beer; rye is spicy, almost minty; oats add a silky smoothness. Rice is sometimes used to lighten the body of beers, and maize as a cheaper ingredient, though one that can impart an unpleasant stickiness.

VARIETIES OF BARLEY

Two varieties of grape may produce dramatically different wines; the distinctions between barleys are less obvious, but the brewer is still interested in the selection of variety, the region of cultivation, and the season.

Two races of barley, distinguished by the number of rows of grains in each ear, are used in the making of beer. Many brewers prefer two-row barley, and feel that the six-row varieties have too much husk character. Some brewers feel that the influence of the husk adds to the flavour of their beer. As farmers seek better yields, new varieties of both races are constantly being bred. Many brewers prefer spring barley (sown in March and harvested in July and August), feeling that the winter varieties (whose season is from October-November to June) are too harsh. Again, some take a different view, feeling that winter barley adds character, especially to ales..

Farmers were once commonly also brewers. Grain is perishable, and was hard to transport in the days of horse and cart. There was much work on the farm in summer, but less in winter. During the cold months, the grain could be fermented into beer (and then perhaps distilled into spirits). There are still farmhouse breweries in Belgium. Girardin, which grows wheat, is the best example. Others are recognisable as having been farms, even if they are today exclusively breweries. There are also monasteries that have both farms and breweries. The rhythms of farming, harvesting, brewing, maturing and drinking are also remembered in the tradition of seasonal beers. Agricultural and religious seasons tend to coincide, of course. In those days, Belgium grew enough barley to quench its thirst.

WHERE BARLEY IS GROWN

Fine malting barley is cultivated mainly in the Northern Hemisphere, notably between latitudes 45 and 55. It likes cool weather, gentle sun, rich but well-drained soil, and reasonably flat land.

Today, the cultivation of barley for the brewer is having a minor revival in Belgium: around Gembloux (between Brussels and Namur); in the province of Liège; and in the area between the city of Antwerp and the border with The Netherlands.

Far more barley is imported. Belgium is surrounded by barley-growing countries: France (with cultivation in the region between Orléans and Paris, and in Champagne); Germany (especially Lower Franconia); The Netherlands (Dutch Zeeland); Denmark; and England (East Anglia).

While the grape is delicate, and disinclined to travel, barley is much more robust. Indeed, it will not give up its sugars, or the enzymes needed in their fermentation, until it has gone through the process of malting. This may be done in the country of cultivation, or closer to the brewing of the beer. It takes place in an establishment known as a maltings. Wherever barley is grown for malting, they can be seen, though many of the smaller ones have been turned to other uses (in Britain, one is a celebrated concert hall). The older maltings are very distinctive buildings. They usually have at least two or three storeys, with vents on the roof, pulleys to hoist the grain, and shutters to control the temperature. Belgium still has six or seven maltings, well known throughout the world of brewing for the quality of their products. Today, maltings are usually free-standing, though in the past many shared a site and ownership with a brewery.

TURNING GRAIN INTO MALT

Grain is steeped in water, allowed partially to germinate, then dried, in the process of malting. The end product is known as malt. It is the raw material not only of beer (a fermented drink) but also whisky (its distilled counterpart).

These barrels at the Lambic brewery of Frank Boon accommodate wild yeast fermentations.

The procedures of malting take about ten days in total. The steeping, in tanks - with several changes of water, and aeration to allow the grain's embryo to breathe - is much the same in all maltings. The steeped grains may then be spread on a stone floor, and turned by rakes to ensure that they remain aerated and separated while they begin to germinate. Or they may be placed in shallow, ventilated boxes, or in rotating drums. The floor system is the most traditional, and some maltsters feel it produces the best results. Its disadvantages are that it is very demanding in space and labour, and the method is most commonly found in rural Bohemia or the whisky country of Scotland. For 30 or 40 years, the Belgian brewer Artois had a magnificent six-storey floor maltings in the city of Leuven, but the company announced in 2001 that this would be either closed or sold.

MALT, COLOR AND FLAVOR

Just as the length of contact with the grapes' skins influences both colour and flavour in wine, the drying of the malt does the same in beer. A very gently kilned malt will be pale in colour and delicate in flavour, and make a golden, beer. A malt that has been "stewed" will provide a more reddish colour and a sweeter, slightly biscuity, or even toffee-ish, flavour. A malt that has been roasted will be dark brown or black, and may have a flavour reminiscent of dark chocolate or espresso coffee. The kilns at a traditional maltings are not dissimilar in outward appearance from those at a pottery. Where very dark malts are made, there will also be drums like those used by coffee roasters. Even the smell is similar to that of coffee being roasted.

A maltings may make just the very pale type, or as many as a dozen variations, each with its own regime of moistures and temperatures. Some are known by the name of the beer-style they produce: Pilsener Malt, Pale Ale, Vienna, Munich (in ascending order of kilning). Others are described by their characteristics: Aromatic Malt, Biscuit, Chocolate, Roasted, and there are many variations on these themes.

Some beers are made with just one style of malt, many with two or three. Speciality beers may employ as many as eight, though that is unusual. A beer made from several malts may have an especially complex, subtle, colour. In the scale used by brewers, a golden beer using only pale malts might have 6.5 International Units of Colour. A stout could have 150-200.

Few maltsters in other brewing nations makes as many variations as the half-dozen in Belgium. Caramelised and aromatic malts are especially important in the flavors of many Belgian speciality beers. The Belgian producers of these malts also have a growing reputation elsewhere in the world.

INFUSION AND DECOCTION

At the brewery, the malt is cracked in a mill, then soaked in hot water for an hour or more to release its fermentable sugars. The duration and temperatures of this mashing procedure vary according to the brewery and the style of beer being made. It may be a simple infusion, at just one temperature, or there may be series of steps. There may even be a decoction, involving transfer between two vessels at different temperatures. When the sugars have been released, the liquid - the "juice" of the barley - is strained into the brew-kettle. This "juice" is known by brewers as wort. The term has its origin in the Germanic word for "root". This "juice" is the root of the beer.

The "juice" is very sweet, and that is why it needs the subsequent seasoning of hops. It would not be a very refreshing drink "straight", though I have been served it hot, laced with whisky, as an alternative to coffee, and found it most sustaining.

THE BREWHOUSE

The simplest brewhouse has just two principal vessels: the mash-tun, where the infusion takes place, and the kettle. In an artisanal brewery, perhaps one that had its beginnings as a farm, the mash-tun may be an open, circular vessel, made from cast-iron, and looking like a spare part from a steam locomotive. Inside may be a stirring device that would look equally happy on an early harvesting machine. The kettle may be nothing more than a copper tub, heated underneath by gas flames, or by internal steam coils, and sometimes bricked-in.

This type of brewhouse is still to be found in Belgium, but there are few elsewhere in the world. Belgium and the adjoining areas of Northern France are one of the last homes of truly artisanal brewing. Franconia is another, and there are a handful of such breweries in Britain. Very old brewhouses, and the techniques of beer-making that they demand, will often resemble one another within

Jupille has state of the art equipment

a particular area. There was probably in the past a local engineer who did the design work for all the breweries in his district, as though they were railway stations on a country branch line. This was no doubt an influence on regional styles of beer.

The more instantly recognisable brewhouse is the one where both the principal vessels are of a similar, dome-shaped design, in copper. These are reminiscent of one of Jacques Cousteau's bathyspheres (or a creation of Jules Verne?). This style of brewhouse is still being built today, though often in stainless steel, and in more angular designs. There are also modern brewhouses where the vessels are walled-in, perhaps behind tiles, with hatches and sight-glasses that make the whole thing resemble a huge launderette. Others mimic a food-

processing plant, and some would not look out of place on the Starship Enterprise. In recent years, the trend has been back to traditional shapes, but in a more angular style.

Some very stylish brewhouses, more than 100 in various countries, have been produced since 1845 by the Belgian company Meura, an international name in the industry. Belgium has some of the oldest working breweries in the world, and some of the most technically advanced. There is a small exhibit on brewhouse design, old and new, at the Brewers' House, on Brussels' Grand' Place. There are no fewer than six brewhouses from different periods in an astonishing museum at the Martens' brewery, in Bocholt, in Belgian Limburg. The collection of equipment there occupies about 5,000 square feet on three or four levels. How did it start? In the 1970s, Jean Martens was faced with the need to replace a worn-out mashtun. He could not bear to discard it. The rest is history, in more senses than one. In 2001, Jean, aged 81, showed me round with the true pride of a Belgian brewer.

Yeast

Some countries have only lager cultures, other favor ale. Belgian fermentations can be winey, sour, even rose-like.

Wild yeasts that reside on the skin were the first agents of the fermentation that turns juice into wine, with all its complexities of flavour. Some wines are still made in this way, others by the addition of a yeast that has been cultured for the purpose.

For much of the history of wine-making and brewing, the practitioners were unaware of the existence of yeast. Wine-makers knew that a transformation took place, but were not aware that it was caused by a scarcely-visible micro-organism on the skin of the grape. Neither did brewers realise that the more resilient grain, once its sugars had been liberated by malting and mashing, was receptive to visits from yeasts that were airborne, or resident, in the brewery.

This was how beer fermented in Mesopotamian times, and this simplest of methods never completely vanished. There is some evidence that the technique survived around the cities of Düsseldorf and Danzig (now Gdansk) until the early 1900s. Today, Belgium, particularly the area to the immediate west of Brussels, is the last part of the developed world to hold on to this technique, which is used in the production of Lambic beers. That is one reason why Lambic beer is prized. Once, all beer must have been similar to Lambic. Today, it is unique to Belgium.

WINEY-TASTING BEERS: SPONTANEOUS FERMENTATION

The other reason why Lambic is prized is its distinctively winey, acidic, complexity. This derives from the continued use of airborne and resident wild yeasts. This is known as spontaneous fermentation. These products are sometimes labelled in Flemish Bier van Spontane Gisting and in French De Fermentation Spontanée.

(Gist means yeast. With the Flemish swallowed "g" the words resemble each other phonetically. Yeast, gist, the bubbly beer-style Gueuze, and the words gas and ghost may all be related: referring to something "invisible" that rises from below. The Germans have a quite different word for yeast - Hefe - but that, too refers to lifting, as in "heave" or "heft"). No doubt the French levure leavens bread, as well as raising the head on beer.

In the developed world, the makers of Lambic are the only brewers still to pursue spontaneous fermentation, which they have taken to a high level of craftsmanship. Lambic is the most traditional brew anywhere in the world that is recognisable as beer.

The only other brews made by spontaneous fermentation are some turbid, porridgy, "native beers" of many Third World Countries. Lambics are immensely complex beers, whose production can last for three years or more; the nearest process is the production of fino sherry, with its reliance on the wild yeast called flor. Even the smells in a Lambic brewery and a sherry bodega are similar. It is no insult to the cultures of Africa and Asia to say that their native beers, fermented in a matter of hours, are far less refined products. Nor, despite the name, are they recognisable as beer.

One of the elements in a controlled fermentation is temperature. Lambic breweries grew up before this was possible, but Belgium is a temperate country, never far from the sea. The following three styles of fermentation originally used ambient temperatures, but now employ both cooling and heating.

Time is another element. The Lambic family can spent as long as three years in fermentation and maturation. A lager can take three months. An ale may be ready in three weeks.

SOUR BEERS: BRETTANOMYCES, LACTIC AND ACETIC FERMENTATIONS

In the days when all beer was spontaneously fermented, and yeast was not understood, a variety of wild yeasts and other micro-organisms would reside in a brewery. At the time, all fermentation and storage vessels were made from wood, often open to the atmosphere. These were a much more amenable home for wild yeasts and other micro-organisms than a modern brewery, with its closed stainless-steel vessels.

Within the "zoo" of micro-organisms, a pecking order would be established, based on the survival of the fittest and the primacy of the most vigorous. As the micro-organisms caused fermentations, some would be rendered inactive by the alcohol they created. Some yeasts are more alcohol-tolerant than others. Some organisms cannot work without oxygen; others can. For these reasons, there can be a sequence of fermentations, as one yeast or micro-organism falls away and another takes over.

Typical participants in such a sequence might include several yeasts in the family Brettanomyces, and lactobacilli and acetobacters.
The first creates aromas and flavors sometimes said to be reminiscent of a horse-blanket, or perhaps hessian or hop-sack; the second a lactic character; the third an acetic, vinegary note.

Acidity can make for an undrinkably sour beer if it is not controlled, but in an equilibrium, it can also create stability, as it does in the preservation of foods by pickling. Lactic fermentations are employed in the sharply refreshing wheat beers of Berlin, and Brettanomyces in some porters and stouts, but the use of such elements is at its most widespread in Belgium, especially in the production of Lambic beers, but also as part of the regime in some top-fermenting beers, notably the Old Brown ales and "sour" red ales of East and West Flanders. In the wide world of brewing, these fermentation techniques are little known, but they are a very specific aspect of the Belgian brewers' art. They are also a bridge between spontaneous and top fermentation.

FRUITY-TASTING BEERS: TOP-FERMENTATION

When beer ferments, its surface begins to foam. As this foam bubbles up, it can overflow. Some fermenting vessels have a lip so that overflowing foam can be directed into a waiting vessel. This system seems to have evolved in medieval times. When the bubbling had stopped, brewers would tip the foamy overflow into the next batch. Empirically, they discovered that this made for a more reliable and consistent fermentation next time. The foamy liquid seemed to have miraculous properties, but they did not know how it worked. English brewers called it "God Is Good". The overflowing foam actually comprised millions of fresh, vigorous, yeast cells, but the brewers did not know that. The word "yeast" had not yet been coined. Brewers did not know what yeast was, and it was not properly understood until the mid 1800s. Meanwhile, the brewers who employed this technique had advanced from spontaneous fermentation to an empirical, unknowing, procedure of yeast selection. The collection of yeast from the top of the fermenting vessels gave this technique its name. In Belgium, a beer that is top-fermented will often be labelled in Flemish as Hoge Gisting and in French as Haute Fermentation. Top-fermenting yeasts, known as *Saccharomyces cerevisiae*, are used in the production of wheat beers, ales, abbey beers, stouts and other specialities. They are sometimes known simply as ale yeasts. These cultures. typically produce fruity, spicy, flavors. These should be noticeable in any top-fermenting beer, not just those that actually contain fruits or spices.

Top fermentation... yeast being skimmed off the surface by hand.

FLOWERY COMPLEXITY: RE-FERMENTATION IN THE BOTTLE

While both the Germans and the British have some beers that enjoy a secondary fermentation in the bottle, and there are a growing number in North America, this technique is unusually widespread in Belgium. In labelling such beers, the Germans often refer on the label to yeast (Hefe) or turbidity (Trub) without specifying whether there was a further fermentation. The English-speaking world usually favours the term bottle-conditioned, the Belgians refer to it as "Re-fermentation in the bottle" (Hergist in de fles / Refermentée en bouteille). The secondary fermentation can be brought about by bottling the brew unfiltered, but this requires great skill. If too much yeast remains in the brew, the fermentation could be too great, and the bottle might explode. Or there might be too much yeast for the amount of nutrition available in the residual malt sugars. The yeast would die and leave an unpleasantly gritty flavor.

One solution is first to let the brew settle in a tank, so that much (but not all) of the yeast precipitates before the bottling. This is like decanting the brew even before it is bottled. Another method is to centrifuge the brew to remove much of the yeast, leaving enough for the secondary fermentation. A third is to filter the brew, then add a measured quantity of fresh yeast.

Some brewers use the same yeast for both primary fermentation and bottle-conditioning. Others prefer in the bottle a yeast that will compact, to avoid cloudiness. There are other reasons to use a different yeast in the bottle: it has to work in a smaller space, with less oxygen, in an environment where it may be inhibited by alcohol, and it has to stay alive for a long time, so as not to leave those "dead yeast" flavours.

In most countries, bottle-conditioning went out of style because brewers found it easier to filter and pasteurise their beer, and consumers grew accustomed to a bright, clear, pint. Belgian brewers developed the skills to perfect bottle-conditioning, while bartenders and consumers know how to pour these beers without necessarily casting a haze.

While bottle-fermented wheat beers like Belgian Wit/Blanche are usually poured with the yeast in suspension, Lambics and other styles are served more gently, as though they were being decanted, so that the sediment is left behind.

The advantages of bottle conditioning are twofold: the secondary fermentation preserves the freshness of the beer; and distinct flavors are created. These can very complex, typically flowery, sometimes notably rose-like.

CLEAN-TASTING BEERS: BOTTOM-FERMENTATION

For most of the history of brewing, work was possible only in winter. During the warmer months, there were just too many wild micro-organisms in the air and too great a danger of sour beers. In March, an unusually large brew would be made, to be kept as a provision and drawn upon during the summer months. The summer lay-off would also allow farmer-brewers to attend to their agricultural work. After the barley and hop harvests, the new brewing season would start in late September or early October. Traditional Lambic breweries still operate in this way.

Bottom fermentation: first came dark Munich and amber Vienna lagers, then the Czech city of Pilsen created the world's most well-known style.

When the Munich brewers stored their beer for the summer, some did so in nearby caves in the foothills of the Alps. In time, they noticed that the caves not only kept the beer in good condition, but also seemed to impart a stability to it. This was because, in the cold, the yeast sank to the bottom, out of harm's way. This method came to be known as lagering, after the German word for storage. Storage is first mentioned in 1420, in the minutes of Munich town council, but it was not understood until much later.

Yeast was first viewed under a microscope by the Dutch scientist Anton van Leeuwenhoek, in 1680. In the 1700s and 1800s, the work of the French chemists Lavoisier and Gay-Lussac and the German Liebig furthered knowledge in this area. In the 1830s, the Bavarian brewer Sedlmayr began to develop a methodical technique to make bottom-fermenting beer. Those early Bavarian-style lagers were dark brown and they were quickly followed, in 1841, by an amber Vienna-type and, in 1842, the golden product of the town of Pilsen. Brewers' growing ability to make paler malts, precipitate their yeasts - and for the first time make a clear, bright, beer - meant that a translucent, golden, product was an attractive novelty, especially at a time when opaque metal or stoneware drinking vessels were being replaced by mass-produced glass.

It was still not until 1857 that a real understanding of yeasts was resolved, by Pasteur, and in 1883 the first single-cell, bottom-fermenting culture was isolated, by Emil Hansen, at the Carlsberg brewery in Copenhagen. Bottom-fermenting yeasts became known as Saccharomyces carlsbergensis.

In order to work properly, these yeasts need low temperatures. Where Alpine caves were not available, ice could sometimes be cut from lakes, but it was the development of artificial refrigeration that enabled lager brewing finally to spread worldwide. Today, golden lagers represent an international style of beer. Many consumers know no other.

SERVING TEMPERATURES

A beer fermented and matured only with the higher cycles of temperature will express its flavour most fully at around 13°C (55°F). A strong, rich, example like Chimay Grande Réserve might even benefit from being served warmer, at around 15-18°C (59-64°F). The palate of such a beer is destroyed if it is served heavily chilled.
Bottom-fermentation classically rises to only 9° C (48°F), and is followed by anything from one to three months' lagering at, or around,

0°C (32°F). Once beer has been lagered, it seems to express its flavour best at cooler temperatures, ideally around 8-9°C (45-48°).

STRENGTH

The potency of beer is an equation between its original content of natural sugars (sometimes known as DENSITY, or ORIGINAL GRAVITY) and the extent to which these have been fermented into alcohol. Just as wine-makers have the Brix scale to express sugar content, so brewers have a number of measuring systems. In some countries, these systems, rather than alcohol content, have traditionally been used in labelling. Even alcohol content can be expressed in two different ways: by weight or volume. Because alcohol is lighter than water, the weight system produces lower figures; volume is easier to understand.

The same sample of an internationally-known brand of Pilsener beer, for example, could typically be described as having 12 degrees in the Balling scale (Czech Republic), a similar rating in the German Plato scale, 4.6-4.8 degrees in a Belgian system, 1048 original gravity (British), 4.0 per cent alcohol by weight and 5.0 by volume. The weight system is used in the laws concerning alcohol in the U.S., where a majority of states does not permit potency to be indicated on the label. These states take the undemocratic view that the consumer is not to be trusted: he might buy only the strongest beers. In a minority of U.S. states, Canada, the European Union and many other parts of the world, alcohol by volume is indicated on the label.

While the measures of sugar content (otherwise known as "original gravity" or "density") are of interest to knowledgeable beer-lovers, the consumer is probably happy simply to know the product's alcohol content.

No topic is more subject to myth and legend. Drinkers swear that one country's beers are stronger than other's, but that is not true. Every brewing nation has beers at a wide variety of strengths. The most that can be said is that an imaginary average beer, based on total consumption, would have 4.7 per cent alcohol by volume in Germany and Belgium, 3.7 in Britain and 4.5 in the U.S.

Belgium's average is derived from a pattern of consumption that is more varied than in any other country. Belgium has many weak beers and an unusually wide, readily-available, and well-patronised selection of strong ones. Whether they do so consciously or not, Belgians seem to pick the beer that suits the moment. Interbrew reckons that the average Belgian beer drinker samples eight styles of beer in a year. How many Germans get beyond a regular Helles, Pilsner or wheat beer? How many Britons cross loyalties from Lager to Bitter to Stout?

One of Belgium's many civilised habits is its production of table beers. Long before "no-" and "low"-alcohol brews, Belgium had light beers that could be served to the family, including the children, at the dinner table. Although this category has declined, there are still about 80 of these beers. These are usually lagers, both pale and dark, and they range in alcohol content from 0.8 to 3.2 by volume. A child accustomed to the choice of such brews at table is less likely to be excited into irresponsibility in his or her teens, when beers of a more conventional level become available. Beer is a part of civilised life in Belgium; it is not a rite of passage into an adult garden of temptation and sin. Belgians would do well to retain this understanding, and perhaps even teach it to others.

Most everyday beers in Belgium are a little under, or occasionally just over, a 5.0 per cent mark. These include well-known Pilsener-style beers like Stella Artois, Maes and Jupiler; ales such as Palm, Ginder and Vieux Temps; and the "white" wheat beers like Hoegaarden.

Belgium has scores of stronger beers, in a broad range from 6.0 to 10.0 and plenty more potent than that, with brews like the yellow-top version of

Revival of table beers: Alken-Maes launches its "Maes Nature" in 1999.

Trappist Westvleteren (11.0-11.5) and Bush (12.0-12.2, and similar to a British barley wine) at the top end. The British, Germans, Swiss and Americans have all produced individual beers that are more potent, but none of those countries has anything like the Belgian variety of styles among its strong beers.

Potency is not a measure of quality. On a hot day, a beer that is quenching but light in body and low in alcohol might be just what is needed. With dinner, a brew that is moderate in both alcohol and body might be perfect. Before or after dinner, something slightly more assertive may be preferred. Nor do body and strength always coincide. It is easy to make a low-strength beer that is full in body, though it is more difficult to produce a very potent one that is light. Most very strong beers are heavy, and therefore hard to drink in any quantity. All the same, a Kasteel Beer with a book at bedtime is another civilised habit. Nowhere to drive. Nowhere to go but to sleep.

Lock the castle gate, and have a strong beer before bedtime... Kasteel Bier has a sedative 11.0 percent alcohol.

Spices, herbs and hops

Coriander, Curaçao oranges, paradise... a touch of the tropics.

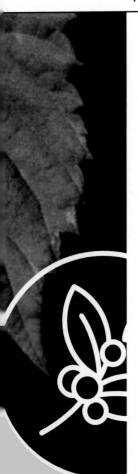

Flavouring ingredients were once added to all drinks, to mask imperfections, add aroma, balance the natural tastes, and in some instances as a preservative.

The first wine-makers added herbs, spices, flowers, berries, fruits or tree-barks to their products. Wines spiced with camomile, quinine bark and rhubarb are still made today, but we know them as vermouths. Today's wine-makers prefer to give the grape a balancing, dryish, aromatic, character from the oak of the cask. In ancient times, clay amphorae did not have that effect. Some brandies are still spiced with essences of nuts or fruits. Gin is a spirit aromatised with juniper berries, coriander, orange peels and other "botanicals". Liqueurs are spirits with spices, herbs, nuts or fruits added. Once, all beers had such flavourings.

There is some reason to believe that the ancients used honey and dates. As brewing spread west and north into Europe, juniper, bog myrtle and alder twigs were among the indigenous flavourings that came into use. There is in Belgium the odd revivalist juniper beer, usually intended to evoke the jenever gin of the Low Countries. The older use of juniper twigs, with berries, as a filter, a contributor of aroma and flavor, and a preservative survives among farmhouse brewers in Estonia, Finland, Gotland, Sweden and Norway.

With exploration and the establishment of colonies in Asia, Africa and the Americas, more exotic ingredients were employed. Belgium and The Netherlands were one country in the early colonial period, and very active in the spice trade. The Caribbean island colony of Curaçao became famous for its small, bitter oranges. These fruits were regarded as a luxury, and featured in the paintings of Flemish and Dutch masters. Sometimes, they were shown with vessels containing unidentified drinks.

The custom of adding herbs, spices and fruits to beer survived longest in Belgium, never altogether vanished there, and is most strongly associated with that country. Tropical ingredients like coriander, grains of paradise and ginger were especially used. In recent years, the practice has enjoyed a revival in Belgium and been rediscovered in some neighbouring countries and North America.

I once visited the very old-established wholesale herbalist Robert Meyskens, in Quévrain, near Mons. He showed me faded, handwritten ledgers detailing orders for a wide variety of herbs from a dozen or 20 brewers. Mr Meyskens said that the numbers of brewers among his customers had dwindled to two at the beginning of the 1970s, but had risen again to about 10 by the time of my visit, in 1986. Three years later, he wrote to tell me that his business with brewers was "good". Today, almost every new beer launched is spiced.

In addition to honey, orange peels and coriander, popular ingredients include star anise, licorice, the peppery grains of paradise and ginger. This is especially typical of "white" wheat beers in the style of Hoegaarden, though it also applies to other brews. A few of these are specifically categorised as Kruidenbieren. A Kruid is a herb. In old Germanic languages, a blend of herbs added to beer was known as a Gruit. In modern English, the term grouts is used semi-colloquially for the residue of leaves at the bottom of a cup of tea.

HOPS AS A DELICACY

Hops were known to the Ancients, but it is not certain how they were used. Pliny knew them as a garden plant, whose young shoots were eaten as a salad. In Europe, this custom is still known in Bohemia, Germany, and elsewhere, but thrives only in Belgium. In his book "Food", the late Waverley Root, the Paris-based, American essayist put his finger on it in characteristic style: "The most fervent admirers of the hop are the Belgians." He was speaking gastronomically, but "admire" is the right verb.

The eating of hop shoots, jets d'houblon, is enjoying a revival. The natural season for this succulent, nutty, delicacy is short: for about three weeks, from mid March to the beginning of April, during which time the shoots are normally being thinned. The season has in recent years been extended by forced cultivation in warmed earth.

Like many classic dishes (the pizza of Naples, the eggs and spinach of Florence, the quiche of Lorraine), jets d'houblon had humble beginnings in the desire to utilise every last scrap. The shoots had to be thinned, so why not eat those that were picked? The thinning is done when the shoots are just peeping a couple of inches above the ground. Today, it can be done partly by spraying: thinning by hand has become very expensive, and that is another reason for cultivation under glass. Hop shoots have become a rare and expensive luxury.

The most basic way of serving them is to blanch or poach them in salty water with a seasoning of lemon juice and present them in a soup plate, with one or two softly poached eggs on top, and butter, cream or a simple sauce - velouté, béchamel or a mousseline. Modern-day refinements might include the addition of slivers of smoked salmon. Escoffier recommended croutons of fried bread, and insisted that they be cockscomb-shaped. Like eggs Florentine, jets d'houblon is a simple but delicious snack - or entrée. Like asparagus with scrambled eggs (another dish that is often served with beer), it has the ritual and fun of a short season. Like both of those dishes, it has appetising contrasts of texture between the eggs and the vegetable or salad ingredients.

Since the 1990s, an annual hop-shoot festival has been organised in early to mid March. Visitors are taken by bus to see the shoots being thinned, and later to enjoy a multi-course lunch featuring the magical plant.

THE HOP PLANT

While it is the shoot of the hop that is eaten, it is the leafy cone, sometimes known as the blossom, that is valued for its oils, resins, tannin, acids and aromatic qualities.

Botanically speaking, the hop is a member of the family Cannabinaceae. It shares a common parent with cannabis, and has been used through the ages as a sedative (in herbal pillows), a preservative (where there are isolated reports of its use in embalming and tanning) and a medicine or beauty aid (as in beer shampoos). At least one translation of the Babylonian Talmud talks of the Ancient Jews making beer and using hops, but this rests on the

interpretation of Aramaic words for drinks and plants. The Romans recorded that the hop grew wild among willows, and this was the origin of its botanical name, Humulus lupulus.

More persistent references to the cultivation of hops do not appear until the eighth and ninth centuries A.D., when gardens are mentioned in Bohemia, Bavaria, and other parts of Germany. King Pepin of the Franks (the father of Charlemagne), who was enthroned at Soissons, is recorded as having given a hop farm to the Abbey of St Denis. There is also a significant mention of hops being required by monks in Picardy prior to 822.

The early references do not say why the hops were grown, though there are also plentiful records of beer having been brewed in the same areas at the time. There are vague allusions connecting hops, grain and beer from the beginning of this millennium. The abbey of Affligem, founded in 1086, is credited by one writer with having introduced hops to Flanders, and perhaps to England. In the 1100s, the first undisputed reference to the use of hops in beer was made in the writings of Abbess Hildegarde of Bingen (in what is now Germany).

One account has hops being introduced to the Low Countries by monks in the French-Flemish town of St Omer some time prior to 1322, at which point cultivation began east of Dunkirk, in Poperinge. In 1364, the Bishop of Liège and Utrecht referred to the use of hops in beer as having been in vogue for 30 or 40 years.

The Flemish exported hopped beer to England in the 1400s. It is a short sea crossing from Flanders to the East of England, and the two regions already had a history of trading in wool. Engineers from Flanders and Holland had also worked on draining the lowlands of East Anglia. At the time, the English were still making beer without hops. Initially, there were protectionist measures against hopped beer, but these were swept away by Henry VI. Hopped beer had given the Flemish fat faces and bellies, and could cause death, said an English writer of the time (curiously, he had a Flemish-sounding name: Boorde). It became popular nonetheless. In the 1500s, Flemish immigrants started growing hops in England.

On the borders of the hop-growing counties of Kent and Sussex, in a church at Playden, near Rye, there is in the floor a stone slab dating from about 1530, with an inscription showing a crossed staff and fork (used in mashing, and a symbol of brewing) and two casks. A Flemish-language engraving says that this is the tomb of Cornelis Roetmans. No doubt he was a brewer. By the 1700s, the Flemish hop-growing industry was suffering severely from English competition.

Hops had by then also been introduced to the New Netherlands, in North America. Hops followed the development of the United States, beginning in what is now New York State, migrating to Wisconsin, in the Midwest, and thence to California. Today, they are mainly grown in Oregon and Washington state, and across the Canadian border in British Columbia.

Uses of hops: the shoots are a seasonal delicacy in Belgium.

The abbey of Affligem may have introduced hops to England.
Between early March and late August, the vines can reach 18ft (6 metres).

HOP VARIETIES

Today, different varieties of hops are used according to the style of beer being made. The variety native to Bohemia, and grown around the town of Zatec (Saaz hops, in German) are prized for their delicate, flowery, bouquet. It sometimes reminds me of camomile. They are classically used in the finest Pilsener-style lager beers. Several similar varieties, most notably the Hallertau Mittelfrüh, are grown in Bavaria.

While the Saaz and Hallertau-Mittelfrüh are used principally to impart aroma to the beer, other varieties contribute dryness, or bitterness. One of Bavaria's favourite bittering hops is Northern Brewer, which is also grown in Belgium, and originated from Britain (hence the English name). Germany grows, mainly in Bavaria, between a quarter and a third of the world's hop crop. Flanders contributes less than one per cent of the world's crop, but has a rich hop lore. I have even tasted a Flemish gin called Hopjenever, made by a firm called Verhofstede, in Nieuwkerken-Waas, near Sint-Niklaas. I found it hard to detect the hop aroma and flavour, but loved the eclecticism of the idea.

Although varieties of hop are internationally recognized, they still emerge with a different character depending upon the country in which they are grown. Hallertaus cultivated in Belgium are, for the example, the "secret" ingredient in one well-known speciality beer made in the United States. The Bohemian Saaz and the Northern Brewer were the parents of Record, a variety that was first grown in Belgium. This has some of the aroma of a Saaz or Hallertau, but a more assertive bitterness and fullness of flavour.

Although the Record might be regarded as the principal Belgian variety, Brewers' Gold is also grown. This hop, which has a sweetish perfume, originates from Britain. Belgian ale-brewers often use British varieties of hop, notably the earthy, oily, powerfully aromatic Golding of East Kent. This is both grown in Belgium and imported. In recent years, Belgian growers seem also to have favoured a variety called Challenger, scenty and clean, with suggestions of lemon-peel and quinine. Belgium grows fewer hops than Britain, but the latter is small in world terms. Britain is, though, noted for hops that perform well in ales. British hops have also been used to parent varieties in North America, Australasia, and Styrian Slovenia.

Hops like shelter, a temperate climate, with light rain and moist soil. They tend to thrive at fairly similar, and corresponding, latitudes in the Northern and Southern hemispheres, and they are grown in several other countries, including Japan and the Soviet Union.

The principal growing region in Belgium is still around Poperinge, and there is a smaller district around Asse and Aalst, between Ghent and Brussels.

Just off the Roman road from Boulogne to Cologne, and part of the lands of the abbey of St Omer until the French Revolution, the country town of Poperinge is keenly aware of its history. It has three Gothic churches, a British military cemetery, and the house where the philanthropic organisation Toc-H began, but most of all it is a hop town.

There are only 12,000 inhabitants, with another 8,000 in the adjoining five villages, but its population was doubled in the days when seasonal hop-pickers would arrive each September. Local engineers were active in pioneering mechanical methods of hop-picking, which were shown at the 1958 World Fair in Brussels. After more than 100 years as a weighhouse and pressing room for hops, a sturdy building in the town centre was assigned in 1975 to become a national museum of the industry (71 Gasthuisstraat). It is open during the holiday season (check hours with the local tourist board: tel 057-334081; fax 057-337581; e-mail: toerisme@poperinge.be; internet: http://www.poperinge.be).
The floors are still stained with the green resins of the hop cones, and the collection of equipment and photographs provides a vivid peep into the past.

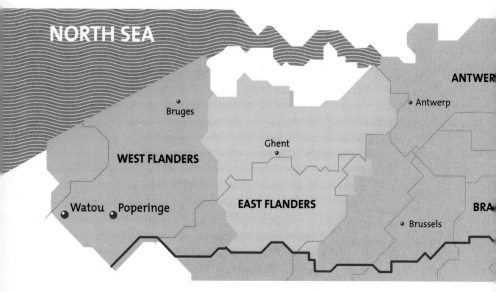

The far Western corner of Flanders is hop country. Poperinge is the „capital". Taste the shoots, and the beer, in Watou.

Poperinge's Palace Hotel, its dining room decorated with hop blossoms, has a hearty kitchen featuring local dishes, and about 100 beers (34 Ieper Straat; tel 057-333093/fax 3335350). In season, I once ate delicious jets d'houblon there. They were served as an intermediate course - an entrée in the European, rather than the American, sense. "Would you like the Beef Poperinge to follow?" I was asked. "Of course ..." This turned out to be beef garnished with hop shoots. Perhaps I should have gone for another local favourite, Hennepot, a casserole of rabbit, chicken and veal. The dessert was a further

Poperinge speciality, Tarte Mazarine, a very sweet, syrupy, cinnamon-flavoured cake similar to a rhum baba. Perhaps this confection was named after Cardinal Mazarin (1643-61), successor to Richelieu, at a time of French influence in the region.

For Poperinge's local crop, the Flemish language uses the word hop, which has Germanic origins, but the term Hommel (deriving from the Latin Humulus) is also employed locally, especially to describe the cone or blossom. This confuses visitors, as Hommel is also Flemish for bumble-bee. D'n Hommelzak is a tea-room at 10bis Paardenmarkt, in the centre of Poperinge, and d'Hommelkeete a stylish restaurant at 3 Hoge Noenweg, on the outskirts of the small town.

HOP COUNTRY / WATOU

Born and raised in Poperinge, Stefaan Couttenye spent his childhood vacations in Watou, where his great aunt had a butcher's shop. He grew up to be a chef, spending formative years in Antwerp, at the "Sir Anthony Van Dyck", a restaurant famous for its

Honouring the hop... the Couttenyes prepare to feed a hungry guest.

haute cuisine. In 1983, he returned to Watou, and opened a restaurant called t'Hommelhof, where he specialises in cuisine à la bière. The restaurant, which has cottage-like atmosphere, is in a building that was a brewer's house, on the main square (17 Watou Plein; tel. 057-388024; fax 388590).

Among many delights I have enjoyed there, I especially recall his interpretation of the classic Flemish fish soup Waterzooi, prepared with the coriander-tasting Watou's Witbier.

Lobster poached in white beer, with herbs...at the Hommelhof.

This beer is made by one of the town's three breweries, Van Eecke, which is just round the corner from the main square. The Van Eecke family has owned its brewery since the 1840s. It was founded as the estate brewery of a local chateau, and dates from 1642. A former brewery of a similar period stands opposite, now functioning as an art gallery.

Van Eecke's real speciality is a hoppy, golden-bronze, ale called Poperings Hommelbier. This beer is made from a blend of winter, summer and aromatic pale malts, at a starting density of 16 Plato; soft water, from the brewery's own well; Brewers' Gold and Hallertau hops, both grown in Poperinge; and top-fermented with a very attenuative yeast that precipitates quickly. It is primed with white sugar, and re-yeasted for a fermentation in the bottle. The finished beer has 7.5 per cent alcohol by volume and 40 units of bitterness (see THE HOP IN THE BREWERY), though it tastes lighter on both counts. Some drinkers feel, and I am inclined to agree, that it has a faintly honeyish yeast character - or is this thought deposited by the bumble bee? The beer certainly has a great deal of hop aroma and flavour, and is very refreshing and cleansing when served lightly chilled.

Hop country speciality...though the bitterness of the blossom is balanced by the honeyish yeast character.

There also seems to be a honeyish yeast note, and some wineyness, in the brewery's complex abbey-style beers, under the name Het Kapittel (the name means a "chapter" of monks). These beers are said originally to have been created to a recipe supplied by the Trappist monastery of Mont des Cats, just across the French border. It is believed that the monastery in France brewed until the beginning of this century, and it still makes cheese.

Instability in France at one stage led the monks of Mont des Cats to establish a refuge, called Notre Dame de St Bernardus, on the Belgian side of the border, along with a dairy farm. The monks made cheese, and developed a local market for it. When the brothers returned to France, a Flemish family of cheese-makers took over production, establishing a dairy in Watou. After World War II, the family turned their dairy into a brewery, also called St Bernardus. The stimulus for this was a request to produce beer for another Trappist abbey, St Sixtus, in nearby Westvleteren. This arrangement has now ended, and the St Bernardus brewery makes its own range of fruity, creamy, abbey-style beers. The brewery also incorporates a small but stylish bed-and-breakfast hotel (tel 057-388860).

The witch from the woods... riding a mashing fork at brewery De Bie.

Watou additionally has a tiny micro-brewery, called De Bie, making a dry, orangey, strong ale known as Helleketelbier (after a local

woods) and a sweeter, pruney, chocolatey one called Zatte Bie ("Drunk Bee" - a Dutch brewery uses the same epithet). De Bie's tasting room, Café d'Hellekapelle, opens on Friday evenings at 6.00 and weekend afternoons. The brewery can be visited on weekend afternoons (26 Stoppelweg; tel 057-388666).

On Watou's second square, De Kleine Markt, is a statue of a brewer, erected in the early 1980s, at a time when the whole Poperinge area seemed to be awakening to public interest in its heritage. Every three years (1999, 2002, 2005...), on the third weekend in September, a hop pageant is held in the town. On the other years, there is a hop-inspired event on a smaller scale at the same time, with a wide selection of brews, and regional cheeses. Once again, information is available from the tourist board. The local hotels, hostel, cottages and farms fill quickly, so arrangements should be made early.

Farmers also have their own private celebrations to mark the conclusion of a successful harvest. Wherever it is grown, the hop is very susceptible to blights and pests, and the farmers feel they have a permanent struggle against the Devil. At the end of the harvest, the devil somehow metamorphoses into a lovable rogue (rather like England's Guy Fawkes). Some farmers burn a straw figure called the "Hop Devil", and serve their harvest workers a ceremonial meal called a Hommelpap. The word Pap derives from a typical meal for small children, though this is not served. A statue of the Hopduvel stands in the town centre of Asse, in the more easterly growing region. The Hopduvel also gives his name to one of Belgium's best beer cafés, in Ghent (10 Rokerelstraat; tel. 09-225-3729).

THE HOP IN THE BREWERY

Only the cones of the hop are used by the brewer. They may be supplied in their natural form (pressed and dried, in sacks known as "pockets"), or compacted into pellets (vacuum-packed in foil, like coffee), or as an extract (a jam-like liquid, in cans). The cone is the simplest form, and some brewers feel that it is the best. In pelletized form, the cones are less exposed to air, and therefore to staleness through oxidation, and are easier to handle, but some brewers feel that the compacting diminishes the qualities of the leaves. Extract is even easier to handle, but is farthest away from the original cone.

When the hops are added to the boiling brew in the kettle, their flavours and aromas are taken up, and their additional qualities as a natural anti-infectant and clarifying agent come into play. Some brewers boil for only an hour, most for 90 minutes. Speciality beers may take a much longer boil.

Hops added at the beginning of the boil will confer the greatest dryness or bitterness. Those put in later will impart more aroma. Hops may be added in the kettle only once, or two or three times. If whole cones are used, the boiled brew will be run through a strainer to remove the leaves. Some brewers add further hops in the strainer. As the hot brew drains through them, it picks up further aromatics. When the brew has spent some days in fermentation vessels, and been moved on to maturation vessels, more hops may be added. This technique is known as "dry-hopping", and is intended further to enhance aroma. One or two brewers in Belgium use this method, though it is more common in Britain.

*Brewers like to cup their hands, rub the cones in their palms, and appraise
the aromas before approving the hops for use.*

Some brewers use the same hops at every stage, but most will choose different varieties for bittering and aroma. These are sometimes known as "kettle" hops and "finishing" hops. All of these variations in procedure will be based not only on the preferences of the brewer but also on the type of beer to be made. By using a formula based on the quantity of hops used, and their acid content, brewers can measure the bitterness of their beers according to an international scale. A very bland beer might have only 10 or 15 International Units of Bitterness. An assertively dry and full-flavoured beer could have 40, 50, 60 or even more.

Working brewers often choose a hoppy beer for their own consumption, but believe - perhaps because they have been told as much by their marketing colleagues - that the public prefers something blander. By making propaganda for bland beers, the brewers thus persuade the consumer that he or she should really be buying mineral water.

The Lambic family

Finos, Chardonnays? The most wine-like, and surprising, of beers.

Anyone who appreciates the fresh apple fruitiness of a New World Chardonnay; the grassy, stony, edge of a true, Burgundian, Chablis; the toastiness of Champagne; or the refreshing life-force of a yeasty fino sherry; should enjoy exploring the Lambic family of beers, the rare speciality of Belgium's Zenne Valley.

The sherry comparison might be most obvious in the hard-to-find unblended, barely-carbonated, Lambic. Flavours resembling those of the Chardonnay grape are more likely in the blended, sparkling, version known as Gueuze.

(Spellings vary: Geuze is also used. as are Lambik and Lambiek. The river is the Senne in French).

Neither Champagnes nor Chardonnays, but a range of classics...
examples of Gueuze at its finest.

"Hard but not harsh," says the wine-writer Hugh Johnson, describing the ideal Chablis.. Hard but not harsh; bone-dry, but not astringent. Drinkers who find Lambics too assertive may simply be suffering from the shock of a taste that they did not expect in a beer. Or they may be drinking a Lambic that is excessively acidic. Occasionally, a Lambic is too tart, but more examples have been blunted by sweetening. The best start soft, but harden toward an extraordinarily long finish. These are the Belgian brews that can most shock the consumer, and they are certainly the most wine-like.

Both fino sherry and Lambic are the products of fermentation by their own distinct cultures of wild yeasts. Like a fino sherry, a Lambic is a product that has been aged for some years yet is notable for its freshness of flavour. The Andalusians drink a small bottle of fino with fishy tapas, and knowing Belgians snack on a Lambic with sharp, soft, local cheeses and radishes. I once shared a fino with the famous "nose" Don Jose Ignacio Domecq, at the family's bodega in Jerez, and the conversation turned to my interest in beer. No sooner had beer been mentioned than Señor Domecq asked me if I was familiar with Lambic.

Not only are there similarities in the fermentation process between fino sherry and Lambic, and in colour perhaps between the palo cortado and the beer (when it is fully matured), but also in aroma and taste. In the Belgian magazine "Revue", in 1986, I found myself comparing the pinkish tinge of some Lambics with the Arbois wine of the Jura, described by A.J. Liebling in his classic "Between Meals" as, "the colour not of the rose but of an onion-peel, with russet and purple glints." I later learned that the grape of the Arbois, the Savaguin, collects a great deal of yeast, and is also used in the region's Vin Jaune, which is fermented with a "flor" yeast, like sherry.

Jean-Xavier Guinard, a North American brewing scientist and devotee of Lambic, finds similarities in taste and texture between the mature brew and the classic Jura wines. He takes up the theme a couple of times in his book "Lambic" (1990), one of a series on classic beer styles published by Brewers' Publications, of Boulder, Colorado. In his book, Guinard also quotes from an article I wrote in the American magazine "Zymurgy" in 1982. What I felt then, I still believe: "The Lambic family are not everybody's glass of beer, but no one with a keen interest in alcoholic drink would find them anything less than fascinating. In their "wildness" and unpredictability, these are exciting brews . At their best, they are the meeting point between beer and wine; at their worst, they offer a taste of history."

It is a family based on one type of brew, Lambic, but also including a blended version, called Gueuze; the sweetened Faro; and styles like Kriek and Framboise, in which cherries and raspberries are added. Between Belgium's two main languages, and the various dialects of Flemish, these names appear in a variety of spellings.

THE NAME LAMBIC

Much mystery surrounds the name of this most mysterious among beers. One explanation is that the name derives from that of Lembeek, a small town in the area of production.

Lembeek is at the point where a smaller river meets the Zenne. The "beek" part of the name is Flemish version of the German "Bach" or northern English "beck", meaning a stream, creek, or small river.
 The "lem" segment may be an old Flemish reference to the "lime" tree. This is supported by a shrine to the town's patron saint, Veronus (grandson of Charlemagne), in which he is shown holding a twig of lime. The theory is dented by the fact that the lime tree is usually known in Flemish as the linde (as in "linden"). It is more commonly accepted that the town is named after limey or loamy soil (leem). The "Lime Creek" theory has recently been challenged by a suggestion the first syllable was corrupted from Leen, a word referring to loans (English also has the word lien) and rights to property: the Lien on the Beck.

Lembeek was a Neolithic settlement on a piece of land almost encircled by a sharp bend in the river Zenne. The Celts protected this peninsular town by walling it off, and later it was an independent "city state" between the duchies of Brabant and Hainaut. During this period, Lembeek granted its farmers the unusual right to combine the brewing of beer with the distilling of genever gin. A farmer would have used the same part of his premises for both activities. Did the Spanish rulers in the 1500s and 1600s simply call such a premises a distillery - an alambic? Was that corrupted to Lambic? The earliest known written reference - in French, in 1791 - supports this theory.

There is an appealing thread to this notion. Distilling is said to have been developed by the Arabs and introduced by the Moors into Europe, and to have spread north from Spain to the Low Countries, where grain and juniper were first turned into gin. It is a tenuous thread, though. Yet another theory is that the name derives from Lambere, the Latin verb to sip, but that notion seems far fetched.

Lembeek had a Guild of Brewers 500 years ago, and became an important centre in the region of production of Lambic beers - the Zenne Valley and the countryside to the west, known as Payottenland. The Zenne, which rises in Hainaut, sneaks under Brussels, eventually joining the river Dijle, which flows into the Schelde.

Along the river, and in the country districts to either side of Brussels, farmers grew barley and wheat, and provided beer for the growing metropolis. Like all brewers in medieval times, they used spontaneous fermentation, and they never abandoned that method. This part of Brabant is perhaps the most conservative corner of the brewing world, even more traditionalist than Bavaria (with yeasts that make phenolic wheat beers), Berlin (with lactic fermentations) or Burton (with its technique of linked wooden barrels like a sherry solera).

The beer did not all come from Lembeek, but neither was the first Kentucky whisky made in Bourbon County, or the greatest blue cheese of England produced in Stilton itself.

Lembeek's brewer-distillers were gradually driven out of business by restrictions on spirits, culminating in tough laws in the early 1900s, at a time when the whole of the developed world was going through a temperance phase.

The restrictions on gin did not benefit Lambic. Spontaneous fermentation produces beers of modest alcohol content, and the disenfranchised spirit-drinkers turned to stronger styles like Trappists and Scotch Ales, helping Belgium gain its reputation for potent brews.
Today, Lembeek, little more than a town-square perched on top of a hill, has 4,000 people and, down by the river, one brewery, run by the revivalist Frank Boon. As a city-state, Lembeek had its own army, and four "regiments" have been maintained, the distinction passing from father to son. These men are paid a small stipend by the municipality to lead a ritual on the Monday after Easter. At 3.0 in the morning; they blow bugles to alert the citizens, who must assemble at 8.00 to walk the bounds of the town. The religious start from the church, the less devoted from the town hall, and the walk rambles for 20 kilometres, stopping at each café in the town. Where cafés once stood, the householders man tables loaded with Lambic and genever gin, purchased communally and dispensed free. The consumption of these precious fluids was held to ward off bubonic plague and rabies, though the pilgrims also kiss a shrine to St Veronus to make doubly sure. This being Belgium, the walk stops for lunch.

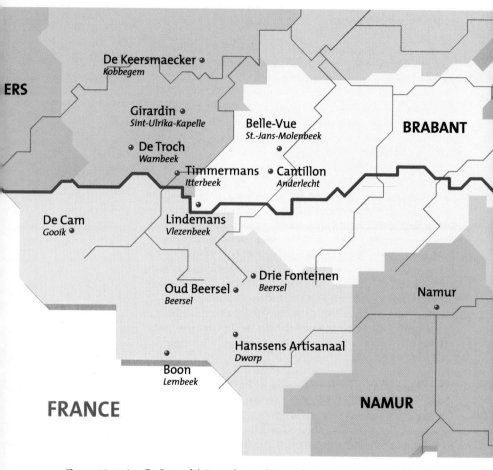

The most Easterly breweries in the Lambic region are Belle-vue and Cantillon, on the edge of Brussels. The region fans out westward, within Flemish Brabant.

To Brussels' East, the tradition of brewing Lambic in the Zenne Valley has died, though the beers in blended form are still served in the cafés of Jezus-Eik to strollers in the forest of Soignes on a Sunday afternoon. Today's production area is on the Western side of the city, from Anderlecht to Beersel, Lembeek and wrapping round Brussels in a district known as Payottenland (deriving from the Flemish word for "patriot").

Bruegel lived on this side of Brussels, in its Flemish Old Town, and wandered in the villages of Payottenland. The church in "The Parable of the Blind" is clearly Sint-Anna-Pede, between Itterbeek and Schepdaal. Nor, 400 years later, could anyone fail to recognise the Flemings of "The Peasant Dance" or "The Wedding Feast" enjoying a beer in one of the many cafés of the valley, probably within sight of Brussels' skyline.

In "The Wedding Feast", beer of a strawy-russet colour is shown being decanted from the type of stoneware crock still often used for Lambic today. The same crocks feature in "The Peasant Dance". There are similar images in the paintings of the aptly-named artist Brouwer, who came along in the next century, and no style of beer features more pervasively in Flemish popular art, literature and folklore than the Lambic family. (Nor, arguably, is any theme more central in Flemish culture than the brewing and consuming of beer of any kind).

The beer in Bruegel's „Peasant Dance" is Lambic... and Flemish faces are still recognisable 400 years later.

These themes are explored in a 1955 treatise on "Gueuze and Humanism" by the poet Hubert Van Herreweghen. This begins with a reference to Erasmus, "the great citizen of Anderlecht, great European and great humanist"... and is within a page or two citing Bruegel.
The signposted Bruegel Route is popular with explorers of the Lambic region, but several of the breweries it once passed have closed. There is talk of re-drawing the route to be more brewery-friendly.

None of the breweries is more than 10 or 12 miles from Brussels, yet Payottenland switches from the urban to the suburban to flat farmlands and wooded folds in sudden hills. Every now and then, a Lambic brewery, sometimes disused and a miniature item of industrial archaeology, makes its distinct mark on the landscape. Perhaps the brewery name, and the word Lambic, partially survive in a painted sign on the brickwork. There are ten Lambic breweries in the traditional district; three Lambic blenders; and two breweries outside the district (both in West Flanders) which produce beers in this style.

HOW LAMBIC IS MADE

Lambic is a type of wheat beer, and that distinction already places it among a group of speciality styles. As compared to wheat beers elsewhere in the world, it is unusual in that the wheat used is not malted. No one seems sure why. Perhaps the farmer-brewers simply found they could make beer without this step. That is possible because, as in all wheat beers, a proportion of malted barley is also used - and the latter grain provides the necessary enzymes. The local, small-grained, Brabant wheat is sometimes used. For many years, the coarser winter wheats and barley were preferred, but brewers have recently been switching to summer varieties, with a view to achieving less astringent flavours.

Grain mills are wonderfully durable machines. Timmermans still has some very early equipment, driven by pulleys (facing page).

The ratio of wheat to barley has varied over the years, but was eventually formalised in law. The definition of Lambic was set out in a series of Belgian Royal Decrees in the 1960s and 1970s. These determined that Lambic must be made from at least 30 per cent unmalted wheat; at a gravity of not less than 11 Plato (1044).

Some Lambic brewers use up to 40 per cent wheat and the remainder malted barley. Over the years, some have also added proportions of corn, rice, or even rye.

Lambic beers are typically made from an original density of 1047-1054 (11.75-13.5 Plato, 12.7 is the classic level), and in their unblended form usually emerge with an alcohol content of around 5.0-6.5 by volume. As with many types of beer, much higher gravities were used in the past. A variety of mashing regimes, some very long and elaborate, are used to extract the fermentable sugars from the grains. The classic Lambic method involves making two mashes, and separately heating each in the kettle before they are filtered. A milky-white wort is produced rather than the clear type that is expected by conventional brewers. While these techniques were no doubt arrived at empirically, they are partly necessitated by the use of unmalted wheat and the long fermentation and maturation.

There are further peculiarities at the boiling stage. Far more hops are added than in a conventional brew, perhaps six times as many. Perversely, these are hops that have been aged for up to three years. The object of aging the hops is to diminish their aroma, flavour and bitterness: the very attributes for which they are valued by conventional brewers. In this instance, the hops are being used for their secondary purpose, to protect the beer against unwanted infections and excessive oxidation. In this role, the choice of variety is not especially important. A variety long-gone local variety was once used, but I have seen Belgian-grown Brewers' Gold, British Fuggles and Bohemian Saaz, among others, in Lambic breweries.

While conventional brewers typically boil for an hour and a half, the makers of Lambic have a much more exhaustive process. In their case, the boil can last for more than three hours, and sometimes as many as six.

Then comes the most critical procedure. The boiled wort is cooled in a shallow, open vessel in the loft of the brewery. This vessel, made of copper or steel, will take up most of the floor space in the loft. It will be perhaps seven or eight meters long, five or six wide, but only 30-50 cm deep, so that a large volume of the brew is exposed to the atmosphere. Nor is the vessel filled to its full depth. The room will have windows that can be opened, and louvred vents. Once, all brewers cooled their wort in this way, and the louvred vents can often be seen on the apex of their pitched roofs. In time, brewers learned that this was a perilous method. If the wort remained in the vessel until it was really cool, there was the danger of intrusion by wild yeasts. Conventional brewers sealed their cooling areas, shortened the period in which the wort remained in the vessel, or augmented or replaced this system with heat-exchangers. Today, most use heat-exchangers: enclosed systems, in which the wort is run through pipes jacketed with cold water or a cooling fluid.

Geuze brewing in Bellegem: Omer-Jean van der Ghinste stands proud before his foudres.

The Lambic brewers took the opposite view: they worked with nature, rather than fighting it. They welcomed the wild yeasts, and let them help determine the character of the beer.

In a Lambic brewery, windows and vents are left open, and even the odd tile may be allowed to go missing, in order to allow in the wild yeasts. If he is worried that there is too little activity, the brewer might adjust the vents. As one brewer put it to me: "We can play with the wind." The wort spends the night there, and the yeasts enter and have their way with it.

Some Lambic brewers also hesitate to replace their roofs, or any part of their fabric, in case they disturb resident wild yeasts or other microflora that give a house character to their beers. Every beer, of any type, has a "house" character, but none more than the Lambics.

Once the wort has cooled, it will begin to ferment. The simplest way for the brewer to handle this is to fill the wort into casks and let nature get on with the job. Once, all brewers proceeded in more or less this fashion. As brewers learned to pitch their own yeasts, more controlled systems were developed, like the linked casks of the "Union" system in Burton or the larger stone troughs of Tadcaster (those two towns being brewing centres in England). Today, most brewers use stainless steel vessels, with cooling systems that will control the progress of the fermentation. Very few breweries anywhere in the world still ferment in wood, and only the Lambic-makers in free-standing casks. Here again, the situation developed naturally. In no major city do the Romance and Germanic cultures meet quite as they do in Brussels. It is a city that imports and consumes a great deal of wine. In the days when the wine came in casks, these were snapped up by the local brewers for use as fermentation vessels. There is a parallel in importation of sherry to the English city of Bristol, and the selling-on of empty casks for the maturation of Scotch whisky. Just as a whisky warehouse in Scotland will contain casks bearing the legends Domecq, Gonzalez Byass or Osborne, so the evidence of Port, Rioja or Muscat may be stencilled on the barrel-ends in a Lambic brewery.

Today, less wine is shipped in the barrel, but Lambic-makers can still buy casks that have been used in vinification. As winemakers begin to use more stainless steel, that releases wood to the Lambic-brewers. Regrettably, the closure of Lambic breweries has also released wood for the survivors. There are also coopers in the industry to repair vintage casks.

I have seen casks 150 years old in Lambic breweries, but even those acquired recently soon have their own population of resident microflora. These, too, play an essential part in fermentation. In a brewery that began life as a farm, I have seen more than two thousand casks, divided between 15 cellars and attics. The favoured size is 250 litres (the "Brussels ton"), a fat, short, cask designed to deceive the dipsticks of excisemen during the French revolutionary period. In this size, there is a relatively large surface area of flor yeast in proportion to the beer. The ton seems to produce complex Lambics, though each vessel will perform differently according to its exact shape and age. When Lambic maker Frank Boon gave me tastings from a variety of casks, one seemed lemony, another grapefruit-like; one flowery, another nutty, a third honeyish. The blending of these flavours is central to the art of Lambic.

Like the makers of Port, the Lambic brewers have casks called pipes, which hold 600-700 litres. Some breweries have "foudres" of 3,000-10,000 litres, but these can mature the beer too slowly. One way round that is to keep tapping and topping up as though it were part of a sherry solera. This is also a means to stop the wood from drying. Foudres produce elegant Lambics, according to Boon, In a blended Gueuze, the foudre attacks and the ton rounds.

The casks lie in long cellars or galleries, sometimes cloaked with moulds and cobwebs. Some brewers are hesitant to clean up too much in case they disturb an essential guest. Others argue that the

The Lambic brewer chalks his own code on the barrel ends so that he knows what he has in stock...but his own samplings finally determine the blend.

important wild yeasts are attracted in the open cooler, or resident in the casks, and that the cellars or galleries should be kept clean.

Although the Lambic-makers differ widely on the extent of cleaning that is desirable, they agree in regarding as their best friends what other brewers would view as the creatures of nightmare. One Lambic brewer told me that white moulds on the casks had a favourable influence, but black ones on the walls were insalubrious.

When I showed galleries full of cobwebs at Lindemans in a television documentary, many brewers were astonished at the sight. Although I was well acquainted with such scenes at Lambic breweries, I also remembered the whisky writer Philip Morrice saying that the Linkwood distillery, in Scotland, had once forbidden the removal of spiders' webs. In his book, Guinard talks of Lambic brewers who consider the killing of a spider to be a crime. Why? Because spiders are predators of flies. Fruit-flies are attracted to yeasty wort, and often bring to it unwanted micro-flora. I once noticed fruit flies in a brewery in an apple-growing region of the United States. The brewer said they were a dreadful nuisance, but gave me an odd look when I suggested he install some spiders.

Traditional Lambic-makers do not brew in summer, because the wild inoculation of the wort at that time would be just too unpredictable, and the beer would be sour. They stop sometime between March and May, and re-start in September or October. In the traditional manner, they regard the summer as the time of storage, continuing fermentation and maturation. As the only brewers who still observe this seasonal regime, they measure their fermentations in "summers". Some Lambics stay in the cask for just one summer, at which stage they are still regarded as "young". A Lambic of two or three summers is regarded as mature. Some breweries have far older Lambics among their stocks.

It is not unknown for Lambic to be served when it is less than three months old, but that is not ideal. Beer brewed at the end of the winter brewing season, in March, will make good young Lambic in July or August, the leisurely months when people like to stroll in the villages around Brussels and stop for a drink. Young Lambic can be straw-like in colour and sometimes has a reddish haze (described as Vos, indicating "foxy"). It is often very assertive, perhaps lactic (like a sharp soft cheese), acidic, cidery and apple-like. It is sharply refreshing, though also drying, and arouses the appetite.
Lambic is dry because it is so exhaustively fermented. Paul de Neve, of the brewing family, once described it to me as "the world's first low-carbohydrate beer". This is just as well, since a glass can make you want to eat a horse. Conveniently, it is possible to do that in Belgium.
Mature Lambic has much more subtle colours, sometimes including the onion-like, pinkish-purple tones. It is mellower, more rounded and complex, with fruity (sometimes rhubarby), notes, that hint of Chablis, and its characteristically sherryish flavours. There is no more enigmatic drink.

While most beer (and wine) has a primary and a secondary fermentation, Lambic has at least five phases, forming a chain reaction, including the development of lactic and acetic characteristics.

This helps explain why it is so complex in bouquet, palate and finish. Many brewers elsewhere have traditionally regarded the choice of grains, malts and hops as the dominant factor in the character of their beer, but the influence of yeast and fermentation behaviour on aromas and background flavours is increasingly being appreciated. No beer is as complex in this respect as Lambic.

Are the cobwebs essential? Some Lambic brewers maintain that they are. Others disagree.

While most beer-makers would regard strains of only the carlsbergensis or cerevisiae types as permissible brewing yeasts, at least five major groups of wild yeasts and other microflora are found in Lambic breweries. In one beer, these major groups may manifest themselves in 15 or 20 forms. So far, 86 strains of wild yeast or other microflora have been identified in Lambic beers. These notably

include four oxidative yeasts that form a film on the fermenting beer, similar to the flor on sherry. There are also wild yeasts of the Brettanomyces family, which was once associated with British styles such as Stock Ale, Barley Wine and strong Porter, traditionally aged for long periods in wood. Brettanomyces impart aromas that have been described as "horsey", "leathery" and "blanket-like". They also work very slowly, fermenting more thoroughly than other yeasts, and potentially making leaner beers. About a dozen strains of Brettanomyces have been identified in the Zenne Valley, and two are taxonomically identified with the district: bruxellensis and lambicus.

"Brettanomyces bruxellensis is the richest niche in the micro-biological spectrum of Lambic fermentation," I was once told by Professor Hubert Verachtert, who has done much work on the subject with colleagues at the University of Leuven. Their work is densely argued, yet Professor Verachtert still had a wry smile for many of my questions: "That is a factor we don't quite understand yet ... that might necessitate another Phd study ..." The Zenne Valley still holds its mysteries.

Can a valley so close to a large and partly industrial city retain its own ecology of micro-life? Perhaps only in the sense that everywhere has its own unique eco-system. Certainly every brewery creates its own habitat, and nowhere more obviously than in Lambic country. As casks change hands, and wort is sold to fermenters or blenders, even as brewers visit one another, perhaps the industry has developed its own ecology.

It is possible to make spontaneously-fermenting beer elsewhere, and this has been done on an experimental basis, but the results have recognisably not been the Lambic of the region. While the Lambic-makers struggle in the market at large, there is a growing connoisseur interest in their beers. One or two brewers outside Belgium have attempted to make beers in this vein.

Why, without the heritage, would any brewer wish to practice such a difficult and unpredictable art? For the challenge, perhaps? The

most frightening difficulty is that of accommodating wild yeasts in a brewery that also produces more conventional beers.
Just across the Dutch border, the respected Gulpener brewery, near Maastricht, has since the mid 1980s made a mildly Lambic-tasting beer called Mestreechs Ajt a separate premises.

A similar solution was found in England, where the Samuel Smith brewing company had long ago acquired a brewery called Melbourn, in the historic town of Stamford, Lincolnshire. Brewing

The three tuns are a traditional sign of a brewery...
but especially appropriate if the brew is Lambic.

on the Stamford site may date from the 1600s, and the present premises were built in 1825 but closed in 1974. The brewery has an open kettle, to which Samuel Smith's added an open cooler. In 1992, Lambic from De Troch, of Belgium, was sprayed over oak chips at Melbourn to introduce Zenne Valley yeasts to the atmosphere. They seem to have made themselves at home in this Lowland brewery, with its wooden structures and open beams. The beers made there, flavoured with fruit and juices, have a Belgian accent but a very soft acidity. They are labelled simply as fruit beers.

In the U.S., the Seven Barrel brewpub, in Lebanon, New Hampshire, has used Brettanomyces and lactic cultures to produce a rhubarb-tasting Sour Mash Wheat Beer. In Cleveland, Ohio, the Diamondback brewpub has used raw wheat and yeast harvested from Boon bottles, to make a fruity brew aged in old wine casks.

It is in the style of a Lambic but identified as "Gueuze". In the Swiss-American town of New Glarus, the local micro-brewery makes a powerful fruit beer using cherries grown around the Brussels, Wisconsin, and cultures from Belgium. There have been several similar experiments elsewhere. Straight Lambic is very dry, with very little carbonation. Traditionally, brewers sold it in this form, in wooden casks, directly to local cafés. The outlets cellared it, and sometimes aged it further. In the cellar, the cask would be tapped into a stoneware jug, which would be fetched up to the bar to serve the customers. Few cafés want to be bothered with this, so I is almost impossible to identify cafés where straight Lambic can reliably be found. Some brewers are now beginning to realise that its elusiveness is bad for business, so tide may soon turn. Other brewers no longer supply Lambic in this form, saying there is no demand for it. They may continue to produce genuine Lambic, but exclusively as a component for Gueuze: blended to create a secondary fermentation and sparkle.

THE APPELLATION 'OLD LAMBIC'

The Royal Decrees that determined the minimum proportions of wheat also insisted upon spontaneous fermentation, and minimum levels of acidity.

In 1991, further efforts to define Lambic were made by the Belgian consumerist organisation The Objective Beer Tasters (Objectieve Bierproevers). This group and voluntary organisations in other countries are members of The European Beer Consumers' Union, which in 1991 started to award its own "appellation controlée" to traditional beers in the Lambic family. Products awarded this soubriquet were permitted to use it on their labels. To qualify, a Lambic had be made in the classic way. It had to be fermented only with wild yeasts, and they had to include Brettanomyces Bruxellensis and Lambicus. A Gueuze must be a blended entirely of Lambic, and must have re-fermentation in the bottle, with no filtration, artificial carbonation, sweetening or pasteurisation. This was the precursor to a ruling in 1997, defining "Old" beers of the Lambic family, based on an application by the Belgian Confederation of Brewers to the European Union. The word "old" refers to the method, which is set out as above, but there is also a provision regarding the age of the beers. Any blended member of the family identified in Flemish as Oude, or French as Vieille or Vieux (depending on the grammar of the label) must contain a proportion (unspecified) of Lambic three years old and has an average age of not less than one year.

GUEUZE, THE CHAMPAGNE OF BELGIUM

The soubriquet "The Champagnes of the Beer World" is often applied in general to the tart, refreshing styles of beer that can be made from wheat. The term Méthode Champenoise is sometimes informally borrowed by brewers whose beer has a further fermentation in the bottle. Just as the wine-makers in the Champagne region have made that style of fermentation their speciality, so have Belgian brewers. Comparisons with Champagne can be applied on one or both counts to many Belgian beers, but none more than the Lambic family's sparkling Gueuze.

Being Lambic in origin, this is a wheat beer. It is made by the blending of two or more Lambics to create a secondary fermentation and a Champagne-like sparkle. Sometimes the words Lambic and Gueuze are hyphenated, especially if the product is being served from the cask. This may have been an early form, made with the intention of turning the rather flat Lambics into a sparkling drink. (The British add sugar primings to their cask ales for the same reason, and the Germans Kräusen with wort). It was when they bottled the result that the Belgians truly discovered what an elegant drink a blend of Lambics can be, and today that is the classic manifestation of Gueuze. Because the fermentation builds up considerable pressure, Gueuze is put into the same bottles as are used for Champagne.

THE NAME GUEUZE

It is pronounced almost like cursor, though for such an artisanal product that seems an inappropriately high-tech mnemonic. The word Gueuze may derive from the same root as gas and geyser, and simply refer to the possible consequences of tapping a cask or opening a sparkling bottle, and thus releasing a great amount of carbon dioxide. (In the United States, there is a similar story about Steam Beer).

Another suggestion is that the name derives from political pressure and uprisings in Payottenland against Spanish, or in favour of Dutch, rule. One account specifically pins the name on a Mayor of Lembeek who was politically a Liberal (a "Geus") and who is said to have pioneered the adaptation of the Méthode Champenoise to Lambic beer. This is recorded as having happened in 1870, at which point Belgium had for some decades been an independent country. Coincidentally, Kir (originally white Burgundy and today often, royally, Champagne, with crème de cassis or framboise) is named after a resistance hero who was the Mayor of Dijon.

A much earlier reference, in the 1600s, indicates that Lambic brewers already had some means of naturally carbonating their beers. There is also a suggestion that beer was the drink of the peasants, who were likely to be Gueux in their political sympathies, while the ruling class drank wines from France or Spain.

That most sparkling of brews...only a Champagne bottle can hold it.

The blending of wines to make Champagne pre-dated Dom Pérignon, in the late 1600s, and by the early 1800s, the Widow Cliquot had already developed the means of remuage and dégorgement, which have yet to come to Gueuze, though there have been experiments along these lines in Belgium.

GUEUZE: A BLENDED BEER

The characteristics of the Lambics will be carried over to the Gueuze, but the further fermentation will have created a greater complexity and finesse - as well, of course, as the sparkle. A naturally-carbonated drink can be matured for some time in a cask, but it will be better contained in glass, and Gueuze is usually given some bottle age before it is served. A true Gueuze is dry, tart and fruity, and several have a toasty aroma reminiscent of some Champagnes. Because of the fermentation in the bottle, its alcohol content by volume should be marginally higher than that of the original Lambics, usually around the 5.5 mark.

The choice of Lambics is critical to the palate of the finished product, but also to the functioning of the fermentation in the bottle. The young Lambic in the blend will have more residual sugar, while the old will have developed some interesting yeasts during its chain of fermentations. Having undergone at least five overlapping stages of fermentation (employing at least ten types of yeast

No other style of beer is matured in the bottle for such long periods, or on such a scale, as Gueuze....cellars at Boon.

and microflora) in the cask, the Lambics when blended will proceed through a further three phases, in which four or five of the original yeasts and microflora will again play an important part. Small wonder that these beers are so complex.

While blending is normal in the production of Champagne (and other drinks like Cognac and Scotch Whisky), it is unusual in the making of beer. A big brewer may blend batches to achieve consistency, but not to impart character. One or two British products, including Newcastle Brown Ale, and several Flemish specialities, are made by blending different beers, but not for the purpose of creating a further fermentation.

The Lambic brewer is not only unique in trying to work with spontaneous fermentation but also in his variation on the Méthode Champenoise, in the production of Gueuze. Even the Champagne-maker adds yeast and priming sugar.
Unlike any other brewer, the Lambic-maker has to consider what purpose he should put each cask. Should it be sold as unblended Lambic and, if so, young or old? Or should it be a component of a Gueuze - and, again, at what age? In general, the casks that seem to be developing best will be kept longest. Some brewers feel strongly that the beers which start out best are those brewed in the cool weather of January and February, when the wild yeasts are at their most restrained. How those beers perform subsequently will be in part determined by the weather over the next year or so. There are good and bad years for Lambic: the "vintages" of grain may not vary critically, but the temperatures in maturation do.

Other factors will include the origin and size of the casks into which a beer has been filled, and even their location within the cellars and attics of the brewery. These are factors that also concern, for example, producers of Single Malt Scotch. There are many analogies in the crafts that produce very traditional, artisanal and individualistic drinks. None of these crafts is more esoteric than the making of Lambic and Gueuze beers.

Beyond all the considerations of temperature and wood lies the unpredictable: yeast is a living organism, a life-force, and its behaviour can never be relied upon even in the most conventional of breweries. The proportion of young Lambic to old varies. About 70-30 is quite common, though such a high proportion can produce an excessively lactic Gueuze. The more old Lambic that is used, the greater aroma and, depth and length. A classic Gueuze might have only 15 per cent young Lambic.

The Lambic may be centrifuged or filtered to remove cask sediment, and dead and excess yeast, but sufficient live cells will be left for the further fermentation. How many casks go to make one blend may depend upon the style of Gueuze to be made, and the equipment at the brewery. One brewer told me he always had a

The full range of classic Gueuze is available among 350 beers at the De Heeren van Liedekercke, run by the family De Four. Joost (left) is the beer expert, his brother Tom an inventive exponent of cuisine a la bière. Their pub-restaurant, Denderleeuw, is out of the way but definitely worth the detour.

coupage of between 40 and 50 casks - coincidentally, the same number of Single Malts goes into some blended whiskies. The blending will take place in a large wooden tun or metal tank, and the melange will then be bottled for anything from five or six to 18 months' maturation at the brewery. The bottles are racked exactly as in wine cellars. Not only does a Lambic brewery have many rooms full of casks stacked on their side, it also has cellars full of bottles.

Because some breweries are allowed to retain mould and damp, makers of Gueuze in the recent past preferred not to label their bottles. The labels were inclined to become grubby, or peel. Traditionally, the brewers simply dabbed a little whitewash on the bottle to indicate which side has been uppermost during maturation. Whenever the bottle had been handled, it had been kept the same way up, so that the natural sediment, mainly yeast, would remain undisturbed. Today, it will be labelled: as Old Gueuze.

A sign of a good "vintage" is the way in which the yeast has settled against the side of the bottle during maturation. If the yeast has been working well, it will have formed a shape resembling a fish-bone. A good secondary fermentation will create small, persistent, bubbles, like the bead in Champagne, and a character that is brisk but not aggressive.
In a good café or restaurant, the bottle will be carefully cradled on its side, and brought gently to the table. Cafés and restaurants often cellar Old Gueuze for a further two or three years. At that extreme, some of the beer in the bottle could be seven or eight years old. Some private individuals like to keep their bottles for 18 months before opening them. I have sampled a Gueuze of 45 years. It was surprisingly soft and well-balanced, but with an intense fino character and remorseless dryness in the finish. It was totally flat.

FARO, THE RUSTIC WINE OF BELGIUM

Just as France, Italy and Spain have their rough, rustic, wines, so all brewing nations once had traditions of beers that were quickly and inexpensively made, relatively low in alcohol, and intended for everyday refreshment. These beers could be consumed in large quantities, and were suited to times when manual work was more widespread than it is, today. Some were specially associated with harvest times. Others were high in residual sugar, or sweetened, as a as though to replace energy. In some countries, these were known as "running beers", as distinct from "stock beer"; the one was made quickly, to be drunk immediately; the other, with more alcohol, was stored for long periods as a provision. The two might also be used to make blends..

Faro was big before World War I, but by the 1920s, brewers were mounting this remarkably early example of generic advertising. each brewery over-printed its own name.

Like some rough-and-ready wines (or comparable dishes, such as pasta, fish and chips or hamburgers), the traditionally inexpensive beers can often be very enjoyable.

In the early and mid 1800s, the Lambic family of beers were emphatically the local brews of Brussels, and the version that served as a running beer (the British might say "session beer") was Faro. This style is greatly celebrated in Belgian folklore, and was obviously much appreciated, even if Baudelaire was famously scatological about it.

Faro was sometimes darkened and sweetened with candy sugar or molasses, and on occasion spiced. In the days when it was an everyday beer, it would have been served as an unpasteurised draught, but its turnover would have been sufficiently fast to prevent the sugar fermenting out, or the beer becoming very sour. The cask would have been exhausted within a day.
The distinction between "running beers" and "stock beers" often rests on a very basic process. When a brewer extracts the "juice" from his

grain, he does so by running warm water through it. The first time he runs the water through, he obtains a rich extract. Some speciality beers are made only from these "first runnings". Weaker beers may be made from second and third runnings. (Some Italian espresso bars do the same: offering a choice of "first pull" or second). Faro was originally a blend including the third runnings. A beer made only from the third runnings was known as Mars. This term may have had its origins in the idea of drinking lighter, more refreshing, beers in spring.

Between the late 1800s and the two World Wars, Faro lost its dominance to more conventional (and stable) ales of what might broadly be regarded as a Belgian-British type, and lagers of a Bohemian and Bavarian style. There were also later fashions for the Dortmund and Danish types of lagers. When Faro became less popular, and turnover

dropped, the beer would sometimes go sour beyond its normal. One remedy was for the bar-keeper to hang into it strings of candy sugar. This agent of sweetening, and secondary fermentation, came in a very convenient form. String had earlier been suspended in extract of sugar-beet so that the crystals would form. This is how candy-sugar is traditionally made. Today, the odd café still provides candy sugar and a small tool called a stoemper with which to

Lambic luminaries gather for a book launch. The publication of „Lambi(e)k en Geuze", by Jef Van den Steen, marked a time of renewal in the industy. The beer was soon served.

crush it (like the muddler used in a cocktail bar).

Faro still exists, but somewhat vestigially. With its Lambic acidity balanced by candy-sugar, or sometimes dark malts, it can have some of the characteristics of a sweet sherry. In the traditional Lambic district, examples have in recent years been made by Boon (which has taken a special interest in the style, Cantillon, De Troch, Drie Fonteinen, Lindemans and Timmermans.

Cafés have also been known to blend their own Faro variations. The English counterpart to Faro would by Mild ale. When it was more commonplace, Mild was often served half-and-half with Bitter ale. Irish Dry Stout with ale, a "Back and Tan", would be another analogy Or Irish ale with Barley Wine. In the world of wine, several regions blend brandy and fresh grape juice to make what is variously known as a Pineau, a Ratafia or a Mistelle.

THE NAME FARO

Faro is the name of a town in Portugal. Troops from that region of Iberia were a part of Spanish rule in Belgium. Did they bring with them the dark, sherryish, wine of Faro? Or did they remember it when they saw the dark, sherryish, beer of Brussels? Perhaps the occupying elite drank the Iberian wine, while "The Faro of the People" was the local beer. Such a self-deprecating soubriquet would be typical of those people. That is the most recent theory on the origins of the beer's name. Or was the designation perhaps derived in the same period from the Latin farina, meaning flour, to describe a "wine" produced from grain? In the same way, the British have the term "Barley Wine", though for a very strong beer. In modern Spanish, faro means a light or, colloquially, a bright idea. The British have an expression for becoming drunk: "Getting lit-up". Perhaps that is a clue.

LAMBIC BREWERS AND BLENDERS, WITH TASTING NOTES

The best news in the world of Lambic in recent years has been the establishment of a new brewery, at Drie Fonteinen (previously a blender, café and restaurant); a new blender, De Cam; and the emergence of new generations willing to carry on brewing at Oud Beersel and blending at Hanssens. These four producers, together with Boon, De Keersmaeker, De Troch, Lindemans and Timmermans, are members of a new Guild of Lambic Brewers (Hoge Raad voor Ambachtelijke Lambikbieren, known by the acronym HORAL).

The Belle-Vue ("BV") brewery has endless cellars, but the beer is virtually impossible to find unblended.

Among its activities are a biennial Tour de Gueuze, in which buses circulate between member breweries. In 2000, HORAL also collaborated with the Province of Flemish Brabant in the publication of the book "Lambi(e)k en Geuze", by Jef Van den Steen. This small, illustrated, book, initially published in Flemish, also contains recipes for dishes prepared with Lambic beers, and a short essay on the region.

The very conservative Girardin brewery, and the purists of Cantillon have yet to join HORAL. Because its true Lambic beers are so restricted in availability, and its sales efforts dominated by non-traditional brews, Belle-Vue has not been able to join. HORAL also takes a conservative view of geography: the two West Flanders brewers are not considered as meeting that qualifications.

Geuze Boon, with its gingery spiciness, can stand up (or even lie down) to a carpaccio of of wood pigeon. This combination was devised by chef Karel De Wolf, of De Snip, in Waasmunster, East Flanders.

BELLE-VUE

Where Brussels embraces the neighbourhood of Molenbeek-St Jean, the largest traditional Lambic brewery, built around the time of the First World War, is a landmark. The brewery is on a canal (43 Quai du Hainaut; tel. 02-412-4411), but is also in the valley of the river Zenne.

Belle-Vue was a mass-market label before the brewery was acquired by Interbrew, at the beginning of the 1990s, and is now even more widely available. The international giant has made some welcome, if small gestures toward the beer-lover. There is now a guest bar, in the former stables. It offers a draught beer, with a low carbonation, described as Lambic. This is actually a blend of four or five Lambics, most of them young but some up to five years old, sweetened with candy sugar and served without a great deal of further fermentation. It starts sweet, but has some good Lambic flavours. A bottled product called Sélection Lambic is in fact a Gueuze (it has been given a secondary fermentation, to create a more evident carbonation), with an older average age and no sweetening. It has much more attack, and a very drying finish.

Beers fermented and matured in Molenbeek's many thousands of tuns, pipes and foudres (some made of chestnut, rather than the more usual oak) are quite hard, with a touch of oakiness, some evocatively musty cellar notes and an aromatic hint of mandarin-skin. Some of these vessels yield wonderful Lambics. Unfortunately, almost all of them are blended with much less distinguished beers produced at Belle-Vue's 1970s brewery not far away in Zuun, where Brussels meets St Pieters Leeuw. These blends, the widely available versions of Belle-Vue, are sweetened and pasteurised. They are light in flavour, and sweet, though they do have some late, dry, tartness.

Shirt-sleeve brewer Jean-Pierre Van Roy is a doughty campaigner for traditional Lambic and Gueuze, and very much a maverick in the industry.

BOON

In Lembeek itself. Its origins were on a site that had accommodated a farmhouse brewery and distillery as far back as 1680. in 1977, the owner, René De Vits blended Lambics In 1977, he retired and sold his business to Frank Boon, then a blender. With Frank Boon, I met Mr De Vits in 1986, and he was still wearing the leather apron of a brewer, and living in his former café. He died in 1995.

Meanwhile, Boon had moved to a more spacious building, a former iron foundry closer to the river Zenne, and began to brew. He now runs the brewery as part of the Palm group.

Although, like almost all Belgians, Boon has family connections in the brewing industry, he came in as an outsider, having developed a great interest in beer during his student days. When he entered the industry, breweries were closing due to lack of succession. Either the owners had no offspring, or their children did not fancy such hard work for such modest rewards. No beer takes as long to produce as Lambic, nor is any so hard to sell - it being a complex taste for a consumer to acquire. Boon (his name is pronounced "Bone" (or "Beaune"?) has brought new life to the craft, for which he has become a knowledgeable spokesman. He is a strong believer in certain traditions, and uses an especially rigorous turbid mash, but does not feel that Lambic was ever intended to be as drily acidic as some purists would argue.

His Oude Lambik has excellent complexity, with a toasty, winey, Chardonnay, note. Oude Gueze Boon (at 6.5 per cent alcohol by volume) is spicy-tasting (ginger?), with some sweetness in the middle. His favourite old Lambics are set aside for blending into Gueze Mariage Parfait. "March is the best time to bottle," he says. "All nature is waking up. The warmer evenings arouse the yeast." Oude Gueze Mariage Parfait (with a density of 16 Plato, and 8.0 abv) has a garden-mint aroma and a mild, sweetish, start; the vanilla flavours of American oak in the middle; a gradually emerging intensity; and late acidity. (Visits can be arranged through the Zenne Valley and Payottenland Tourist Board, in the nearby town on Halle, tel: 02-356-42-59)

CANTILLON

In Brussels. Cantillon is a working brewery and museum (56 Rue Gheude, Anderlecht; tel. 02-521-2891). It is not far from the Midi Station, where the Eurostar arrives. From the outside, the brewery looks like nothing more than a lock-up garage. Inside, it is very traditional

The Cantillon family were originally brewers in Lembeek, and came to Brussels in 1900. Their descendant Jean-Pierre Van Roy is a purist and a famously outspoken, opinionated, advocate for very dry Lambics, though his recent examples have been less aggressive and more lemony. While unblended Lambic is usually available on draught only, Cantillon does bottle old vintages, almost without carbonation, under the name Bruocsella Grand Cru.

Visitors to the brewery are offered a sample and can buy bottles or gift packs. There is always something

new. On one visit, I tasted a product called Iris, an all-malt beer, brewed with fresh hops, but spontaneously fermented in the style of
a Lambic. This had a slightly smoky, phenolic, aroma; an oily, nutty,
palate; and a late woody dryness. It was intended to revive a
Bruxellois speciality historically represented by a once-popular
beer called Jack-Op. Cantillon also makes some of the driest, and
most authentic, fruit beers (see Kriek and Lambic). An interesting
variety of wood is used, including Port pipes.

DE KEERSMAEKER (MORT SUBITE)

The famous Brussels café Mort Subite "Sudden Death", not far from
Grand' Place, gives this brewery its better-known and more celebrated name. "Long Life" might be more appropriate. The brewery itself
is to the North-West of the city, at Kobbegem, in Payottenland.
Much of area was once owned by the abbey of Affligem. A family

*Veteran Lambic
brewer André De
Keersmaecker provides
a sense of scale as he
examines the foudres
at Mort Subite.*

called Van Der Hasselt was brewing on the site in 1604. Nearly 400
years later, at a judging for "Beer Passion" magazine, I found myself
in conversation with Bernadette Van Der Hasselt, of the same family, who works on quality control for the brewery.

At the brewery, I was once shown ledgers from 1721. Among the
notes in the ledgers were formulations employing Lambic to cure
ailments among horses and cattle. I also saw a handwritten
document concerning the purchase of a mill, signed in 1780 on
behalf of Archduchess Maria-Theresa, and one from a year later
bearing the wax seal of Emperor Joseph II.

For five generations, the brewery has been run by the De
Keersmaeker family, though in recent years it has been part of the
Alken-Maes group, now owned by Scottish and Newcastle.

The brewery has had a long association with the Vossen family's café in Brussels. The café, built in about 1880, was re-fitted in 1926, and is a classic of the period. It was originally called La Cour Royale. The café was once favoured by staff from the National Bank and journalists from "La Libre Belgique", who played a dice game there. If one was called back to the office urgently, the game would be terminated by "Sudden Death". The café came to be known as MORT

Five generations on... the brewery cherishes documents dating to the 1700s. Despite its name, Mort Subite has enjoyed a long life.

SUBITE (French for "Sudden Death"), and that is today its official name. It is at 7 Rue Montagne aux Herbes Potagères, and still serves the brewery's beers. The Mort Subite was the favourite café of Maurice Béjart, who used it as the setting for a ballet.

The beers at the cafe are the widely-available sweetened, filtered and pasteurised versions. The brewery also produces an Old Lambic with a somewhat herbal note (hyssop, said one devotee). Wort was at one stage also sent to the old Eylenbosch brewery, in Schepdaal, where it was fermented and matured. The Eylenbosch Lambic is now hard to find. It has a nuttier character.

Before World War II, when Lambic beers were losing popularity to ales

The tower structure of the De Troch brewery. Right the office of brewer Jos Raes is watched over by the village church.

and Pilseners, a new brewhouse was designed with those styles in mind. An ale, a Pilsener and even a Dortmunder were made for a time. The brewhouse was finally built after the war. Both the building and the vessels have a 1950s look that seems out of character with the brewery's products. The brewery does not use an open cooler, but achieves wild yeast inoculation by pumping air into a closed vessel. This, again, sits oddly with the wooden casks ("pipes" and "foudres"), the odd one carved with its date of manufacture more than 100 years ago and the name of a long-gone wine.

Mort Subite's Old Geuze (7.0 abv), has a honeyish aroma, with some floweriness; a smooth, oily, body; and a yogurt-like acidity in the finish. It performed memorably when served with salmon in a lemon and honey sauce at a lunch presented by Alken-Maes. The chef was Jan Wirix, whose better known diners have included the King of Belgium. On another occasion, two generations of the De Keersmaeker family and their brewer took me to Sunday lunch at an haute cuisine restaurant next to the brewery. First, they tapped, straight from the foudre, Lambic and Kriek to accompany our meal. We made an odd tableau as we walked through the streets and into the restaurant clutching large pitchers of beer.

DE TROCH

The resident cat once led me on a tour of this brewery, visiting each room in the correct order of production processes. Clearly, he knew the routine. Many breweries and whisky distilleries employ a cat to discourage mice from visiting their grain stores, but few have a feline guide. De Troch's tortoise shell volunteered her services to me while the proprietor was detained by a phone call.

De Troch is at Wambeek, in Payottenland. Parts of the structure date from 1820, when it was a farm and chicory distillery. The handsome little brewery, in brick and pantiles, is built on the tower principle.

This is a typical brewery design, in which bags of malt and pockets of hops are hoisted to the top of the building, which also accommodates a water tank. All the ingredients then flow by gravity through the procedures of mashing, brewing, fermentation and maturation, becoming finished beer in the cellar. The brewhouse at De Troch is one of the very few still to be coal-fired. De Troch produces an Oude Gueuze for the Belgian market. This has oaky, cellar-ish, notes in its aroma and palate, with a dry finish. A version for export markets, labelled "Traditional". A variant under the Chapeau brand-name is sugar-sweet. The company has given much more attention in recent years to very sweet, increasingly "tropical", fruit beers made with juices and extracts.

DRIE FONTEINEN

The favourite meeting place for Lambic-lovers is this café-restaurant, long-standing blender and now brewer in the attractive little town of Beersel, six miles from Brussels. When Beersel was more rural, it was noted for its cherry trees, and there were once a dozen or more cafés blending their own Gueuze and making Kriek. "Three Fountains" (3 Teirlinckplein, tel 02-331-06-52; fax 02-331-07-03) dates from 1887, and has been a blender since its early days. It has been in the same family, the Debelders, since 1953.

The small square on which it stands is named after poet, novelist and playwright Herman Teirlinck who, who was once a regular at Drie Fonteinen, where he instituted a club of Flemish literati. He is credited with having persuaded café-owner Gaston Debelder to persist in the blending of Gueuze at a time when interest seemed to be waning.

„My father,s beer": Armand Debelder and father Gaston. Now Armand brews his own Lambic at their historic literary café.

The café-restaurant is in a 1960s building, with a shop-like facade. The interior has a tiled floor and pale wood panelling, and is set round an island bar made of brick. It is possible to have beer with bread and soft cheese, or a full meal, ranging from stoemp (a Flemish counterpart to bubble-and-squeak) to mussels prepared with Gueuze or guinea fowl with Kriek.

On one visit, I was allowed to taste a Gueuze blended by Gaston Debelder in 1972 and served at the wedding of his son Armand three years later. It was delicate, faintly oily and elegant. When I offered my impressions to Armand, he was anxious not to appear to be taking credit. "It's my father's, not mine. He made it, and I was fortunate enough to enjoy it." The blend contained Lambics from Girardin, Lindemans and De Neve," the latter now long gone.

In the late 1980s, Gaston began to train Armand in the art of blending. By 1991, Gaston was satisfied with Armand's work, and handed the task over to him. "The first time I ever saw tears in my father's eyes was when the Objectieve Bierproevers gave me an award for my beer, in 1993," Armand recalls. The award attracted the attention of the poet Hubert Van Herreweghen's son, Willem, one of Belgium's most experienced young brewers, and a man with a passion for Lambic. Willem became a friend and adviser.

The Debelders had again wondered about the future of Lambic blenders; now, they began to gain confidence. Armand and his brother Guido came to an agreement over their ultimate inheritance: The café-restaurant business would be Guido's; the beer would be Armand's.

In 1998, Van Herreweghen assembled brewing equipment to install at Drie Fonteinen. The mash-tun and kettle were retired from the Jupiler Pils brewery, where they had been used as a pilot plant. A compact, galleried, brewhouse, with open cooler, now occupies part of the old cellars at Drie Fonteinen. There is still room in the cellars for casks, but storage has also been arranged in a nearby building.

Armand has made something of a speciality of using casks from the Côtes de Nuits. While in the past Lambic brewers often used vessels in which wines had been shipped, Armand goes to France, noses barriques and chooses the ones he feels will produce the best Gueuze. He is a stickler for detail, obsessive about natural ingredients and appropriate methods.

Drie Fonteinen Lambic has robust flavours: an apricot-like fruitiness; good, oaky vanilla; a touch of sherry; and excellent length. The café also offers a Faro, based on Lambic matured for a year in a barrique and sweetened with candy sugar. An Old Gueuze I tasted in 2001 had the same fruitiness and oaky vanilla, especially in its aroma, even to the extent that it reminded me of a Burgundy. The same characteristics were present in the palate, with a touch of lemon curd, and lots of flavour development, moving to an appetisingly nutty dryness. Blends containing Drie Fonteinen's own Lambic were not yet available at the time.

GIRARDIN

Farm brewery, on what was once an aristocrat's estate, at St Ulriks Kapelle. The brewery began in 1845, as a part of an aristocrat's estate. The Girardins have owned it since 1882, through four generations. After years of asking, I was permitted to see the brewery in 1993. Louis Girardin was 69 at the time, running the brewery with his wife Jacqueline and sons Paul and Jan, with no employees. His rural conservatism extended to a mistrust of long-haired foreign snoopers. It was a memorable visit, and I was saddened when, while attending a beer festival in 2000, I was told that Mr Girardin had just died. Happily, his family are still running the business.

They grow their own wheat, brew Lambic in winter and produce a Pils in summer. The Girardins use 40 per cent wheat in their Lambic, and still have a mill that grinds the grain between stones, as well as a more modern one with metal cylinders. "We continue to use the stones for some of the grist," Louis told me, "in case it contributes to the character of the beer."

They still have a cast-iron, open, mash-turn and bricked-in kettle, though at the time of my visit they had just installed a more modern (1950s or 60s?) copper brewhouse, bought second-hand in Germany. They had spent a month in Germany dismantling it themselves, then fitted it back home in Belgium. Their advance calculations of the space required had proven correct down to a notch of a couple of centimetres made in a ceiling support.

"If you damage or dirty anything in our brewery, you must pay for it," said Louis. He was only half joking. When I made to lean on a kettle to take a photograph, a cloth was quickly placed beneath my elbows. The fastidious Girardins even have two open-coolers, one in the attic and another at brewhouse level. Why? "The temperatures are different in the two places. Depending upon the weather outside, we can juggle to get the best possible inoculation of wild yeasts."

This is truly craft brewing, and the wheaty, dry, well-rounded, beers have a complexity that is admired by all lovers of traditional Lambic. Louis Girardin first gave me a bottle that had been in his cellar for five months. I thought it had a remarkable combination of intense dryness and smoothness. "No!" said Mr Girardin. "This is too young!!"

A three-year-old was fetched, and I found it one of the most complex beers I have ever tasted. The unfolding aromas and flavours reminded me of talcum powder, freshly-cut cedar sawdust, hay, apples, cider and dry oloroso sherry.

LINDEMANS

The sight of René Lindemans stoking his coal-fired kettle was one of the more memorable images in my "Beer Hunter" series of films for television. The brewery is in Vlezenbeek, not far from the Zenne. When I first saw it, I was charmed not only by its cast-iron mash-tun and bricked-in kettles (a classic brewhouse design in Flanders), but also by the Brabant farmhouse buildings, which date from 1869. The business began as a farm brewery in 1809, and records show that it was paying tax as a brewer by 1829. A year later, farming stopped..

Lindemans now has a more modern brewhouse. It still makes a straight Lambic, but the product is almost impossible to find.
Its Old Gueuze is named Cuvée René, after the owner of the brewery. This beautiful beer has a fresh, leafy, dry, aroma; a textured mouth-feel

("like swallowing clouds") one enthusiast suggests; a beautifully-balanced, fruity, lightly tart, crisp-apple, palate; and a suggestion of palo cortado sherry in the finish.

Lindemans has always had a commitment to traditional Gueuze, and this product was introduced to reaffirm that. The brewery was mentioned in my 1997 book "The World Guide to Beer", and subse-

Dirk Lindemans tends a kettle bought second-hand in Germany. This replaced the kettle stoked by his father René in „The Beer Hunter".

quently approached to supply an American importer. Despite his best efforts, the American market was at that time not yet ready for traditional Gueuze, so sweetened products were offered. In the years since, the brewery has enjoyed considerable commercial success in export markets with sweetened versions of Gueuze, Kriek and other fruit beers. It even has a tea-flavoured beer.

OUDE BEERSEL

The "Beer House" of Old Beersel is mini-landmark, but it remains a local café and brewery rather than a tourist attraction.

Just as many "mom and pop" baker's shops once made their own bread, so cafés made their own beer before the growth of industrial brewing. Such establishments survive in Bavaria and the "Black Country" of England. In the land of Lambic, the Vandervelden family's Oude Beersel is a classic survivor. Its founders would have been surprised, even puzzled, by today's revival of brewpubs.

With its decoratively tiled 1930s facade, announcing "In 't Bierhuis Oud Beersel", the café hides the tiny brewery, which is 50 years older. (230 Laarheidestraat. Café 02-380-44-48; brewery 02-380-33-96).
There were worries about the survival of the brewery when Henri Vandervelden came to retirement age in 1991 and his son did not wish to run the business. In the event, it was taken over by his nephew Danny Draps, who had been involved for several years.

The café serves the Old Lambic, which I find flowery, resiny and piney. The Oud Gueuze has a piney, peppery, aroma; a refreshing palate; and an appetisingly dry, finish.

TIMMERMANS

Near Brussels' Grand' Place, Café Bécasse is a hidden landmark (11 Rue Tabora and down an alley). It specialises in sweetened blends based on the Lambic of Timmermans' brewery, at Itterbeek, West of the Zenne.

There is believed to have been a brewery on the site since 1650, though the present buildings date from 1888. The brewery uses some beautifully-maintained old equipment, including a traditional mash-tun in the madammen style (named after ladies who wiggle when they walk). A turbid mash is still employed. So is a direct-flame kettle (oil-fired) kettle, which may contribute to he maltiness of the beer. Flames can create "hot spots". contributing to caramelisation.

When Germaine Timmermans married Paul Van Cutsem in 1935, her wedding gift from her father was a new open cooler for the brewery. It is still there. A device in the cooler rings a bell in the con-

Called a madammen, after ladies who wiggle when they walk... the swivelling discs in the mash-tune at Timmermans.

At Timmermans, Jacques Van Cutsem taps from a foudre marked with the brewery,s own symbol. A vessel this size seems hardly likely to missing.

cierge's office when the wort reaches the temperature at which it should be run-off. Paul Van Cutsem's son Jacques told me of the times he had been awakened by this bell.

When Jacques Van Cutsem showed me round in the mid 1970s, it was my first sight of a Lambic brewery. I was amazed by the galleries of casks and amused by the piles of discarded cherry stones. I have visited Timmermans several times since, most recently in 2001. Jacques showed me around again, and I was amazed how little had changed. He still has a share in the brewery, but control is in the hands of John Martin's, a company better known for its pale ale. In recent years the company has invested considerably in Timmermans, especially in a pubby guest bar (Tel 02-569-03-58)

A note of fresh cedar seems to be a house characteristic in the Timmermans beers, most obviously in the Lambic. It has been available in recent years at In 't Vagevuur, in Vlezenbeek. Timmermans Oude Gueze, sub-titled Caveau, additionally has a big body; a pronounced maltiness, with some sweetness; and a touch of tangerine in the finish. Timmermans also pioneered "White Lambic".

GUEUZE BLENDERS

Traditionally, Lambic breweries also sold partly-finished beer to establishments that carried out only the fermentation. What they were selling was brewed wort. This is rather like a press crushing grapes for several wine-makers. The breweries also sell wort to blenders. This is more like a vineyard selling wine to a Cognac house. Neither of these

practices is common in the production of other styles of beer, but Lambic is especially shaped by its fermentation, and the related style Gueuze by blending.

Typically, blenders use their own casks. They ferment and mature the wort for between one and three years, in the usual way. The resultant young and old Lambic is then blended and bottled. After several months in the bottle, the blend has melded, and carbonation developed.

DE CAM

In the pretty village of Gooik, in the heart of the traditional region, a 17th-century château farm that long ago accommodated a Lambic brewery "De Cam", rediscovered beer in 1997. The poet Van Herreweghen's son Willem put one of the buildings to use as a Gueuze-blending cellar, the first new one for many years. Willem did this as a part-time activity while working as Director of Production at the sizeable Palm brewery.

Remarkably, he commissioned his own casks for De Cam. Even more strikingly, these were made to a German design of the 1860s. Astonishingly, they were cut down from oak lagering vessels once used at Pilsner Urquell. All 45 of the casks used are in this format. They are racked behind a window, with a freestyle neon sign announcing De Cam. It all seems a long way from Bruegel, and that impression is heightened by the blender, Karel Goddeau, a young man in his 20s, crowned with long blond curls that would look good on a rock singer or footballer.

Talking to his generation: Karel Goddeau proselytises for beer with flavour, especially Gueuze.

Goddeau's "day job" is to work at the Proef brewery, perhaps the most modern in Belgium, where he makes a huge diversity of styles. He has had a passion for Gueuze since he chanced to drink a Girardin at the age of 15 or 16. He went to brewing school for four years, but was disappointed by the lack of reading on spontaneous fermentation. "About four lines in 800 pages. That's all there was on this beautiful beer."

De Cam used the Lambics of Boon, Girardin and Lindemans in its early blends, but now also has its own Lambic, made at Drie Fonteinen. An early bottling of was judged blindfold in a tasting for "Beer Passion" magazine and won rave reviews for its complexity and dryness. I found it thirst-cutting, with layers of intense flavours, notably grapefruit and gooseberry .The beers are available in the adjoining Volks Café De Cam (57 Dorpsstraat. Tel 02-5322132, closed Mondays).

HANSSENS

Originally, a brewery, called St Antonius, established on a dairy farm by a mayor of Dworp, Bartholomé Hanssens, in 1896. St Antonius made brown table beer and Lambic.

The copper kettles were removed by the German Army during the First World War to make munitions, and production ceased. After the war, the business became a blender, and for decades enjoyed an excellent reputation for its Gueuze. In recent years, Hanssens has gained a following in the United States.

Jean Hanssens with his daughter Sidy and husband John. "I want to taste the Region". The future of the enterprise became uncertain in 1999, when the third generation, Jean Hanssens, announced his wish to retire. His daughter Sidy and her husband John emerged as saviours when they realised that the business did not require them to work full-time. Sidy is a secretary in a law office and John an air-traffic controller.

"We could keep our day-jobs and do this if we were prepared to sacrifice some of our social life," he told me. "Nobody else blends on a part-time basis, but it is a way of continuing what my father and grandfather did."

Hanssens fills 70 "pipes" per year, but has far more of these casks in its cellars, given that some of the beer is matured for three years. Four or five pipes go into each blend. Sidy said that she did not work to a pre-ordained recipe, but to achieve a taste. Apart from conceding that that she did not want the Gueuze to be to sour, her best effort to define the intended character was: "When I drink it, I want to taste the region."

She demonstrated the stirring of the blend. This involved her standing on an upper floor, above the marrying tun, and wielding a "swizzle-stick" three metres long.

Among the equipment, much of it antique, she was especially proud to point out the racks in which the washed bottles were dried. "My grandfather designed and built those." There were 30,000 bottles in 16 "caves," She picked out several and we walked directly from the cellars into the family house to do some tasting. Hanssens Oud Gueze has an earthy character, with a complex fruitiness that has always reminded me of rhubarb. Other tasters have argued for melon or even pineapple.

GUEUZE OUTSIDE THE REGION
PRODUCERS OF GUEUZE IN WESTFLANDERS

VAN HONSEBROUCK

Presumably regional sensibilities stopped the production of Gueuze spreading across Brabant's border into East Flanders. That being the case, how does the style come to reappear in farther-flung West Flanders? Though textiles and trade have been historically important in both provinces, perhaps the East is slightly more oriented to manufacture, and the maritime West to commercial buccaneering. Even in such a small country, there are local differences of character.

In the late 1960s and early 1970s, when in several countries the post-war urge to be "modern" and uniform gave way to some rediscovery of cultural heritage, there was in Belgium a new flurry of interest in the Brussels' area's traditional Gueuze beers, and this style was taken up by two brewers in West Flanders. Originally, the Van Haelen brewery of Ukkel, Brussels, supplied Lambic as an addition to the range of the family firm of Van Honsebrouck, in the historic town of Ingelmunster, West Flanders. When Van Halen closed, in 1968, Van Honsebrouck fermented some of the brewery's wort in wood as a starter for its own "Lambic", and created its own micro-climate. From this beginning, Van Honsebrouck became well known for a sweetened Gueuze under the brand-name St Louis. Now, the company has added a product more traditional in style. In 1993, beers of two and three years old were blended to make an unsweetened, unfiltered, product called Gueuze Fond Tradition. The first bottling had a light body; a clean, smooth, very refreshing acidity; and a tart, thirst-cutting, spritzy, finish, with a touch of cellar character. A bottling I tasted six years later had more complexity: slightly vegetal (celery), with a lightly appetising bitterness reminiscent of chicory. I imagine these derived from Brettanomyces. Van Honsebrouck is otherwise known for a "red" ale in the local style of West Flanders; a strong brew called Brigand, in loosely the Triple style; and a "Castle Beer" that the British or Americans might call a barley wine.

St Louis Gueuze and Kriek is sweetened; Gueuze Fond Tradition is not.

BOCKOR

The other brewery in West Flanders to make a Gueuze is that of the family Vander Ghinste, in the village of Bellegem, near another historic town, Kortrijk (in French, Courtrai). This brewery, originally part of a farm, has been in the family since the 1890s. In the 1930s, it had as its speciality a "German-style" lager which it called Bock. The beer was golden, and the brewery eventually became known as Bockor (the "or" meaning gold, in French). Bockor started to produce Gueuze in 1970, originally using in its blend a

proportion of Lambic bought from Heyvaert, in Asse, in the traditional region. That brewery closed in 1981, and Bockor now produces its own beers for blending.

All breweries used open coolers before the invention of heat-exchangers, and Bockor still has one, in an elegant tower characteristically curved to run-off the condensed steam. It uses the cooling vessel only for its "Lambic". It also has, in their own cellar, 16 fixed oak tuns, variously acquired from wine merchants and Cognac houses. These are used for both "Lambic" and a beer in the sour-and-sweet brown-red ale tradition of West Flanders. Bockor's Gueuze is called Jacobins, a name with both ecclesiastical and democratic connotations. The terms derives from a Dominican friary near the church of St Jacques, in Paris. The building housed a club for radical democrats at the time of the French Revolution. The youngest beer in Jacobins Gueuze has been fermented and matured for a couple of months. The oldest has 14-20 months. The finished beer begins tart, and retains some of this character throughout, staying fairly dry and developing a nuttiness toward the finish. It is filtered, but not pasteurised.

FRUIT BEERS, PINK CHAMPAGNE OR ALCOPOP?

The finest, driest, fruit beers of Belgium are the pink Champagnes of the beer world, products of great complexity and delicacy. These are not always easy to find.

Some of the more popular, sweeter, examples are more like alcopops. Fruit beer sounds like a contradiction, and looks like a novelty, but is neither. The Ancients are believed to have used honey, dates, perhaps oranges in their beers, and in Belgium these traditions never died. These products are beers because the principal raw material from which they are brewed is grain. Only later, classically during matura-tion, is the fruit added, to trigger a further fermentation while also adding aroma and flavour.

If only fruit were used, they would be wines. There is a widespread misunderstanding in some countries that "Lambic" means "fruit beer". It doesn't. A straight Lambic contains no fruit. Nor does a Gueuze. The mis-understanding arises because Lambic is the style of brew most often used as a basis for fruit beers.
The use of wheat and wild yeasts in Lambics gives them an acidity that seems fruity. This combines well with fruits, and enhances the complex of dry flavours. The driest, most complex and delicate, fruit beers are based on Lambic.

The flavour of whole cherries is more pronounced in Belle-Vue's Primeur than in its year-round Kriek.

KRIEK AND FRAMBOISE

The fruit most traditionally used in Belgium is the cherry, but neither the Flemish term Kers nor the French Cerise is usually employed to identify it. The fruit is normally known by its Flemish name, Kriek, and only occasionally by its French description Griotte. In English, it might be called a Morello cherry. It is small, almost black, with a full-coloured juice and a sour, or acidic, flavour. The Kriek/Griotte/Morello is a brother to the paler, redder, Montmorency, which is also sour but produces a relatively clear juice. They comprise the family Prunus cerasus. This family and the sweet cherry family Prunus avium are the ancestors of all cultivated varieties. Kriek trees can still be seen in the heart of Brussels, and around the city, especially to the Northwest: in the Schaarbeek neighbourhood, and stretching out toward Ninove. It was natural that a fruit growing in profusion locally would be used, and the intense aromas and flavours of the "Schaarbeek Kriek" are associated with the most authentic interpretation of this beer style.

A complex Kriek is enjoyed by its brewer, Frank Boon, who came in from the outside world, and has done much to reinvigorate the industry.

It was once common for householders, cafés and small brewers to use cherries from private gardens. In the most traditional method, the cherries are allowed to dry, like prunes on the tree. Cherries in this condition are scarce, because the birds enjoy them so much. As Brussels grew, cherries were in shorter supply, and the Schaarbeek Kriek has to a great extent been replaced by the Gorsem cherry, grown around Tienen and St Truiden, in Belgian province of Limburg. Many brewers use less traditional varieties, imported as purée, juice or essence, from Germany, Demark or Poland. Some employ a combination of these sources. The other fruit widely regarded as being traditional is he raspberry. In this instance, the French word Framboise is often used. This can be confusing, as the same term is used in French for the clear, "white" brandy made from the raspberry. In a restaurant, it might be worth making clear whether the Framboises are desired in the form of bière or eau-de-vie. The Flemish for raspberry is used rendered on the label in the plural, Frambozen.

A authentically dry Kriek is the perfect beer with which to greet guests at a summer party or barbecue. It also makes a wonderful aperitif. It has the acidity of a Champagne, the bouquet and delicate flavour of cherries, and a balance of almondy dryness from the stones (an important element), as well as the sherryish background of the base beers. A traditional Framboise fills the air with its bouquet, and is even more delicate in palate and finish. A seducer would be tempted to engage it, and a sexist to deem it the most feminine of beers. The less traditional, sweetened, examples may be less distinguished, but they go perfectly with a sweetly fruity dessert. I have American friends who love them with Cherry Jubilee, the flambeed dish of hot fruit in its own syrup, and ice-cream.

In the world of beer, the nearest tradition is the Northern Germans' habit of adding a dash of raspberry juice to Berliner Weisse, their sharply lactic style of wheat brew. This, however, is not a part of the production process; the addition is made by the bartender. In a springtime ritual, some German taverns make a whole-fruit syrup to add to beer or wine as a "May Bowl".
The Southern Germans used to add a slice of lemon to their spicier Weisse or Weizenbier, but that is hardly the same thing. Nonetheless, these are both interesting drinks. These customs in Germany and Belgium start with a beer that has an intense character, and complement it. Some other countries use a strong flavour to "enhance" a relatively neutral-tasting beer.

The French have been known to add the patent aperitif Amer Picon to lager from Alsace. British women used to add sweet lime cordial to lager beers, and it has become the custom among inexperienced drinkers in the English-speaking world to add a segment of the fresh fruit to some of Mexico's lightest-tasting beers. In Canada is not unknown to add tomato juice to beer, to make a Calgary Red-Eye.

This approaches cocktail country, though a Bloody Mary is a much more satisfactory drink. Among wines, the raspberry vermouths of Chambéry are well-known and delicious. Among liqueurs, cherry "brandies" like that made by Peter Heering in Denmark are nodding acquaintances of Kriek. Among spirits, flavoured gins, vodkas and aquavits are distant relations.

THE LAMBIC FAMILY

HOW KRIEK IS MADE

After the harvest, usually in July, the cherries are introduced to the beer in the cask. The Lambic used may be as young as three months or, more traditionally, 18 months. More likely still is a blend of both. Some producers print on the label or cork two dates: when the old beer was brewed, and when the cherries were harvested.

The most cherryish flavours emerge if the brew stays on the fruit for about six weeks, but some beers will remain much longer. From the viewpoint of fruit character, October is a good time to bottle, but the yeast activity in the beer will be better in March, April or May. The yeast character is important to the further fermentation in the bottle. This is one reason why not only the base Lambics but also finished Kriek may well be blended to include different ages. A small, artisanal, brewery cannot bottle all of its Kriek in a single optimum month, or even one season. If the cherry harvest is good, the brewer will probably make more Kriek than he can sell in a single season, and keep it for future years.

Kriek that has spent long periods in the cask picks up more dryness and bitterness from the stones of the cherries. This can add balance and complexity, especially if a young and older Kriek are blended. After six months or a year, this pleasant bitterness can turn to ast-

ringency, but much depends upon the condition of the cask, and the temperature (as always, the brewer likes cool weather). It is unusual, but not unknown, for beer to stay on the fruit for more than one summer. Some breweries use 300 grammes of cherries per litre of beer, others are less generous. Some also use a proportion of elderberries, for colour and added complexity. Some, having drained the cask but left the fruit inside, will then add a second charge of beer. They will then blend the first and second "extracts". Some will add young Lambic before the bottling. The traditional producer will then mature his Kriek in the bottle for one summer before releasing it. The beer will have had a further fermentation in the cask, caused by the sugars from the fruit, and will then have a period of maturation in the bottle.

In a traditionally-made Kriek, the further fermentation caused by the blendings and the addition of fruit will add to the strength. The strength of the original Lambics will, of course, influence the potency of the final product, which may vary from around, or a little over, 5.0 per cent to more than 7.0.

LAMBIC-BASED FRUIT BEERS, WITH TASTING NOTES

Almost all producers of Lambic, and many brewers who make other styles, use a proportion of their output (often the biggest share) as the basis for a Kriek, a Framboise and perhaps other less-traditional fruit styles. These beers have enjoyed a great growth in sales in recent years.

BELLE-VUE

A Kriek Primeur is launched each April, using younger Lambics and sweeter cherries than those employed in its year-round product. The cherries are harvested the year before, in St Truiden, and the Primeur is intended to greet spring, and remains on the market for about a month. It is not intended to be laid down, and is filtered and flash-pasteurised like the year-round version. The Primeur is a different blend each year, but can have an almost purple colour and a fresh, jammy, cherry character, rounding out to a lightly tart finish. The regular Belle Vue Kriek is fruitier and more iron-ish, than it once was, but still sweet. Lambics of four months are given cherries for a year, then blended with younger beers, "smoothened" with a small proportion of cherry juice, and sweetened with fructose (fruit sugars).

BOON

The classic, unfiltered, Kriek from Boon is no longer called Mariage Parfait. Embracing the new definitions for Lambic beers, it is simply identified as Oud Kriek Boon, and has 300 grammes of cherries per litre. The filtered and flash-pasteurised version and 200 grammes. Boon has a relative-ly complex process, beginning with a two-year-old Lambic, which spends four to five weeks on cherries. This is then blended with one-year-old Lambic and a proportion of a lower gravity Mars-type beer made with darker malts. The end result has a toasty, jammy, liqueur-like, intensity of fla-vours. A sweeter, lighter Framboise is also produced.

CANTILLON

Noted for elegantly dry fruit beers. The outstanding example, called Rosé de Gambrinus, has evolved in its composition over the years. In recent times, half the blend has been Framboise beer; 15 per cent Kriek beer; and 35 per cent one-year-old plain Lambic. Newly bottled, it has a huge fruitiness, already balanced by acidity. With bottle age, the blend develops an austere delicacy. A beer with the Arctic cloudberry, for the renowned Stockholm beer bar Akkurat, had an orange-honey, buttercup-like, note.

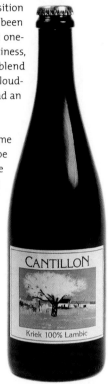

A beer with apricots from the French department Drôme was more scenty. Cantillon has also produced grape (Druiven) Lambics, with the Muscat and similar white varieties from Belgium, Alsace and Italy, and with Merlot and Cabernet Franc from Bordeaux. This brings beer and wine even closer, though the characteristics of Lambic are stronger than those of the grape. I felt this particularly the case with early essays, but more recent examples have had more of a "grape skin" note, especially in the aroma and finish. The red wine version, neatly called St Lamvinus, had a reddish-brown tinge and excellent tannin.

In 2000, I spoke at a dinner in which ten Lambic variations on draft were served, along with brews from Lindemans and Hanssens. Each of the five courses was also prepared with a different Lambic beer. This astonishing tour-de-Lambic took place at Monk's Café, in Philadelphia.

DE KEERSMAEKER (MORT SUBITE)

Considerable research into cherries has been carried out by Mort Subite and its parent company in association with the University of Leuven. Orchards in Limburg are contracted to grow the fruit to its requirements. Bees are introduced to encourage the spread of pollen. Young Lambic spends three to four months on cherries (250 grammes per litre), at ambient temperatures, then there is a long slow melding period, of about a year, at colder temperatures. The unfiltered version has a purply colour; a hnt of cherry skins in the aroma; a big fruitiness in the middle; and a cleansing acidity in the finish. This version is extremely hard to find. The filtered and pasteurised version, made from 100 per cent Lambic, is light but firm, with a pleasant tartness. It is sweetened, but not overwhelmingly.

DE TROCH

A pleasantly tart Kriek has occasionally been released, but more often De Troch offers a sweeter version, with juicy, fruit-fibre, notes, under the Chapeau label. De Troch has become something of a specialist in unusual flavours, made with juices or essences. These include a refreshing, medium-dry peach; a nutty apricot; liqueur-ish pineapple; a plummy mirabelle; and a sweet, chewy, banana.

DRIE FONTEINEN

Schaarbeek cherries are strongly favoured, at a high rate of 350 grammes per litre. A Lambic of five or six months spends a half-year on whole cherries (ie, with the stone), and a similar period of maturation in the cask or bottle. The Old Kriek has a bramble-like intensity, a hint of passion fruit, and a very soft acidity.

GIRARDIN

Such is the delicacy of the Girardin Lambic that to add fruits seems like gilding the lily. The wheat character shows through in the fruit beers, which are scenty and delicate, even in the filtered versions.

HANSSENS

The long admired Old Kriek from this blender is firm and fruity, with a good interplay of sweetness and acidity. A newer product is a whole fruit strawberry Lambic, called Oud Beitje (the second word is a diminutive of the Flemish word for a strawberry. This is reminiscent of a medium-dry rosé wine, with a very light strawberry aroma and palate, against a background of almost wafer-life maltiness.

LINDEMANS

While its Cuvée René offers a fine Gueuze, this brewery seems in the fruit department to have been seduced by sweetness. A wide range is produced (in some markets under the name Foudroyante). Lindemans pioneered Peach Lambic, in which the flavours seem quite harmonious. Cassis Lambic is a less happy combination. The lemony-tasting Tea Beer is a refreshing novelty.

OUD BEERSEL

The resiny, piney, peppery, characteristics of the Oud Beersel Lambic show through in this brewery's Old Kriek, making for an especially dry interpretation of the style.

TIMMERMANS

A dextrously balanced Kriek (filtered) from this brewery: good, dry, "horse-blanket" Lambic aroma; substantial flavours, with maltness and restrained fruitiness. Lambic of six to nine months spends a further 18 on Gorsems cherries from St Truiden. The other fruit beers in the range are sweeter.

FRUIT BEERS FROM OTHER REGIONS

Outside the Lambic region, the production of Kriek and Framboise is especially long-established around Oudenaarde, in East Flanders. There, Liefmans is well known for an assertive Kriek and a gentler Framboise based on its famous brown ale. Liefmans also makes a spiced Glühkriek, to be served hot.

Also in the Oudenaarde area, the tiny Cnudde family brewery makes a beautifully-balanced Kriek, again based on brown ale, from its own cherry trees. Unfortunately for the drinker at large, this supply is sufficient only for the Cnudde family.

The West Flanders brewery Bockor also uses its Jacobins Gueuze as the base for a Kriek. Beer 18 months old spends half a year on cherries. From the wood at the brewery, it has a deliciously tart cherry character, but the version released is much sweeter. In the same area, the Verhaege brewery, at Vichte, also produces a Kriek variation. This Echte Kriek, using cherries from St Truiden, has the aroma and palate of a Kirsch.

In Limburg, the St Jozef brewery, better known for its Pax Pils, uses that as the basis for a soft, fruity Bosbier. This is made from Bosbessen (bilberries, or blueberries), which are also used locally in flavoured genever gin, and in fruit pies. In the Belgian province of Luxembourg, I have tasted a beer made by Fantôme with a dash of raspberry juice.

As Belgian fruit beers have become more widely know, they have inspired variations on the theme all over the world. Many of these are blandly sweet brews aimed at people who "don't like" beer. The most complex fruit beer I have tasted anywhere else is a "Belgian-style Red" made in New Glarus Wisconsin. A mixed culture obtained from Belgium is a key element in this beer, but there is also a certain felicity to the source of cherries: Brussels, Wisconsin.

Lambic brewers gather at the cellars of Drie Fonteinen for tasting on behalf of Beer Passion magazine. The tasters, and the beers, were from breweries and blending houses within the Guild of Lambic Brewers, HORAL.

	Hoegaarden
	Celis Wit
CHAPTER VII	Further producers of White Beers, with tasting notes

White beers

*From Celis to Hoegaarden to Wittekerke...
summer's cloudy coolers.*

Summery, refreshing, wheat beers have been the great success of the last few years in several countries. Unlike some hot-weather beers, the wheat brews combine their easy drinkability with plenty of flavour. The drier examples are as appetising as a gin-and-tonic. The sweeter, fruitier, ones perform well as a dessert beer, especially with dishes featuring oranges, bananas or apples.

Were these attributes considered by the Mesopotamians, who used wheat in brewing? Perhaps not, though they did give their beers to their high priestesses. Wheat beers were clearly valued in Bavaria when it was a kingdom. Only breweries owned by the royal family were allowed to employ this grain. Wheat beers were made all over Europe before the spread of lager-brewing, but they almost vanished after World War II.

Wheat provides crisp, tart, flavours, but it is a difficult grain with which to brew. With its lack of a fully-formed husk, it tends to clog the vessels. In comparison, barley's husks act as a natural filter. For this reason, it is highly unusual for a beer to be made only from wheat. To be identified as a wheat beer in Germany, a brew normally has at least 50 per cent of that grain, sometime more, the rest being barley-malt. In Belgium, 50-50 is more common. The Germans use only malted wheat; in Belgium, it is normally raw.

The most famous families of wheat beers are the Weizenbier/ Weissbier of Southern Germany (and especially from the Eastern part of Bavaria), which sometimes has a phenolic, spicy or fruity (often banana-like) character, deriving from the behaviour of the yeast used; the sharply acidic Berliner Weisse of the North, which is made with a lactic culture; and the Witbier, Bière Blanche (or occasionally Tarwebier or Bière de Froment) of Belgium, typically made with the addition in the brew-kettle of Curaçao orange peels and ground coriander seeds. The Belgian style is especially associated with the Eastern part of Flemish Brabant.

The German Weizen, Flemish Tarwe and French Froment all mean "wheat". Weisse, Wit and Blanche mean "white". In the days when wheat beers were made all over Europe, the term "white" was widely used to describe them. No one is sure why. Some people argue that it was a misunderstanding, arising from the similarities of the words wheat and white in several languages. Others point out that most styles of wheat beer are very pale in colour (though this is not true of all variations). There is a theory that "white" refers to the very pale head on the beer, or on the foam formed during fermentation. Another suggests that the term derives from hazy nature of many wheat beers. The difficulty of producing a clear beer from wheat would have made for a milky colour before the invention of filtration. The fact wheat beers are very old styles may have led brewers to retain the cloudiness as a distinguishing feature. In Germany, young drinkers treat unfiltered wheat brews as the "wholefood" of the beer world, but clear versions are also produced. In Belgium, almost all wheat beer is served unfiltered.

HOEGAARDEN

Today's Belgian examples are all inspired by one beer. In the English-speaking world, this product is labelled as Hoegaarden White. English-speakers tend, understandably, to pronounce it as in Hoe Garden; in Flemish, it sounds more like Who H'Garden. In Belgium, the beer has been labelled Oud Hoegaards, and more recently just Hoegaarden.

Highway design, Belgian-style. Other European countries have roundabouts. The Belgians sometimes add a brew-kettle. This one is in the town of Hoegaarden.

From Brussels, it is less than an hour's journey east, beyond Leuven (in French, Louvain), to Hoegaarden and the scatter of villages around Tienen that traditionally made beers in this style.

Leuven had its own "White" beer, described in detail in a brewing manual of the late 1700s, and produced until 1975. In its last days, I was told there was still a small stock at the bar in the railway station. I went there for a valedictory glass, and asked for the beer, in Flemish, to looks of incomprehension. I tried again, in French, but with no more success. Then the lady behind the bar decided that I required something native to the British Isles. She broke into a smile and said, in heavily accented English: "Monsieur, I have a beer for you." Proudly, she gave me a bottle of Guinness. It was delicious, but not what I had been seeking.

In the middle of Leuven's main market square is the church of St Pieter. The parish saint gives his name to all connected with the town. Its version of "White" beer was known as Pieterman, and occasional revivalist examples have been produced under that name, somtimes with spelling Peeterman. In the village of Neerijse, the De Kroon brewery until recent years intermittently produced a sweet, cidery, and very cloudy, "Double White". In Lubbeek the Verlinden brewery had its own similar example until 1985.

For several decades, though, Hoegaarden has been the place associated with the style. I have been assured locally that Hoegaarden is a village. I would call it a small town. A brochure promoting the local beer extravagantly calls Hoegaarden "a fairly large town", and points out that it has Belgium's biggest rococo church. The church is certainly impressive, and I rather like the bandstand in the middle of the village/town.

Hoegaarden is in a region of rich soil and château farms growing wheat and sugar beet. Although it surely had breweries earlier, they begin to be mentioned in its history in the early 1300s, and in the 1400s a monastery that made both beer and wine was established. By the 1500s, Hoegaarden had a Guild of Brewers. Many of its members were farmers, who brewed from their own wheat and oats. In the 1700s, the town had become a brewing centre, sending much of its beer to adjoining Principality of Liège. In the 1800s, there were more than 30 breweries in and around the town, at the confluence of the Grote Gete and Nermbeek rivers. (Despite the "Grote", neither river is large). In this century, the growth of Leuven as a brewing centre, and the increasing popularity of Pilsener-style beers (not to mention two World Wars and the advent of national marketing) helped wash away much of Hoegaarden's brewing tradition. In the mid 1950s, the last remaining brewer of "White" beer ceased production.

A few years later, several locals were having a chat when one observed, sadly, that he missed the "White" beer they used to enjoy. In the gathering was Pierre Celis, who had lived next door to the old brewery. Celis had often helped out at the brewery, been fascinated by the place, and had come to know something of the production procedures. He was even involved in the selling of a white drink, though a somewhat different beverage: he was a milkman.
The enterprising Celis, then in his early 40s, felt that the tradition could be revived. With some financial help from his father, a cattle-dealer, he bought equipment from another extinct brewery, consulted the town's last brewer of the style, and started making "White" beer once more, in 1966. He called his brewery De Kluis - meaning "cloister", "hermitage" or "monastery" - in honour of the town's 15th-century brewers. It has since become more readily known simply as the Hoegaarden Brewery.

"I thought the older generation of beer-drinkers would support me," he once told me, "but I was concerned about the younger consumers, who would not know what White beer was." In fact, it was the young who supported him, from the start. "The movement to natural products helped. People liked the natural look of a beer with a sediment. I did not make any publicity. It was all word-of-mouth. People started coming to the brewery from Cologne and Paris. Sometimes I had no beer for them. I could not meet demand. One day, a local man said to me: "Do you know, our Hoegaarden beer is being sold on the Champs-Elysées ...?"

The brewery expanded quickly, but put a strain on the financial resources of Pierre Celis, especially after a fire in 1985. Soon afterwards, Celis sought additional investment from Interbrew, which now owns the enterprise.

The Hoegaarden brewery is on an old farm site, and buildings have been acquired and restored as it has grown. One battlemented wall dates from the 1500s, another from the mid 1750s, and more of the structure from the 1830s. An arched courtyard leads to pantiled former farm buildings. Over the centuries, parts of the site have been used, like many farms in Northern Europe, for malting, brewing and distilling. Today, there is also a bar and restaurant, the Kouterhof, specialising in dishes prepared and served with the Hoegaarden beers (tel 016-767433, open every day). Meanwhile, a chain of summery garden cafés under the beer's name are being established around the world. There is even a Café Hoegaarden in Japan.

Pierre Celis, tireless at 76, wears his Taxan-style bolo tie and pours the beer that bears his name. It is now made in Belgium by the Bios brewery, of Ertevelde.

The early "White" beers of Hoegaarden seem to have been made with not only wheat but also a small proportion of local oats, and this tradition has been continued by some producers. While the wheat contributes its own fruity tartness, the oats perhaps add a pleasantly oily smoothness. Certainly this particular blend of raw materials has its influence on the complexity of flavour of the "White" beers.

There was a tradition in eastern Brabant of spreading green malt on the roof to dry. This very simple method would probably have produced very pale beers. I have also heard of brewers in the past using figs as an adjunct, again to produce notably pale beers. A pale hue was perhaps seen as being attractive and "pure" in the days before brewers knew how to make clear beers.

The original "White" beers were produced by spontaneous fermentation, in wood, and some brewers continued with this method. Old people remember the beer being very sour - and needing to be sweetened. Brewers used herbs and fruits for that purpose - coriander seeds and Curaçao orange peels have become the recognised seasoning in this style of beer. These, again, make their own contribution to complexity.

When some brewers began to pitch yeast, they would have used top-fermenting strains, as the lager method was not known. Both in Germany and Belgium, "White" beers are made with top-fermenting yeasts, and in each case a living culture may be left (or added) in the cask or bottle. There are particular top-fermenting yeasts that work well with wheat, or mixtures of grains, or have adapted to do so - and each of those will add its own element of complexity. Often, one yeast is used in primary fermentation and another in the bottle for the secondary stage-adding yet another dimension. In both Berlin and Hoegaarden, people remember burying bottles in the earth to keep them cool while the beer "ripened". The German types of "White" beer do not employ oats, or spices.

Hoegaarden is brewed from roughly equal parts of raw wheat and malted barley. The gravity is a conventional 12 Plato (1048), and the beer has an alcohol content of 3.8 by weight, 4.8 by volume. It is not intended to be a hoppy beer, but it does have some Kent Goldings for dryness and Saaz for aroma. The spices are milled before being added. The brewery is very secretive about this aspect of production. There was in the early days talk of a third, "mystery", spice. If it exists at all, I wonder whether it is cumin seeds.

The brewhouse is of a relatively traditional design, in a mix of copper and stainless steel, set in a very compact arrangement in an attractively blue-tiled room. The brewery has a very advanced yeast-propagation system, and in the Hoegaarden it uses different cultures for primary and secondary stages. Primary fermentation, at 18 °C (64.4 °F)-26 °C (78.8 °F). It then has three to four weeks' warm conditioning in cellar tanks at 12 °C (53.6 °F) to 15 °C (59 °F) before being bottled with a priming of sugar (glucose) and a dosage of new yeast. Once bottled, the beer has a secondary fermentation of about ten days at 25 °C (77 °F), in a temperature-controlled room. The beer has a very pale, whitish-yellow colour, and is very hazy. It has a dense, white head. In aroma, it has wheaty, apple-like, tartness; herbal-spicy notes, with perfumy coriander; zesty, orangey fruitiness; and honeyish sweetness.

It is normally served chilled, in which condition it is at its most refreshing, but it most fully expresses its flavours at a natural cellar temperature of perhaps 11-12 °C (51-53 °F).

With the growth in popularity of "White" beers, they have been increasingly served fresh, on draught, as a summer quencher. In my view, today's examples are not hopped and spiced with such care, or matured quite as gently, as those of ten years ago. I believe that in those days they were softer, more suited to being stored for a few months, or even years, and served with a dessert, as the beer world's answer to an Orange Muscat. A really good bottle of a Belgian "White" beer is delicious with an orange sorbet, lemon meringue, or apple pie (especially the very sweet, treacly, spicy, American type).

Hoegaarden in 1995 added a winter version, called Speciale, available from September to March. This is stronger (13.5 Plato; 1054; 4.5w; 5.7v), with a greater emphasis on barley malt (55 per cent). The malts used include a nuttier, crystal, type, and the result is a sweeter, "warmer" interpretation. The spicing is the same, but the slight changes in the balance of the base beer seem to accentuate the citric zestiness in Hoegaarden Speciale.

Hoegaarden Grand Cru is also a spiced beer, but made solely from barley malt and to a yet higher gravity (18.4; 1076; about 7.0w, 8.7v). It has a hazy, peachy, colour and a notably fragrant aroma. Its palate is peachy, too, and sweetish - though never excessively so. Its fruity notes - not just suggestions of peach, but also of mango and honeydew melon - and its warming finish, make it a fine, liqueur-like, digestif. Some devotees prefer this beer at six months old, and it will evolve to some degree for three to four years.

Between the two World Wars, a brewery in Hoegaarden was known for an amber ale, possibly spiced, called DAS. This brewery was acquired in 1960, and later closed, by Artois, a precursor of Interbrew. In 1996, Interbrew launched a similar new beer at the Hoegaarden brewery. Using an older spelling, this is known as Hougaerdse DAS. It is a flame-coloured, hazy, ale, very aromatic, with juicy, fruity, flavours hinting at orange and apple, and a late dryness in the finish. Hoegaardse DAS is made to a gravity of 11.5 Plato (1046), from Pilsner and crystal malt, with 20 per cent maize to lighten the body. It is hopped with Lublins and Styrians, and spiced with coriander and Curaçao orange peels. Fermentation is with the very fruity yeast to make Interbrew's Ginder Ale, and there is a secondary in the bottle. The new beer is intended as a light, refreshing, ale within the Hoegaarden family. Its popularity has helped bring renewed attention to ales in Belgium.

A much darker, stronger ale from Hoegaarden is Verboden Vrucht/Fruit Défendu (meaning, of course, "Forbidden Fruit"). This beer, which has 9.0 per cent by volume, has a claret colour, a very dense head; a spicy aroma; a full, soft, body; and a beautifully balanced palate, with rich, sweet suggestions of coffee and apricots giving way to drier, almondy, almost quinine, notes in the finish. Very assertive at first, then soothing.

The label is based on Rubens' painting of Adam and Eve. When the beer was first exported to the United States, the Bureau of Alcohol, Tobacco and Firearms (a curious conjunction, surely?) sought to ban it on the grounds that the label was indecent. The importer protested: "How dare you say such a thing? That is a Rubens, a great work of art given to the world by the Flemish people!" The bureaucrat pondered this point, then replied: "Did Adam really tempt Eve with a glass of beer? I thought he used an apple ..."

As Interbrew's specialist in bottle-conditioning, Hoegaarden also produces Julius (see Strong Golden Ales) and the Triple version of Leffe (see Abbey Beers).

For all the diversity of beers the brewery has created over the years, the name of Hoegaarden remains especially, associated with its White beers, a product that has inspired at least 30 other brewers in Belgium, almost as many in The Netherlands, the odd one in Britain...and a great many in North America.

CELIS WIT

The popularity of Belgian-style wheat beers in the United States was given a fillip when, in 1992, Pierre Celis opened his own brewery in Austin, Texas. The Celis brewery produced a soft, fruity, full-flavoured, White, and a range of Belgian-style specialities.

His White beer almost immediately won a cult following in the United States, but Celis had difficulty in justifying the considerable investment in his beautiful brewery. In 1995, for the second time in his life, Celis sought the assitance of a larger brewing company. His brewery entered into an alliance with the American giant Miller. This proved an unhappy marriage, and in 2000-2001 Miller withdrew, leaving the future of the brewery in doubt.

Meanwhile, Celis White was introduced to Belgium. Initially, it was produced by the De Smedt, brewery (now known as Affligem), of Opwijk. More recently, it has been made by the Bios brewery, of Ertevelde. The Belgian version seems slightly maltier than the Texan "original".
The tireless and inventive Celis embarked in his mid 70s on another dream: the production of a beer matured, like Champagne, in caves. (see Grottenbier, Page 304)

FURTHER PRODUCERS OF WHITE BEERS
WITH TASTING NOTES

BLANCHE DE BRUXELLES

Produced in Brabant, at Quenast, near the river Zenne, by the Lefebvre brewery, also known for a Saison and its Floreffe abbey-style beer. The brewery is only about 15 miles from Brussels. The white beer named after the city is soft, sweetish and grainy, with some apple-skin notes and a gingery dryness in the finish. In some markets labelled as Manneken Pis or Student.

BLANCHE DE NAMUR

Appetizingly herbal and dry, especially in the finish. From Du Bocq, of Purnode, in the province of Namur. This brewery produces a wide variety of beers, including Saison Régal.

BLANCHE DES HONNELLES

A stronger-than-average (6.0 per cent), very orangey, interpretation from the family micro-brewery that produces Abbaye des Rocs, in Montingies, Hainaut.

BLANCHE DES NEIGES

Full-coloured, sweetish, white beer from Huyghe, of Melle, near Ghent. This innocence of this contrasts with the threatening name of the brewery's strong ale Delirium Tremens. See also Floris.

BRUGS TARWEBIER

A 1930s advertisement for August Vanneste's "Three Monks" brewery, in Bruges, mentions "Spécialités de Bière Brune et Blanche". In 1983, Paul Vanneste's "Golden Tree" brewery became an early revivalist. His "Bruges Wheat Beer" is very soft and notably aromatic, with notes of pineapple and honey. The beer is now part of the Alken-Maes range.

DENTERGEMS WITBIER

Another early revivalist, from the Riva brewery, established in 1857 by the family De Splenter, and still in their hands. The brewery is in Dentergem, West Flanders. This spritzy, refreshing, beer has fresh apple notes and a touch of lemon-honey in the finish. The names Wittekop and Riva Blanche have also been used.

FLORIS GARDEN

Light, sweetish "White" beers from the Huyghe brewery. Unusual in that they come in flavours: an almondy, vanilla-ish Griotte; a strawberry Fraises that tastes of ice-cream; Passion, resembling flowering currant; "Ninkeberry", with apricot, mango and peach; Honey, flowery and sweet; and a smooth, creamy, Chocolat, spelled without the final "e". Floris and Ninke are the children of brewing consultant Roger Mussche.

HAECHT TARWEBIER

An older spelling is used by the Haacht brewery, near the village of the same name in Brabant, to describe its wheat beer. This tart, dry, quenchingly acidic, example emphasises wheat-beer characteristics and is only lightly spiced.

LIMBURGSE WITTE

Brings back the rounder flavours of the first revivalist wheat beers. Dense, creamy head; lightly spicy, fruity, nose; very soft, clean, orangey honey palate. Made by the Limburg brewery St Jozef (known for its Pax Pils), and marketed in partnership with neighbours Martens (renowned for its Sezoens).

MATER WIT

Named for the village near Oudenaarde that is home to the brewery Roman. Mater Wit has the aroma of sherbet, flavour of boiled sweets, and the quenching qualities of fresh lemonade.

MORT SUBITE WITTE LAMBIC

Smooth and creamy, leaving good Brussels lace. Dry, Complex flavours, but the coriander is the most assertive element, gradually developing toward a quite bitter finish.

STEENDONK

Unusual touch of cinnamon in the spicing. Herbal dryness is balanced with sherbety notes and smooth, sweeter, flavours reminiscent of melon. As the name suggests, a joint venture between Steenhuffel's respected Palm brewery and Breendonk's Moortgat, the latter famous for Duvel.

SUPER-FAGNES "LA BLANCHE"

Refreshingly tangerine-like in its aroma and flowery palate. Peels of sweet oranges and lemons are used. In addition to the usual coriander, there is also cumin. Served on premise at an elaborate, tourist-oriented, brewpub in the Ardennes, at Mariembourg, near Couvin (Braaserie des Fagnes, 26 Route de Nismes. Tel 060-31-15-70. Fax 060-31-19-40). A wide range of beers is made, in a very modern. well-equipped small brewhouse, open to view. Equipment from the defunct De Gauquier brewery (1858-1977), which operated in the town of Chimay, has been installed in a mini-museum.

TIMMERMANS LAMBIC WITTE/BLANCHE: The first Lambic-based white beer. This is a hazy, young (six-to-12 months), Lambic spiced in the kettle with coriander and sweet orange peels. Pale candy-sugar is also used. The winey Lambic flavours are still evident, including some crisply toasty notes, but it is a very easily drinkable, beer, with a quenching gingery note (though that spice is not used).

TITJE: Fruit and herbal notes in the bouquet; tart, dry and thirst-cutting in the palate and finish. The name is an intentional double-entendre. A Titje is, in the local patois, a citizen of Enghien, a town near Silly, in Hainaut. This beer is made by Brasserie de Silly, better known for its Saison.

TROUBLETTE

The haze in beer is sometimes referred to as "trouble", and that word has the same root as "turbulent" or "turbid". A white beer can justifiably celebrate its turbidity. This one has an extremely perfumy. sweet lemon, aroma; a very smooth palate; and a fruity acidity in a dry finish. Styrian and Saaz hops are used in the regular Troublette. A "Bio" (organic) version employs Spalt hops, and seems fruitier and slightly less dry. Hops are very hard to grow organically, and Spalt (albeit excellent) is one of the few varieties cultivated in this way. These beers, along with a range of strong ales, aremade by the micro-brewery La Caracole, whose own name celebrates the snail symbol of languid Namur. The brewery was founded there in 1990, but four or five years later moved beyond Dinant to the Ardennes village of Falmignoul. There, La Caracole has lovingly restored the premises and equipment of a brewery believed to date from at least 1766, and silent since 1971. Remarkably, the kettles are still wood-fired. "It is easy find wood in the Ardennes," brewer Jean-Pierre Debras told me, "the problem is finding it dry. If it is too damp, it burns slowly and the kettles gets too hot. It is easy to overcook the pale beers, and give them too much caramelisation of flavour and colour". Not a problem Debras and partner François Tonglet could have anticipated when they first met, at the age of 12 or 13, in the school choir.

VLAAMSCH WIT:

Also labelled as Blanche des Flandres and Flemish White. This beer has an orangey aroma, with its sweetness turning to dryness as the palate develops herbal notes. Very light and refreshing. Produced by Van Honsebrouck, of Ingelmunster, West Flanders. This eclectic brewery appears in several chapters of "The Great Beers of Belgium".

WATOU'S WIT:

Definite coriander emphasis in this slightly darker (a pink tinge?), foamy, white beer from the West Flanders brewery Van Eecke, famous for its Poperings Hommelbier.

WITTEKERKE

The name, meaning "White Church", has a suitably pastoral appeal, but is derived from the title of a Belgian television soap opera about an imaginary village or small town in Flanders. Characters in the series are depicted drinking this beer. The beer is produced in Bavikhove, West Flanders, by the De Brabandere brewery. Wittekerke contains oats, with the consequent smoothness. It pours with a dense, creamy, head, and has an attractive, opalescent, greeny-gold, colour. It is very aromatic indeed, with a clean, teasing, perfumy fruitiness and a faintly herbal tartness. The body is light but smooth. The flavours are rounded, with much subtlety and complexity. At first it seems spicily dry, but there is also a light, underlying creamy sweetness. Wittekerke Speciale is a stronger , wintry, counterpart.

It has a hiny of pears and cream in the aroma. There is a dryish creamness in the palate, too, deveoping a yogurty acidity in the finish.

Kuurnse Witte is an unusually strong (6w; 7.5v) companion brew, named for a nearby small town. Kuurne's self-mocking donkey symbol is on the label. For a beer of its strength, this is astonishingly easy to drink. It is lemony, winey and tingly.

Soap opera's suds...the cast of the Wittekerke tv serial raise a glass in the brewhouse.

Brown beers
From a brew with which to prepare (and accompany) a beef stew to an après-ski winter warmer.

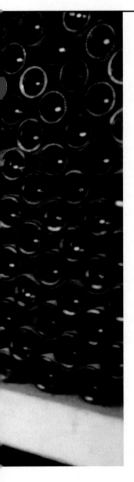

No corner of the brewing world is as strongly associated with truly dark brown ales as Flanders. This is especially true of East Flanders, and notably the area around Oudenaarde. This old city, with many springs, has long been a centre of brewing. It was also the most famous centre of Flemish tapestry-making in the 16th century and is noted for its Gothic architecture. The city's power derived from its occupying a strategic position on the river Schelde. The small hills rising from the valley are known rather grandly as The Flemish Ardennes.

At their best, ales in the Oudenaarde style have a teasingly smooth, almost feathery, fluffy, body (from water low in calcium, high in sodium bicarbonate); a dry, complex, caramelish, maltiness; a winey, nutty sherry, Montilla note (from long periods of maturation at ambient cellar temperatures); a light but distinct interplay of sweetness and sourness; and a spritzy finish.

To my palate, this is the perfect style of beer with which to make the classic beef carbonade. The beer is as typically Flemish as the dish. In his Carbonade Flamande, Escoffier suggests either an old Lambic or a Stout. These are extremely different styles, and a Flemish Old Brown falls between them at equal distances. It is not as tart as the one or as burnt-tasting as the other in its dark malt character. Its lactic acidity seems perfectly to tenderize the beef, and that Montilla character adds piquancy to the cooking liquid. While preparing this dish, I enjoy a glass of the beer, which serves as a perfect pick-me-up in the late afternoon. Then I put my Carbonade in the oven and let my appetite become aroused while the dish cooks slowly for three hours, in time for a wonderful dinner.

Like Lambic in the making of Gueuze, the Old Browns traditionally are blends of young and old beers. This is also true of several similar beers with a redder colour that are made mainly in West Flanders.

This blending can be a means of creating a secondary fermentation, but it is also a way of combining and balancing flavours. In the days before refrigeration, when no one brewed in summer, a stock would be laid down for those months. By the autumn, the last of this beer would have become winey and acidic, and might be blended with, fresher, sweeter, new beer to enliven its flavour. Eventually, "old" beers were produced purely as an ingredient for blending. While the Lambic and West Flanders brewers traditionally use wooden vessels for aging and blending, iron or steel are usual in the East Flanders breweries.

LIEFMANS

By far the best known Old Brown is today brewed by Riva, at Dentergem, in West Flanders, but fermented, matured, blended and bottle-conditioned at its original home, Liefmans, at Oudenaarde, in East Flanders. Riva, which was founded by its present proprietors' family in 1896, now owns Liefmans, which has tax documents showing that it existed in 1679. The Liefmans family owned the brewery from around 1770 to 1905. There are a couple of oblique links between the Liefmans brewery and the performing arts. One was Leon van Geluwe, manager of the Royal Conservatory of Bruges; his son Pierre bought the brewery in 1905 after hearing at a dinner party that it was for sale. In typically Belgian fashion, the company history still recalls the

Hand-wrapped bottles are something of a Belgian tradition. Among breweries that present their beer in this way, Liefmans is the best known.

"Three centuries of craftsmanship"... the rustic brew depicted in the sign has become a sipping beer for the connoisseur.

restaurant where the dinner took place, the Pomme d'Or. Some of the equipment from the time of the van Geluwe family was retained when the brewery moved to its present site by the river Schelde in the 1930s. For its period, it was a very old-fashioned brewery, and hard to operate. The mash-tuns were too small to fill the needlessly large, open, square, wood-clad, kettles, which look like huge, two-storey, crates. It may have been the difficulty of heating these vessels that led to the routine of simmering the wort overnight, though in earlier days some Flemish beers were boiled for 30 to 40 hours. In 1968, the brewery employed 77 people to make a modest 25,000 hectolitres per year.

In the 1970s and 1980s, former ballet-dancer Rose Blancquaert-Merkx provided the second link with the performing arts. She managed the brewery for some years, fought hard to maintain the character of its beers, and gave them a certain cult status. After the Riva takeover wort from Dentergem was phased in, and the Oudenaarde kettles were last used in 1991. At that time 21 people were employed, still a huge number in relation to the output.

Liefmans' tawny brown beers are brewed from three malts: Pilsner-type, crystal and roast. They are hopped with Goldings and Saaz, in one addition, and boiled for two hours. Fermention is in open copper vessels with the house yeast (which has for decades been cultured at Liefmans, although its origins can be traced back to the famous Rodenbach brewery). I will always remember Madame Rose, the former ballet-dancer, donning a pair of clogs and climbing into one of the tanks: "You should see what cleaning they need," she told me, firmly. The brown beers are produced in three versions: Odnar (3.2 per cent alcohol by weight; 4.0 by volume); Oud Bruin (4.0w; 5.0v); and Goudenband (in recent years increased from 4.8w; 6.0v; to 6.5w-7.0v to 8.0w-8.5v). In the making of Goudenband ("Gold Riband"), beer of around four months old is blended with stock two or three times that age. The blend is centrifuged, primed with invert sugar, given a dosage of the original yeast and bottle-conditioned in the brewery's cellars.

Although loyalties to local styles are firmer in Belgium than some countries, they have diminished somewhat. Goudenband, once very much a local beer, is now more widely sold - but as something special. That is why its strength was increased, to make it a sippin' beer. When this change was first made, the beer was uncharacterisically rich and sweet. Riva now seems to have found a surer touch. Goudenband has regained some of its characteristic sour wineyness, iron, saltiness and toatiness. These notes will develop with a few months', or even years', cellaring. The brewery still sells ten-year-old bottles of the older version, and some cafés have it at 25 years.

Why would Riva persist with the troublesome business of brewing in Dentergem and fermenting in Oudenaarde? "The Riva beers cannot risk accidental exposure to the Liefmans' yeast," I was told when I first asked this question. Now, it seems possible that in the future a small new kettle might be installed at Liefmans.

The boilerhouse of the old brewery has been turned into a 200-seat beer-bar. This is known as the Zaal ("Hall") de Baudelot, after the traditional wort-cooler that features in the decor. The idea is to present Liefmans as a "house brewery" (Tel 55-311392; fax 55-3194860) as well as a museum and art gallery, which can be visited on a Schelde river trip.

For the benefit of visitors who are not committed beer-lovers, Liefmans has introduced what is intended to be an "easier" beer: a paler, orangey-coloured, hazy ("natural") brew, at a lower strength (4.4w; 5.5v), but produced from the same malts (obviously in a different ratio) and the "house" yeast. This beer, called Jan van Gent, is lightly toffeeish, with a "peaches in syrup" fruitiness and faintly yogurty finish.

Once a ballet-dancer, then a custodian of Liefmans: Madame Rose Blancquaert in eminent, and playful, company with fellow Knights of the Mashing Fork.

Riva has invested millions of Belgian Francs in tank capacity at Liefmans, much of it dedicated to a whole-cherry Kriek based on the Oud Bruin. The fermentation of the fruit, and some sugar priming, boosts this to 5.2w; 6.5v. Thirteen kilos of cherries and 0.2kg of juice (to enhance aroma) are added per 100 litres, and the fruit stays on the beer for at least six months.

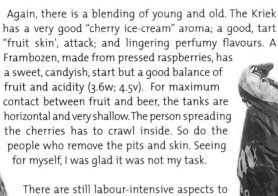

Again, there is a blending of young and old. The Kriek has a very good "cherry ice-cream" aroma; a good, tart "fruit skin', attack; and lingering perfumy flavours. A Frambozen, made from pressed raspberries, has a sweet, candyish, start but a good balance of fruit and acidity (3.6w; 4.5v). For maximum contact between fruit and beer, the tanks are horizontal and very shallow. The person spreading the cherries has to crawl inside. So do the people who remove the pits and skin. Seeing for myself, I was glad it was not my task.

There are still labour-intensive aspects to work at Liefmans. four people hand-wrap bottles with tissue-paper, each managing a good 3,000 per day. Over-sized bottles are a specialty. I was temped by a 12-litre Balthazar, but was told that it had been reserved by a doctor.

Liefmans' medicinal Glühkriek, intended to be served hot in winter, is a highly original beer. Its spicing with cinnamon and clove is very evident, though the anis is sensibly restrained. Although it is very spicy, these flavours are well balanced with rich fruit, iron and acidity. Liefmans has also assisted in the development of a similar beer, Quelque Chose, made by Unibroue, of Quebec.

The notion of beers made for mulling causes the odd raised eyebrow, but these are very enjoyable, complex, brews, and no stranger than an après-ski glühwein.

FELIX

Where an arm of the river once flowed, and a Jesuit abbey stood from the 1200s, is a second Oudenaarde brewery, tracing its origins from the 1600s. It makes an Oudenaarde brown, under the name Felix. At one stage, the brewery was owned by a man named Felix, but it has been in the hands of the Clarysse family since World War II. Although the odd abbey wall still stands, the present brewery's buildings date mainly from the 1970s. The beer is very soft and sweet, with a toffeeish tinge, though it does also have a touch of tartness.
The brewery also produces a perfumy Kriek, a white beer and an abbey-style beer.

ROMAN

East of the town, but still within the community of Oudenaarde, at Mater, is the brewery of the family Roman. The village and the family names may have their origins in Roman times; Mater is on the old road from Cologne to Dunkirk. The brewery is more recent, having been established by the family in 1545, as an inn and farm. The 14th generation is now active.

Roman times?
The family business
dates from the 1500s,
but much of the
present brewery is from
the late 1800s and early
1900s. An open-day at
the brewery draws
a crowd.

Earlier generations looked sternly from picture-frames on the wall as Louis Roman led me through a tasting with his sons Lode and Carlo. I was given a printed family-tree just to make sure I got things right.

When I asked why Roman's brown beers were less tart than those of some neighbours, I was told - as though such distinctions applied only yesterday - that this was a result of their being on the "German" side of the Schelde in the 1300s. The German Emperor issued an edict that beer be made with hops. The other side of the river was controlled by the French, who ruled for beer with herbs and spices rather than hops.

The brewery has imposing buildings set round a courtyard, with flower-beds, a Romanesque stable block, and a tiled hall occupied by beautifully-kept ammonia-compressors, steam engines and early power-generating equipment. Its copper brewhouse dates from the 1930s, but must have been very modern at that time. Different cellars, and five yeasts, are used for the various styles of beer.

Until the 1950s, the company made only brown beers. Roman Oudenaards (4.0w; 5.0v) has a dark cherry colour; the aroma of oranges in boxes; with zesty flavours developing against a background of smooth, sweetish malt, chocolatey flavours and roastiness. The Burgundy-coloured Special Roman (4.4w; 5.5v) is also spicy and chocolatey, but toastier and more textured, with hints of crisp tartness at the edge of the tongue. The brewery has also on occasion produced a Dobbelen Bruinen (6.4w; 8.0v), rounder and firmer, with cocoa, bitter chocolate and warming alcohol in the finish.

Roman has a strong ale called Sloeber (see Wicked Beers), and is becoming well known for its Ename range (see Abbey beers). The brewery's extensive portfolio has also included a bronze Christmas Beer (6.4w; 8.0v with "sweet oloroso" honey and flower notes.

CNUDDE

North of the town, but also in the community of Oudenaarde, in the village of Eine, is the charming brewery of the Cnudde family. Looking at its mini-industrial style, I was reminded of a 1700s woollen mill in England. In fact, the brewery was built as recently as 1919, and somewhat restored in the 1950s.

It was established by by Fons Cnudde, then run by his son Omer and grandson Louis. When Louis Cnudde became ill in the early 1990s, there was some doubt about the future of the enterprise. Now, while Louis' widow still occupies the white-pained, shuttered house on the site, her three sons run the brewery.

Classic 1930s kettles, beautifully kept, at the Roman brewery near Oudenaarde. Their proud guardian is brewmaster Jozef Snauwaert. Pepper pot hop strainer, a very unusual design at the Cnudde brewery (right)

Each has a "day job". Pieter is a lawyer, Lieven teaches maths, and Steven is an engineer. The three brew together, eight times a year, on a Saturday. There are no employees.

The beer is sold only in Eine, at the village's ten cafés. Next door to the brewery is a very basic café called the Casino. The café has a skittle alley, a card school, a moto-cross club and soccer scarves hanging from the ceiling. When I was there, each day's placings in the Tour de France had been posted on the wall. I could have stayed all day - drinking Cnudde beer.

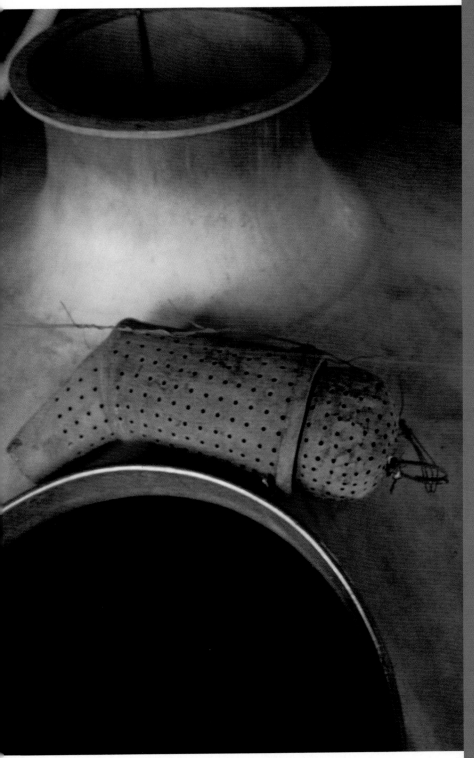

Café Casino, at Eine, the kind of local where a drinker wants to stay all day.

It is brewed in a very simple way, from Pilsner malt and cara-mel, with Northern Brewer and Styrian hops, the latter strained in a device like a pepper-pot. The character of the beer is undoubtedly influenced by the lack of refrigeration in the brewe-ry. The wort passes from the 60 -hectolitre kettle to an open cooler, made of copper, in the gable of the roof, then to a Baudelot. This latter system, looking rather like an old-fashioned radiator, is filled with cold water while wort flows over the outside. The wort is cooled - but also exposed to the atmosphere.

Primary fermentation is in stainless steel. Rodenbach is a sizable, and in many ways modern, brewery, but with a huge difference.

Cnudde Oudenaards Bruin has a claret colour; an alcohol content in the range 3.2-4.0w; 4.0-5.0v; and a fresh, light, cleansing dryness, with hints of iron and a faint tartness. I had the sense of drinking an honest, straightforward village beer from less self-conscious times.

Both the brewery and Mrs Cnudde's house face on to a small orchard with about ten cherry trees. There are enough cherries to make one brew of Kriek each year, and this is kept for the family. The beer goes on to the cherries in plastic vessels. I tasted a two-year-old brew that was tawny red and sour-ish, with a beautiful balance of fruit, pits and beer.

Also in the garden is a sculpture of a buffalo. This American symbol of robustness appears in several places in the Oudenaarde area, recalling the heroism there of the U.S. military, especially the Ohio National Guard, in World War I.

OTHER BROWNS

Not far away in the little town of Zottegem, East Flanders, the Crombé brewery for decades produced a pale brown ale, with a pinkish tinge, and a well regarded Kriek. Behind a café and a family home, through an arch, the bre-wery is a hidden antique, dating from 1798. It even has the remnants of its own hop kilns. It has operated intermittently in recent years, and some of its beer has been produced by the Strubbe brewery, in Ichtegem, West Flanders. Several other small breweries in East Flanders and Flemish Brabant make sourish brown ales, and there are dozens of dark brews of other types produced in Belgium.

An example blended with Lambic is made under the name Jack-Op by Belle-Vue. A similar style of beer was traditionally made on the other side of Brussels, in and around the town

of Aarschot. In recent years, this style was briefly revived by the Biertoren brewery, of Kampenhout, a small town about a dozen miles north of Brussels. Unfortunately, this revival did not succeed. The beer, along with the brewery's Campus range, is now made in East Flanders, by Huyghe, of Melle, near Ghent.

A quite different style of brown ale, brewed to the east of Brussels, is Gildenbier. This was originally the local style of Diest, and is now a speciality of the Haacht brewery. This is a very sweet, caramel-tasting, brown ale, which seems soft and innocent for a brew of 17 Plato, 5.1w; 6.3v. This unusual beer is brewed from three malts, with dosages of candy sugar in the kettle and the maturation vessel. It may seem overpoweringly sweet, but it is wonderful with a chocolate dessert.

A quite different style of brown ale, brewed to the east of Brussels, is Gildenbier. This was originally the local style of Diest, and is now a speciality of the Haacht brewery. This is a very sweet, caramel-tasting, brown ale, which seems soft and innocent for a brew of 17 Plato, 5.1w; 6.3v. This unusual beer is brewed from three malts, with dosages of candy sugar in the kettle and the maturation vessel. It may seem overpoweringly sweet, but it is wonderful with a chocolate dessert.

A bigger brother to this brew has been given more emphasis since the 500th anniversary of the Holy Roman Emperor Charles V. This beer, which was already in the range, is called Keizer Karel (in Flemish) or Charles Quint (in French). It is slightly drier and stronger (5.6w; 7.0v), has a firm, smooth, body, a suggestion of licorice, and a warming finish. It is sometimes served in a four-handled ceramic mug.

CHAPTER IX Rodenbach
Further producers of Red Beers

Red beers

The burgundies of Belgium...
with the acidity to be truly food-friendly.

There was an outcry on the internet, especially from North America, when a rumour spread at the beginning of the new millennium that the Rodenbach brewery might drop its Grand Cru. This beer is so sophisticated and complex in character that its appeal is limited to connoisseurs, but its supporters are articulate and vocal. It is regarded as a world classic, even if it shocks the unwary, and seems "old-fashioned" to some consumers in its native Flanders.

The owners of the brewery quickly moved to assure consumers that Grand Cru was not in danger. When I visited Rodenbach to see for myself, in 2001, the brewers were pondering the development of an even more sophisticated version.

Rodenbach Grand Cru is the outstanding example of a style of beer that has no name. Beers in this style are produced by nine or ten breweries. They have a brownish-red colour; and are made

Primary fermentation is in stainless steel. Rodenbach is a sizable, and in many ways modern, brewery, but with a huge difference.

primarily from barley malt (though they can be as acidic as a Berliner Weisse wheat beer, without quite the drying finish). The classic examples are fermented with mixed cultures, and aged for long periods in wood, but large fixed tuns rather than casks.

Some of these brewers, and many beer-lovers, make no distinction between the Old Brown style traditional in Oudenaarde and East Flanders and the sharper-tasting, redder, interpretation more frequently seen in West Flanders, especially in the towns and villages around the old linen-textile city of Kortrijk (Courtrai, in French).

When I first encountered the latter, in the mid 1970s, I identified them simply as Red Beers. This was clearly an insufficient description, and I later added the word "Sour", I am tempted by "Sweet-and-Sour", but that sounds too much like a dish on a Chinese menu. The sourness is tartly thirst-cutting. I once wrote that Rodenbach was the most refreshing beer in the world. This comment, reproduced in my handwriting, at one stage found its way on to the packaging. On my most recent visit to brewery, I was casually informed that a film crew was in the building. Would I please repeat my opinion on camera? This time, I decided to specify Rodenbach Grand Cru. Served lightly chilled, it is refreshing in the manner of a young Beaujolais. At a natural cellar temperature, it assumes more Burgundian robustness.

When they talk of "The Burgundies of Belgium", the Flemings are referring to their entire cellar-full of beer-styles but, in

colour, the allusion perfectly fits in this case. The most authentic examples of this West Flanders style gain their colour from specific types of dark malt, with a slight contribution from the oak, and perhaps some Maderization. Some also add a dash of fruit juice or caramel. The best have a balance of light maltiness, fruitiness and acidity, with some tannin. It is the acidity especially that makes them so food-friendly. A famous old advertisement for Rodenbach beer said simply, if confusingly: "It's wine ...". Variations on the theme have Burgundian names like Bourgogne des Flandres, Vlaamse Bourgogne and Duchesse de Bourgogne.

Running the brew out of the kettle... but a new brewhouse was installed in 2001.

RODENBACH

By Belgian standards, Rodenbach is a middle-sized brewery (with a capacity of around 250,000 hectolitres a year), and that is a diffiult place to be. Like most traditional beer countries, Belgium has plenty of breweries, and the most successful are either large (making mass-market beers economically) or small (producing specialities).

The avenues of oak tuns are inescapable, a maze from one room to the next, but their importance goes beyond the historic and aesthetic.

Rodenbach survives because it is uniquely equipped to make its world classic beers. No other brewery making Flemish red ales restricts itself to this style, and none of them has remotely as many oak tuns. Nor has any other brewery elsewhere in the world. The word "unique" is largely misused, but it applies to Rodenbach. To justify its existence, Rodenbach has to fill its forest of oak. Apart from influencing the colour of the beer, the oak vessels shape its aroma, flavour, texture and overall character. A brewery that maintains and proudly uses them is a national treasure. A knowledgeable beer-lover compiling a list of the world's most distinctive breweries (from a viewpoint of equipment, production methods and their end result) might settle for three, four or five, or insist upon ten. Choices would vary, but Rodenbach would be in everyone's list.

In the days when everyone drank their local type of beer, it made sense to have a brewery of this size devoted to the style of West Flanders. Today, Rodenbach survives by selling its beer as a (large) speciality not just in its home province but throughout Belgium and increasingly in other countries. The brewery is in the town of Roeselare (Roulers, in French), which is a canalside inland port but hardly a metropolis.

With its tiled housing and brass railings, the 1920s brewhouse has an imposing, if marine, look.

In Ireland, the port city of Dublin is bigger - and the capital - and the Guinness brewery far larger (though less visually surprising). It has oak tuns, though fewer of them. It springs to mind as a rare example of a large brewery making a beer with a character that can shock the novice (less with sourness than burnt and bitter flavours). There is even a parallel in that both breweries were originally owned by dynastic families.
Some people believe that Rodenbach's techniques of aging and blending were taken from the porter and stout brewers of

The world's most refreshing beer? Rodenbach's sharpness is very quenching, but the Grand Cru has the edge.

Britain and Ireland. I think it was initially the Flemish brewers who taught the islanders about such matters, though knowledge did begin to flow the otherway after the Industrial Revolution.

The Rodenbach family themselves had a colourful and distinguished history. They traced their roots to Andernach, on the Rhine, near Coblenz. In 1747 or 1750, during the rule of the Austrian Empire, Ferdinand Rodenbach came to Roeselare as a military surgeon. He wrote scientific papers on medicine (in German), became a local physician, and married a Flemish woman. In 1820, a member of the family, Alexander Rodenbach, bought a small brewery that already existed in the present site in Roeselare, at Spanjestraat. ("Spain Street" - the whole history of Belgium seems to be wrapped up in the brewery). In 1836, the brewery was sold to another member of the family, and that year has since been regarded as the foundation date of the present enterprise..

The founder, Alexander Rodenbach, was the most remarkable character of all. He had been blinded in an accident at a fairground shooting gallery when he was 11, but this did not stop him laying the foundations of a great brewery, devising a rudimentary form of braille, becoming a politician, and taking part in the movement for Belgium's independence. Alexander's brother Constantine was ambassador to Greece, and is buried in front of the Parthenon. In the 1870s, Eugene Rodenbach went to England to study brewing techniques there..

No one knows in which English breweries he worked, but it is interesting to note the Greene King's Strong Suffolk is the only British beer to be made by a process of aging in fixed oak tuns. If there were no North Sea, Rodenbach and Greene King would be relative neighbours. Since I pointed out these links a decade ago, the two breweries have established a friendly relationship. Like the (Graham and Sir Hugh) Greenes of that brewery, the Rodenbachs are also a literary family. Georges Rodenbach wrote in French, and Albrecht - who is remembered in a statue in the town - in Flemish.

The Rodenbach brewery itself is like a great monument to the art of beer-making. On one side of the street, set into a couple of acres of garden wooded with pines, horse-chestnuts and weeping willows, is a 19-room château built in 1891 for the director of the brewery. The garden slopes away to a lake, about 30 metres in diameter, which is fed by 70 small wells. There are trout in the lake, and their well-being is a good indication of the purity of the well-water, which also serves the brewery. Across the street, a maltings more than 100 years old, a circular structure, the height of a four or five-storey building, with a conical tower, is the centre-piece of the brewery. The maltings was closed in 1974, and has been turned into a small but care-fully-conceived museum. That project took two years, including the complete restoration of the tower. More recently, a full-scale visitor centre has been opened, showcasing more of this remarkable brewery.

Industrial archaeology is a feature of Roeselare, which has historically beenan important trading centre for agricultural produce in West Flanders. The people of the region are consi-dered in Belgium to be hard-working and financially prudent. What Alexander Rodenbach bought was the St George Brewery. Englishmen know George as their national saint, but he was also the inspiration of breweries in several countries (another of my favourites is St Georgen-Brau, noted for its Kellerbier, in Franconia). The convention of naming breweries after saints was once widespread. At Rodenbach, a spectacular relief of St George slaying the dragon, dated from 1836, decorates the wall of the present-day malt silos, built in 1962. The com-pany became part of the Palm group in 1998, and shortly after-wards work began on a new brewhouse.

Rodenbach beers are made from two- and six-row varieties of winter barley malt and a reddish, crystal-type malt of the style sometimes described by Continental Europeans as "Vienna". These malts comprise more than 80 per cent of the grist, and the rest is corn grist. A version of decoction is used. Several varieties of hops are employed. These have included Northern Brewer, Target and Yeoman, and especially Brewers' Gold, which is spicy but low in bitterness. Like all tart beers, the Rodenbach

brews are not intended to be very hoppy. Tartness and bitterness do not meld well. It is, though, important that the hops help preserve and clarify the beer during its long period in wood.

The principal beer was originally called simply Rodenbach. It is now known as Rodenbach Klassiek. This is made by the old method of blending "young" and "old" brews. The young beer is brewed to a gravity of 11.4-11.5 Plato (1045-6). The beer intended for aging has 13.3 (1052-4).

When I first visited the brewery, it was using an open cooler and copper fermenting vessels, but these have long been superseded by more modern equipment. Primary fermentation is in cylindro-conical vessels. As brewing science has developed, so Rodenbach has looked more closely at its yeast, which has been in use for about 70 years. The first time I visited the brewery, I was told that the yeast, which is top-fermenting, contained three strains. By my next visit, five strains had been identified. Since then, the yeast has been more analytically examined, at the University of Leuven, and it is now considered to embrace 20 cultures, including a range of lactobacilli.

This handsome malting tower, more than 100 years old, is as tall as a four or five-storey building. It has been restored as a small museum.

Seventy-five per cent of the blended product is "young" beer, though even this has four weeks of warm conditioning, during which period it undergoes a secondary fermentation and some lactic character begins to develop. This takes place in horizontal stainless steel tank stanks. The beer destined for maturation has seven to eight weeks' warm conditioning in vertical stainless steel tanks.

This beer goes on to spend 18-24 months in wood. During this time, there is a third sequence of micro-biological activity, both aerobic and anaerobic. The brewery regards this as a third fermentation. The lactic acid, and some acetic, develops in the beer; there is an influence of micro-organisms resident in the wood; some Brettanomyces activity; and most significantly, the development of more fruity, "ripe apple" esters and roundness of flavour. A degree of evaporation also has an influence on the character of the aging beer. In recent years, the brewery has been slightly shortening the secondary fermentation and giving more attention to the third with a view to achieving a milder and fuller flavour. To the same end, work has also been done on the choices of tuns from which the beers are blended. The wood, with its tannins and caramels, makes a direct contribution to the beer's palate and colour. I once expressed surprise that the wood would continue to impart character after constant employment, and it was explained to me that the inside of each tun was scraped after every use.

Would this not eventually result in the tuns being too thin to be safe, I asked? I was told that the walls of the tuns varied between five and ten centimetres in thickness, that each scraping would remove a fraction of a millimetre, and that even the most exhaustively used would have seen only 50 or so brews. The oldest vessel is 160 years old, and many have been in place since the earliest days of this century. When the brewery expanded at one stage, some were acquired from a competitor that was closing. They are variously made from oak from the Vosges and from Poland. The brewery has three coopers to maintain them, working with numbered staves, hoops, reeds and beeswax.

The tuns make a remarkable sight: the smallest containing more than 100 hectolitres, and the largest six times that size. One hall contains nearly a hundred, and there are twice that many arranged in ten smaller rooms. In the biggest hall, there are five lines of 20 tuns each, with narrow paths between them. The halls are heated if the ambient temperature falls below 15 °C (59 °F).

Although much of the matured beer is used in the blending of the Rodenbach Klassiek, some is held back to be bottled "straight" as Grand Cru. The Klassiek is a complex, tasty, sweet-and-sour, refreshing beer, with suggestions of Madeira, passion-fruit, oakiness, and hints of iron. The Grand Cru is more assertive all round, very slightly bigger in body and darker in colour. Both beers are so tart that they are sweetened slightly with caramelised sugar before being bottled (and then stabilised by flash-pasteurisation). Neither is intended for laying-down, though they do have relatively good keeping qualities.

Some of their admirers would welcome an unsweetened, unpasteurised, version, perhaps to a slightly higher gravity, with the age of the Grand Cru. Like several "old" beers, the Grand Cru has its own distinctive freshness - a paradox in brewing. Although the whole point of these beers is their tartness, some drinkers sweeten them with a dash of Grenadine syrup. For its 150th anniversary, the brewery made a sweeter version named Alexander Rodenbach, after its founder. This blended the freshness of the Grand Cru with a cherry essence, but the product was dropped in 2000. The Palm group had meanwhile been joined by Boon, which produces a more traditional cherry beer.

Rodenbach Klassiek has an alcohol content of 3.7 by weight (4.6 by volume). The Grand Cru has 4.8 (6.0v). They are normally served in Belgium in the range of 8-12 °C (47-53 °F).

There was a time when the Rodenbach beers were advertised as an accompaniment to the shrimps from the nearby coastline. The theme was dropped for fear that people would only order the beer when they planned to eat shrimps.

I have had some wonderful meals prepared and served with the Rodenbach range, not only in its native country but also prepared by Belgian chefs in London and New York. In the beer's home town of Roeselare, the restaurant Den Haselt (53 Diksmuidse Steenweg. Tel 051-225240; fax 241064) makes a feature of using the proud local products.

The old brewhouse: maritime or culinary? Brewing is a form of cooking, and chefs love Rodenbach.

Rodenbach Grand Cru
was used to prepare
this rabbit dish, with a
„confiture" of onions.
A couple of lobsters
joined the fun.

At Den Haselt, I once had an elaborate Rodenbach meal that began with Aperitif Grand Cru (comprising 90 per cent beer, the rest being equal proportions of Amer Picon and Crème de Cassis). The appetisers included oysters marinated in Alexander, a cup of prawn soup made with Rodenbach, and rabbit paté in a cherry confiture flavoured with Alexander and honey. Then there was goose liver with apple, served with Rodenbach. This was followed by monkfish with celery, presented with Grand Cru.

Then rabbit with langoustines, offered with Alexander. Finally came a sorbet made from Alexander, a custard flavoured with Rodenbach and a sabayon Grand Cru. On another occasion there, I was served a bread made with Grand Cru and almonds;

ris de veau in a sauce made from Rodenbach, and a passion fruit meringue flavoured with Alexander. On a more recent visit, the dessert included strawberries poached in Rodenbach, flambéed in pastis and dusted with pepper.

Rodenbach goes especially well - in my view - with shellfish dishes and salads; the heavier Grand Cru (with that hint of iron, as in a Cheval-Blanc) is a perfect accompaniment to liver, rabbit, and game birds like quail; Rodenbach Alexander was, of course, a natural dessert beer.

As Klassiek and Grand Cru become more cosmopolitan, it is easy to forget that they were once the everyday beers of the region. Then, on the odd gable or corner, an old advertising sign for Rodenbach - or a rival - offers a reminder.

FURTHER PRODUCERS OF RED BEERS

BAVIK

A new twist was given to the style in 2001 when this brewery issued a limited release, in the United States, of a beer at 5.2w (6.5v), tentatively called Petrus Aged Pale. This is made only with pale malts, and is unblended. It has 24-30 months in wood, and emerges with an "old gold" to bronze colour; an oaky aroma; hints of sherry (a Palo Cortado nuttiness?) and fruit (pears?) among a depth of flavours; the classic sourness in the finish; and an intentionally low carbonation. A "white" Red Beer? The temptation might be to compare it with a "white" Zinfandel, but the beer is much more robust in flavour and body. My preview of the finished product was at a restaurant with a decidedly winey name, Bistro Merlot. The beer stood up well to a slightly smoky trout mousse and peppery anchovies. I wonder how a Merlot would have performed?

OUD BRUIN

The brewery does have a more conventional Flemish Red Beer. At one stage, there was a version with the derivative name Ro-Bav. This was dropped in the 1960s but, a couple of decades later a new interpretation emerged with the name Petrus Oud Bruin.

The was inspired by St Peter, "the oldest Pope," explains chief executive Ignace De Brabandere. Then he adds: "...and the

holder of the keys to heaven". The name did once prompt a visit from the Bordeaux château Pétrus, but apparently it was very friendly.

Petrus Oud Bruin is blended from two specially made pale beers and one dark, the latter aged for 20-24 months in wood. The brewery has three cellars of wooden casks, each with nine 60-hectolitre vessels. A fourth cellar, the one primarily used, has beautifully maintained casks of 220 hectolitres each. These are about 50 years old, bought a couple of decades ago from France, where they first held white wine and then Calvados.

The beer has a big head; mahogany colour; a full flavour, with rich, soft, chocolatey notes, vanilla oakiness, dessert apple fruitiness, passion fruit and restrained acidity. It has 4.4w; 5.5v. In a local restaurant, I was served goose liver and smoked duck on a salad with a Petrus vinaigrette, mopped up with raisin-bread toast.

Although the Oud Bruin is a small product in volume, it is still emphasised in the company's literature, and the name Petrus has been taken as a rubric for a Speciale (ale) and a Triple. (see appropriate chapters).

The brewery takes its name from its home village of Bavikhove, West Flanders. It is in the fourth generation of the family De Brabandere. They were originally farmers in Bavikhove, and moved into brewing in 1894. The application to the town council for permission to build a brewery is still proudly displayed in the guest bar, along with a family tree and a glass case one or two metres wide containing a copper model of the present, 1950s, brewhouse.

The wooden tuns at Bavikhove (facing page) have their own angle on the art of being imposing... and in 2001 brewer Kris Van Acker produced a startling new beer. Above: Ignace De Brabandere heads the family firm.

BOCKOR

This brewery, also known for Jacobins Gueuze, produces in the local style a beer that has had various names but is currently known as Bellegems Bruin. This is a blend of a "Lambic-style" brew (made with a proportion of wheat), aged in oak, and an ale made from pale and darker crystal malts.

The end result has a good Burgundy colour. It is light and refreshing, with a good firm, crisp, tartness and touches of passion fruit or iron. It has an alcohol content of 4.4w; 5.5v or slightly more. The brewery is in Bellegem, West Flanders.

BOURGOGNE DES FLANDRES

A beer proudly promoted by Michel Van Houtryve, whose family have been in the brewing industry for seven generations, from the 1700s. They introduced Bourgogne des Flandres in 1911. After their brewery, in Bruges, closed in the 1950s, Bourgogne des Flandres was produced by distant relatives in the Verhaege brewing family in Vichte, West Flanders.

They have continued that tradition with their own Duchesse de Bourgogne (see below). The name Bourgogne des Flandres is now applied to a bittersweet, smooth, licorice-ish, brew of 4.0w; 5.0v that is a blend of a specially-made top-fermenting dark ale and Timmermans Lambic.

FACON

Neighbour of Bockor, in the village of Bellegem, West Flanders. The family-run brewery Facon, dating from 1874, still has its original cast-iron mash tun and bricked-in kettles, silent and ghostly. Today's beers are made in a much less attractive brewhouse installed in 1986. Dating from the same period as the original brewery is a family house next door. There, watched over by framed paintings and odd items of Art Nouveau, Jean-Michel Facon took me through a wide range of beers. The brewery's entrant in the local style is labelled Facon Ouden-Bruin and Vieille-Brune (the village is very near the language line). It is a blend of young and old beers, but without wood maturation. It has a brownish-red colour; a touch of Madeira on the nose; a quite sweet palate; and some balancing acidity in the finish. It has an alcohol content of 3.8w (4.8v).

LEROY

Near the town most of the world knows as Ypres (in Flemish, Ieper) is the village of Boezinge (pronounced to rhyme with "Boozing"). The Leroy brewery there has links of family ownership with Van Eecke, of Watou, also in West Flanders. The Leroy brewery has its origins in 1720, and was rebuilt in 1920 as part of a row of small businesses and houses. I tasted the beers in what appeared to be the front room of the family house. Leroy is best known for its lagers, but it does also have top-fermenting beers. Among them is a beer in the local style, named after a famous salesman for the brewery (a parallel with the Irish whiskey Paddy)

The beer is called Paulus. This has its own culture, and is matured "for years" in metal tanks. It pours with a rocky head; has an attractive claret colour; and is quite sweet and full-bodied for the style. It has an alcohol content of 4.8w (6.0v).

Front room tasting panel: Brothers Wim (left) and Philippe Leroy (centre), with veteran sales manager Paul Priem, sample their range.

STRUBBE

In the village of Ichtegem, West Flanders. This brewery was founded in 1830, but its imposing brick facade looks 100 years younger. In fact, that part of the building dates from the 1950s. Its brewhouse, with traditional copper kettles set into a brick trim, overlooks the parish church. Strubbe has kept alive several beers from breweries that have closed. It also make something of a speciality of spiced beers. Its own Ichtegems Oud Bruin is made with a proportion of caramunich malt, and aged hops, and additionally flavoured with licorice root. It is soured for 18 months in metal vessels open to the atmosphere. It has an alcohol content of 4.4w (5.5v). This beer is also the basis for a Kriek.

VAN HONSEBROUCK

This prolific brewery in Ingelmunster, West Flanders, has in the local style a beer called Bacchus: light and refreshing, with some caramel notes, and a spritzy tartness in the finish. The beer, at around 3.6w; 4.5v, is a blend, including stock aged in wood. The brewery has nine oak vessels. The aged beer in Bacchus is also the basis for Kriek "8".
This beer, of 8,0 per cent, is velvety and bittersweet, with berry-fruit and medicinal notes.

VAN STEENBERGE

This brewery, more than 200 years old, is also known as Bios, from the Greek word for life. "My grandfather liked the classics, and he was a microbiologist," explains current incumbent Paul Van Steenberge. The microbiologist also isolated the culture that is used to ferment a claret-coloured beer called Bios, sub-titled Vlaamse Bourgogne. This "Flemish Burgundy" is a blend of young and old beers, the latter aged in coated iron tanks. The finished product has a slightly syrupy start and a late lactic dryness. The brewery is set in two or three hectares of ornamental gardens, with a pretty ironwork bridge over a pond with ducks and swans. It is in Ertvelde, not far from Ghent, in East Flanders.

VERHAEGE

The Verhaege family have been making beer sinced the 1500s, and had a château farmhouse brewery before moving to the present site, in Vichte, West Flanders, in 1880. Other members of the family established breweries in Zulte and Waregem. During World War I, the Verhaeges refused to brew beer for the occupying forces, and in consequence the Germans dismantled their kettles. A new generation of the family has in the last half-dozen years focussed on speciality beers, of which the brewery has a large and flavoursome range.

Today, a privet hedge separates a family house from the brewery, which announces itself on whitewashed walls overlooking pots of geraniums. The original maltings and brewhouse still stand, though neither functions. Today's brewhouse dates from the 1960s, but three of the beers are aged in far older oak tanks, of which there about a dozen.

One of these beers, called Caves, is a Gueuze-like brew but with a fuller colour and nuttier, creamier palate. Another, Vichtenaar, named after the town, is in the local style. It has an alcohol content of just over 4.0w (5.0v); a cherryish colour; a big, iron-ish, bouquet; a fruity start; then Madeira and toffee.

A beer called life, from a garden brewery... Bios, from Van Steenberge

A third, the slightly more florid Duchesse de Bourgogne, at 5.0w (6.2v0, pours with a very good lace; and has a smooth, rich, texture; with a very interesting interplay of passion-fruit and chocolate; and a long, dry, acidic, finish. This is blend of beers eight and 18 months old. The beer is named after the Duke of Burgundy's daughter, Mary, born in Bruges in 1457. When she became Duchess, she was seen as a champion of the people of Flanders.

ZULTE

This village in East Flanders once had a brewery producing an excellent sour red beer. I visited the brewery in the 1980s, but it closed soon afterwards. Its beer has been produced in recent years by Alken-Maes, but in a grainier-tasting, less complex, more lactic, interpretation.

Saisons

Robust country beers for the summer season, the picnic, the cheese and charcuterie.

Another style much appreciated by the most knowledgeable American devotees of Belgian beers. On both sides of the Atlantic, Saison Dupont is the best-known, and inspiring, example. One or two Flemish brewers have whispered to me that, after their own beer, Saison Dupont is their favourite. It is otherwise not well known in Flanders. Saisons are a Wallonian style, and a relatively minor speciality even there. They are produced especially in and around the western part of the province of Hainaut. Saisons have typically been made by a handful of mainly very small and artisanal breweries. Some of these breweries show their origins as farms, and one or two others speak of the small beginnings of the industrial revolution.

Saisons were regarded as a distinct family of beers by brewing scientists in the late 1800s and early 1900s. These beers were originally produced to a variety of strengths, including "children's", "family", "double" and "royal" (Regal), but they were especially associated with the summer season. The beer had to be sturdy enough to last for the summer months, when brewing was impossible, but not too strong to be a harvest quencher.

Apart from region of origin, those two characteristics help characterise a Saison today. It is a medium-to-strong summer ale, traditionally with a distinctively yellow-orange colour; highly carbonated; well-hopped; dry and fruity, with a thirst-cutting acidity and a crisply quenching finish. It is hard to define by technical specification or method of production. Over the years, many techniques have been used.

Hard water is often used. High mashing temperatures are sometimes employed, to produce a substantial degree of un-fermentable sugars, giving a firm edge to the beer. In the past, some brewers allowed the wort to develop a degree of natural lactic acid before the boil. Or this may have happened afterwards, in the wort-cooling. Some breweries used the Baudelot system, in which the wort was exposed to the air, and any wild micro-organisms present, as it flowed over the outside of pipes containing cold water. Some of the beers gained acidity during maturation, usually in mild steel tanks. In some instances, the refreshing acidity was imparted by a blending of young and old beers. These brews are sometimes flavoured with dry-tasting spices and in the past were often dry-hopped. Their flavours also suggest the use of some very characterful yeasts.

Saisons are usually presented in corked Champagne bottles, with a secondary fermentation, and they can pour with a dense, rocky, head.; I am sometimes asked how Saisons compare with the Bières de Garde made across the border. The answer is that the French style at its most typical is not at all crisp or summery: it is softer, more rounded, richer, sweeter, and maltier, sometimes with a licorice note.

A TOUR OF SAISON BREWERIES (FROM BRUSSELS)

LEFÈBVRE

From Brussels, the main road south-west has scarcely passed Lembeek, and is still in the Zenne Valley, when there is a glimpse of the massive quarries at Quenast. The stone dug there was once used to make cobbled streets, and today provides ballast for the trans-European express railways. Its digging created a monumental thirst that could be slaked only by beer. There was

Farmhouse brewery or early industrial. The transition is evident in the style of building, with a hoist to load sacks of barley or malt in an attic-like "barn".

a brewer called Lefèbvre in Quenast in 1797, at the time of the French Revolution. No one is sure whether he was a forbear of Jules Lefèbvre, gamekeeper, farmer, maltster, brewer and publican.

When the men came to dig the stone, in the 1870s, Jules "The Keeper" built a new brewery, and established cafés at every exit to the quarries. He prospered, and his son was able to build a baronial house, almost a château, next to the brewery, by the river Zenne. "At the end of the First World War, British troops were billeted here, to wait for the Peace of Versailles," I was told by a member of the family. "The officers were English and Scots; the men were Indians. They drank Scotch whisky and seemed happy, then they fell silent. There was an epidemic called Spanish Flu. They began to die. One went home for Christmas and never came back. My grandmother used to talk about this."

The house still stands, but only fragments of the brewery. After the First World War, the family bought another brewery, high on the side of the valley. It still operates. In 1994, Pierre Lefèbvre and his son Philippe, the fourth and fifth generations in the brewery, told me how the direction and intensity of the wind affected the fire under their kettle. If the fire was high, the hot spots on the surface of the kettle would caramelise the beer to a greater

Fifth and sixth generations: Phlippe and Paul Emile Lefèbvre. degree. The way the draughts were manipulated would influence the flavour of the finished product. This truly was artisanal brewing. "We cannot put on the label a note to apologise for the lack of wind on the day this particular brew was made,"

Pierre observed to me wryly. The old brewhouse still stands as the basis for a museum, but Pierre has retired and Philippe has gleaming new vessels in stainless steel, heated by steam. When I called in 1997, Philippe's son Paul Emile, wearing a bright red baseball cap, was working in the brewery. I was told he would soon be off to brewing school, representing the sixth generation in the family business.

In the great days of the quarry, the brewery sold immense quantities of an ale named after the blue-grey, porphyritic stone. There are fewer workers today, the cafés have become private houses, and the men go home to watch television. A hint of the famous Porph Ale can be found in Saison 1900, the date of which recalls the height of production. This is a firm-bodied, dryish, Saison of 14 Plato (1056), 4.0w; 5.0v, with a good malt background; a citric palate; and crisp finish. The brewery also makes its white beer, a pioneering honey brew called Barbār and spicy products for the abbeys of Floreffe and Bonne Espérance. All of these beers have a secondary fermentation in the bottle. Quenast is just in Brabant, but right on the border with Hainaut.

SILLY

Just across the border, near the town of Enghien (in Flemish, Edingen), is the village of Silly, which sounds perfectly sensible in French. This village, on the river Sille, grows sugar-beet and wheat. In the centre of the village is a café proclaiming the beers of the family Meynsbrughen (who seem to have fiddled with the spelling of their name over the years). Next door, behind a restored façade, is a cobbled yard that looks straight into the brewhouse. It is still very much an agricultural brewery.

Farmer Nicholas Meynsbrughen established the brewery in 1850, and his family still run it. All of its beers have a very soft fruitiness, reminiscent of nectarine. Its Saison de Silly (4.0w, 5.0v) also has a distinctive wineyness and tartness. This beer is made by the blending of a pale brew with a darker one that has been aged for about a year in a metal tank. Some devotees feel that Saison de Silly is the example most loyal to the tradition, though it does not have refermentation in the bottle. The brewery's other products include pale and dark versions of its maltier, stronger (6.4w, 8.0v) Double Enghien and a potent, smooth, spritzy bronze ale called La Divine (7.6, 9.5v). This area is noted for its loyalty to the local bières spéciales. "It's the Jeu de Balles that causes the thirst," I was told by the patron at

The Enghien beers are part the range of the brewery at Silly.

Café Titien, in nearby Bassilly. He was talking about Pelotte, a game that appears in odd pockets and in various rather different forms, along the European seaboard from Friesland to the Basque country of Spain - and, as Jai-Lai, from Cuba to Florida to Connecticut. There was a league-table on the wall. The Jeu de Balles has also led to the practice of long-distance egg-throwing. In 1990, one of the locals threw an egg 63 metres, and it landed in The Guinness Book of Records.

ELLEZELLOISE

"Worth the detour." as the Michelin Guide would say. A slight diversion toward Flanders, but still just inside the province of Hainaut, and near the town of Ronse (Renaix). Where the Flemish Ardennes spill into Wallonia, they are just called the collines. "La Bière des Collines" is the slogan of this brewery. It is on a lone hillside, and takes its name from the nearby village of Ellezelles. (75 Guinaumont, Ellezelles. Tel 068-45-31-60. Fax 068-54-37-16). As a mascot, it adopts from local folklore a witch called Quintine.

A brewer's son, Philippe Gerard had 25 years in the industry, latterly with Bush (see below) before setting up his own business."Brewing is my job, my hobby, my passion," he told me. "My own brewery, my own beer...that was my dream."

He bought a farm in 1985, and spent eight years seeking out second-hand equipment that could be adapted. The result is a beautifully-fitted copper brewhouse set into a brick base. The kettles are open to a café with eight tables, each of which was decorated with a vase of flowers when I called. Bench seating adds to the rustic mood. A local cheese, flavoured with the beer, is served.

The whole arrangement is in the gable of the roof, with open beams. There is also an outdoor terrace, and beer is available to take away in swing-top bottles. The first brew was in 1993, and in 2001, Gerard started building more storage space, in a sympathetic, barn-like, construction. The farm is a listed building.

Philippe is helped by his wife Jacqueline and their children David and Dimitri, who are both in their 30s.

The beers are neither centrifuged nor filtered. The hop varieties are English Kent Goldings and Styrians, throughout. When I was tasting them, I wrote in my notebook: "Good honest beers." Only later did I realise that this phrase had been used to define the local style by Marc Rosier, of Dupont (see below).

I also wrote: "Robust". and "straightforward." Quintine Blonde has an earthy, creamy, aroma; a malty dryness; and lots of appetisingly hoppy finish that suggests more than the specified 38-39 units of bitterness. (6.4w; 8.0v).

Saison 2000 has an attractive bronze colour; a big, creamy, head; a lightly, nutty, very fruity, palate; and a dry, spritzy finish. (5.2w; 6.5v). What makes it a Saison? In Gerard's view, it can more easily be taken as a summer refresher than his other beers. It is more attenuated, and therefore leaner; it is lower in alcohol, but still quite big.

Witches are popular symbols in Belgian brewing One called Quintine seems to heading for the brewhouse at Ellezelles.

Quintine Ambrée has a fuller, reddish, colour, with a return to a pronounced emphasis on malty dryness. Munich malt is clearly very influential. (6.8w; 8.5v).

The brewery also has the excellent Hercule Stout: creamy, coffeeish, with spicy. Sambuca-like, notes. (7.2w; 9,0v).

PIPAIX

Farther down the road, beyond Ath, the municipality of Leuze has two breweries producing Saisons, in the villages of Pipaix (which also has Bush Beer) and Tourpes.

Saison de Pipaix can trace its history back to a farm brewery in the 1780s. The present brewery is still powered by an 1885 steam engine, its piston thumping and exhaling steam as, through a web of pulley-belts, it drives the mash-mixer and rakes. As the mash progresses, the open tun fills the room with steam. Some of the equipment dates from either side of the First World War, and some buildings from the period just after the Second. The brewery remained within one family until the mid 1980s, when the owner became ill and felt he could not continue.

It was in a very dilapidated condition when it was rescued by two young schoolteachers who were already making beer at home. Jean-Louis Dits taught history, and felt strongly about the traditions of the region. He and his wife, Anne-Marie Lemaire had earlier started an association to promote local products. Anne-Marie taught biology, which is a good basis for the science of fermentation.

They continued to teach, while putting the brewery back into operation and firing its kettle at weekends, once a month. They called it Brasserie à Vapeur - a true "Steam Brewery". The brewery had made a Saison at the time of its closure, and this was revived. Jean-Louis, working with two or three malts, allowed the mash to gain some lactic character before a long boil. He used Kent hops, matured the beers for several weeks in mild steel tanks, then bottled them without filtration.

The first time I visited them, they talked of the pleasure of "making something you like". Soon afterwards, I was horrified to hear that there had been an accident at the brewery, as a result of which Anne-Marie had died. Jean-Louis paid tribute to her in a book which produced to tell the story of the brewery. Their two daughters still help in the brewery, and one would like eventually to run it.

In recent years, Jean-Louis has re-married. His wife, Vinciane Corbisier, and her family have a shop supplying materials to small brewers, bakers, cheese-makers and cooks. When I visited them, Vinciane prepared a meat-loaf spiced with coriander, sweet orange peel and cloves. "Jean-Louis is crazy about spices," she laughed.

He has become noted for his use of them. Saison de Pipaix, which has a very fresh, orangey, character contains six "botanicals", including anis, black pepper and a medicinal lichen.

We sampled three or four vintages, including the first he ever made. At nearly ten years old, it had a huge orange aroma, a good head, a fine bead, and an almost abruptly dry, herbal, palate (5.2w, 6.5v).

Like a cook trying new dishes, Jean-Louis makes a "special" almost every time he brews. Some of his beers contain ash leaves, an ingredient mentioned by the Bénédictine Abbess Hildegarde (1098-1179), whose writings on natural history contain the first definite reference to the use of hops in brewing. Hildegarde was Abbess of Rupertsberg, near Bingen, not far from Mainz, Germany. She did not tell us what ash leaves tasted like, but Jean-Louis reckons they are dry on the side of the tongue, and I agree.

A very round, smooth, beer called La Cochonne had chicory root among its botanicals; all of the beers are primed with fructose made from chicory, a very Belgian ingredient. Later that day, at the nearby Taverne Les Iris, we were served Saison de Pipaix with a magret de canard.

The duck was served in a sauce made from the same beer, with cream and shallots. Further dishes were prepared with a variety of styles from the Brasserie à Vapeur, and with beers from the other two breweries in the area.

In his early days, Jean-Louis was greatly helped by the owners of the Moinette farm and Dupont brewery.

DUPONT

This farmhouse brewery, on a country lane in the village of Tourpes, dates from 1850 or earlier, and has been in the Dupont family since 1920. It was originally acquired to dissuade a family member from emigrating to Canada.

The original Duponts' grandson, Marc Rosier, runs the business with his two sisters and various family members. Marc's nephew, Olivier Dedeycker, is the brewer. In 1995, the adjoining Moinette Farm added to Dupont's offerings bread (sometimes containing spent grain), and a range of cheeses (including one appetisingly spiced with finely-chopped hops).

Dupont,s postcard campaign offered a good view of the open mash-tun. Vessels like this were once very typical in farmhouse breweries, and a few still survive.

Dupont's beers are full of life, and notable for their hop character, with East Kent Goldings to the fore. They have a big, rocky, creamy, head; a sharp, firm, refreshing, attack; a restrained fruitiness; and a long, almost tangibly dry, finish. They are beautifully-balanced, complex, examples of truly artisanal brewing. The family obviously has a very robust yeast, and knows how to handle it.

The most widely known of the beers is Saison Dupont, subtitled "Vieille Réserve". This is made to a gravity of 13-13.5 Plato (1052-54), entirely from Pilsner malt; hopped twice, with Goldings and some Styrians; fermented with the very attenuative house yeast; filtered and re-yeasted with the same strain; primed with sugar; and bottle-conditioned for six to eight weeks at 23-24°C (73-76°). It emerges with 5.2w; 6.5v, and usually pours with some haze.

The others products include an organic version of the same brew, which is less assertive; and stronger pale and dark beers under the name Moinette. (In French, Moine means monk, and the farm is on what is believed to have been an abbey estate).

Between the hoppy, dry, Moinette Blonde and the perfumy, sweeter, Brune, is La Bière de Beloeil, dedicated to a nearby castle. There was once a brewery at Beloeil, producing a beer called Saison Roland. The Dupont brewery has also made a beer comprising 40 cent malted wheat, and with 10 principal spices (including woodruff) and at least as many minor additions. This complex brew is creamy and flowery, with suggestions of buttercup and potpourri. It is sold under the Latin name Cervesia, and dedicated to a Gallo-Roman site in the area.

In 1996, a powerfully hoppy, lemony-tasting, beer for New Year was added. The brewery is forever producing new specialities. "Taste this," Mr Rosier would suggest, every time I sought to probe the secrets of his beer. "In your view, just how should a Saison taste?" I would demand. "It must be a good, honest beer. It should have character. It is essential that it has soul," he would reply, with Gallic imprecision.

BLAUGIES

South of Mons, the town of Dour, and the village of Blaugies itself, recurrent signs by the road offer butter and honey, and point to the local brewery, which is almost at the French frontier.

Finally, a wooden sign somehow fixed to a privet hedge, next to a handsome garden gate, and a greeting from a St Bernard dog, reveal the orchard, cottage and garage-brewery of Pierre-Alex Carlier and his wife Marie-Noelle Pourtois. He teaches physiotherapy, she taught general science, and they became interested in brewing after stumbling upon a recipe in a 1926 home-management encyclopedia. "The recipe didn't work," recalls Marie-Noelle, who does the brewing.

Spelt like this? Two teachers whose lives were changed by an encyclopedia.

Other manufacturers of brewing equipment did not take them seriously, but Belgium's Meura, accustomed to making kettles 50 times the size, was pleased to a supply a seven-hectolitre system. The couple's parents helped with the considerable cost of a bottling line.

I sampled the brews at the Carlier-Pourtois' front-room table. The first, from a recipe of Marie-Noelle's grandmother, is an adaptation of a low-alcohol beer once made for coal-miners in the Borinage. That brave effort at temperance was encouraged by local followers of John Darby, the Anglo-Irish founder of the fundamentalist Plymouth Brethren. The revivalist version, at a nose-thumbing 4.6w; 5.8v, is called Darbyiste and has a deep gold colour. It is made with a proportion of fig juice as a source of additional fermentable sugars. The figs are not evident in the flavour, which is light, lemony and dry.

The entrant in the local style is Saison D'Epeautre, taking its name from spelt, a grain of the wheat family. This grain was traditionally sometimes used in Saisons, and accounts for 30 per cent of the grist in this instance. It may contribute to the very pale colour and firm body of this beer, which is grainy, crisp and perfumy (4.6w; 6.0v). A fine revival.

One of Marie-Noelle' forbears was a local bandit called La Moneuse. His name is given to a nuttier, amber brew of 6.4w; 8.0v. An orangey, rummy, version with Demerara sugar is made for Christmas.

DU BOCQ

In the province of Namur, at Purnode, this brewery makes a variety of styles. Its Saison Régal has for its strength (4.8 by weight, 6.0 by volume) a surprisingly light, but firm, body (it is very well attenuated), and a teasing balance between fruitiness and aromatic hoppiness. Similar beers are produced under the names La Bergeotte, Cuvée du P'tit Lu, La Houlette and Val d'Heure. Like several of its neighbours, this brewery has more labels than beers, and that irritates purists, but no one would deny that it makes some tasty products.

Du Bocq, established in 1854, would have been a sizable brewery in its day. Its chunky, whitewashed buildings, in early industrial style, back on to a small garden that faces the village church. The whole arrangement peeps out of a steep hillside in a valley among the Ardennes. Opposite is the half-timbered house of the owning family. The hillside road winds toward the brewery, crosses another, and that is about the size of Purnode.

FANTÔME

A village brewery that grew quickly in its early days...du Bock is surprisingly prolific.

In the Belgian province of Luxembourg, Dany Prignon is a beer-lover who works for the local tourist office. Feeling that his area had too few gastronomic specialities (by the rich standards of the Ardennes in general), he started to make beer in Soy (Brasserie Fantôme, 8 Rue Preal) and helped establish a brew-pub in nearby Durbuy (La Ferme au Chêne, 115 Rue Comte d'Ursel) facing the river and Château at Durbuy.

Different beers are made at the two breweries, but their "house" character is to be yeasty, fruity and sweetish. Fantôme, named after a local ghost, makes vintage-dated Saisons, differing each year, with variations for summer, autumn, winter and spring.

SEZOENS

Flanders has no counterpart to Saisons as a style, but it does produce one beer that is intended to serve the same purpose, and proclaims as much with graphic personifications of winter and summer on the label. Sezoens (pronounced s'zoon) is made by Martens, of Bocholt, in Belgian Limburg. It is a beer of outstanding character and individuality, and its name is, of course, a protected trademark.

It is a bright, golden, top-fermenting beer of remarkable hop character, especially in its palate. It has the taste of fresh hops, wonderfully flowery and lingering. Sezoens is very refreshing, but even better as an aperitif.

I had in the past understood the hop varieties to be Northern Brewer, from Germany, and Saaz. On my most recent visit, I was told that Sezoens was being hopped entirely with Tettnangers, from Germany, but the choice of variety is only part of the story. Sezoens is dry-hopped, not once but twice. That two-handed approach is most unusual. The first dry-hopping is at the beginning of maturation, which is for two to three months, at 0 °C (32 °F). The second dose of hops is two to three weeks before maturation ends. The beer is filtered. Sezoens has a gravity of 12.5-13.5 Plato (1050-54) and an alcohol content of 4.8 by weight, 6.0 by volume. It is very well attenuated. The result is a light, very firm, body; a clean, dry palate; a restrained fruitiness; and that hoppy dryness. There is so much hop flavour that I was astonished to see an analysis rating the bitterness at only 30 units.

The brewery first made a seasonal beer in 1860, and at that time it was presumably unfiltered. Sezoens evolved, and has for many years been well known as a filtered brew. This "modern" version found itself being identified as Classic when the brewery recently added a bottle-conditioned alternative. The filtered Classic has its cleanness and firmness; the version with re-fermentation in the bottle is softer, fruitier and spicier.

Although they are the same brew, they emerge almost as two products in their own right, and show just what a difference bottle-conditioning makes. In 1989, the brewery launched an amber-red counterpart called Sezoens Quattro. This odd name is intended to suggest The Four Seasons.

Again, it is a very distinctive beer, with a faintly coffee-ish start; then a clean fruitiness; and finally a quite intense and lingering hoppy dryness. This is a beer with a lot of flavour development. It is well-

Limburgse Witte accompanied the Victoria perch, but Sezoens, in its Quattro form, starred with main-course ostrich, both as an ingredient and an accompaniment. The original Sezoens played both roles with dessert crèpes.

hopped in the kettle, but there is no further addition during maturation. Less of a refresher, but even more of an appetite-arouser. I have seen it categorised as being in the German Altbier style, but it reminds me more of the beer world's answer to an Italian aperitif.

I once had a memorable meal in which goose-liver pat was served with Quattro; plaice prepared and offered with Martens' Pils; rabbitcasseroled in Quattro; and warm cheese pancakes flavoured with Sezoens.

Belgian ales

The most sociable of brews for an evening with friends... and one is not enough.

A majority of the country's specialities are technically ales but, within Belgium, this term suggests famous brews like De Koninck and Palm. Brews like these were created to be bright and translucent (albeit copper or bronze), and not too strong to drink all evening.They were also sometimes identified as Spéciales Belge. These beers were Belgian brewers' initial reply to golden lager, when it first arrived from Germany and Czechoslovakia in the 1920s. The best of Belgian ales are restrained in carbonation (not too gassy or filling), and have enough flavour and dryness to be more-ish. One is rarely enough. The idea is to drink two or three, perhaps with friends, ideally in a good café. They are the most sociable of beers.

The spaceship. This is a brew-kettle, not a fermenter. Despite its futuristic appearance, it produces a very traditional-tasting beer.

De Koninck and Palm are particularly well known, but ales in this style are made by many Belgian brewers, especially in a central strip from the western part of the provinces of Antwerp and Brabant all the way south to Charleroi.

These are brews of a conventional gravity (usually around 12 Plato, 1048) and strength (about 4.0 by weight, 5.0 by volume); made exclusively or primarily from barley malt (rather than wheat or any less usual grain);seasoned with hops (though some are spiced)); fermented with a top yeast; and matured without the use of wood or any other very old technique. They are usually served filtered. In the European system of units of colour, most are in the 15-25 range; in bitterness, 19-30.

They sound ordinary, but some are outstanding brews that no beer-lover would readily miss.

Bronze or copper ales of conventional strength are widely made in several parts of the world, and that each has a different emphasis of style. In the United States (especially the West Coast), such ales tend toward assertive hop aroma and bitterness; the "Pale" Ale or "Bitter" of England does the same but much more gently; Scottish ales lean toward darker, richer, malts; the Belgian examples are yeasty, spicy-tasting and soft; and the Germans, as typified by Düsseldorf Altbier, are smoother.

THE ALES OF ANTWERP

DE KONINCK

A Belgian classic. De Koninck is the name of the brewery and its principal product. It is the local brew of Antwerp, and widely consumed there as an everyday drink. No other city in Belgium has quite such a familiar relationship with what might elsewhere be regarded as a speciality brew.

Mighty Modeste Van den Bogaert... one of the opinionated individualists who have made Belgian brewing different.

In a hotel in Antwerp in the mid 1970s, I inquired where was the nearest spot to be sure of a draught De Koninck. Hotels scarcely ever feature a local beer in their own bars (preferring to offer some less characterful international brand that the guest could have found without leaving home). This was no different, but the lady on reception was clearly pleased to have been asked. "Our famous Antwerp beer ... even an Englishman knows it!" she beamed.

The place where she sent me - a tiny, tiled, café on a street corner - had such appetisingly fresh De Koninck that I lost a day there and have never been able to find it again. The visitor who is not quite so feckless should secure a fresh De Koninck among the student drinkers, the mirrors and marble-topped tables at Café Den Engel, on the Grote Markt. Or in the quieter comfort

Part of the old copper brewhouse survives. Once, it served as as hop-jack, in which the blossoms could be strained.

of the city's oldest café, Quinten Matsijs, at 17 Moriaanstraat (corner Hoofdkerkstraat). The café dates from 1565, and is perhaps just a little too well-kept. At Quinten Matsijs, it is possible to play a game called Ton, involving the throwing of discs into holes, on equipment that is 300 years old. If the De Koninck arouses an appetite, there is Gezoden Worst (Antwerp's local pork sausage), and Beuling (black or white puddings). Temptation lurks in every corner. The café even offers a ticket on which glasses of De Koninck are recorded. Buy ten and you get the next one free. Ten? It is a perilously drinkable brew.

I once asked at De Koninck why the brewery had stuck with ale when so many of its rivals had switched to Pilsner-style lagers.

"I don't know. Maybe we could never afford it," mused Modeste Van den Bogaert, the imposing figure who runs the brewery with his family. A recent official history of the brewery recognises that, had it switched to Pilsner, it would have been washed away by bigger companies.

The enterprise takes its name from Joseph Henricus De Koninck, who owned a beer-garden which in 1833 gained its own brewhouse. The site was then at the city limit, near the area where criminals were hanged, and where a toll-post marked the road into the community of Berchem and on to Mechelen. The toll sign showed an upright hand, which is now part the brewery logo. The original owning family linked with the Van den Bogaerts in 1919.

The classical facade on the Mechelse Steenweg looks as though it might accommodate a bank, but stylised ears of barley in the doors hint at something equally liquid. Behind the facade is a decoratively-tiled hall housing a 1996 brewhouse with a passing resemblance to a space rocket (though somehow a wheelbarrow is still needed).

Behind, the old brewhouse sleeps amid whitewashed brick buildings set round a courtyard. One, with the appearance of a traditional malt barn, forms the facade on the side street Boomgard straat.

De Koninck beer is made only from malt, with no adjunct of maize or other brewing sugars. The malts are a blend of Vienna and Pilsener types. The hop accent is Saaz. The gravity is 11.8 Plato (1047). The hops are added three times.

In 1981, I asked Mr Van den Bogaert how long the brewery had used the same yeast. "About 15 years," he said. I should have consulted my notes before visiting the brewery again in 1990, but I didn't. I asked the same question ... and got the same answer.

Was the yeast a single-cell pure culture, I asked? "I wouldn't swear to it," replied Mr van den Bogaert, enigmatically. I believe it is, indeed, a pure culture, though it certainly has plenty of character. Many breweries have had their yeast longer than they can remember. All cultures adapt to their habitat, so every brewery's yeast to some degree develops its own character. Only in recent years have brewers begun to appreciate just how important their yeasts are to the background flavour of their beers. I would say the De Koninck yeast is very important indeed. It imparts a highly distinctive, and delicious, character. Perhaps Mr Van den Bogaert does not wish to be too analytical about his yeast: it is like trying to establish why a joke is funny, or how two people come to love each other.

The De Koninck beer spends seven to eight days in fermentation (up to 25 °C, 77 °F) and cooling, then has about two weeks' cold conditioning.. The finished product has 4.0 per cent alcohol by weight, 5.0 by volume. De Koninck has a dense, rocky, head that leaves lacework with every swallow. It is a subtle, soft, dryish, ale, with a beautiful balance. It begins with maltiness, lightly toasty; then comes the yeasty fruit and spice (one taster was reminded of cinnamon); and finally a most delicate Saaz hop character in the finish.

The famous Bolleke now has offspring, but it is clearly head of the family. Head shoulders, in fact.

Many beers taste best on draught, and this is famously true in the case of De Koninck. For the drinker willing to track the source, the best place to sample it is the café Pelgrim (which may be closed on Sundays), opposite the brewery, at 8 Boomgaard straat. This is very much a traditional café, with dark wood dadoes, and sporting trophies on display.

For as long as anyone can remember, the brewery has supplied buckets of surplus yeast from its fermenting hall to the café, where it is served in shot-glasses. Some old people like to drink it "straight" as a tonic. Others tip it into their beer. It looks like milky coffee, and seems to add a bitter, espresso-like, taste. Several other cafés have taken up the practice. Because De Koninck's yeast makes such a magical contribution, there is something especially celebratory about this ritual.

Other beers have their own glasses - in Belgium, almost every one does - but there is also a special ritual to the serving of De Koninck. Over the years, the beer has been presented in a num-

ber of glasses, but the two most common are a flute and a goblet. Each has its own lore.

The flute, which holds 25 centilitres, is thought suitable only for women. It is ordered in Flemish as a Fluitje, a word that has phallic connotations. A woman announcing that she would like a Fluitje is likely to be greeted with mirth. Fluitje rhymes, more or less, with flout. The -je diminutive adds a "yuh" sound.

The goblet is known as a Bolleke, which is a diminutive of "ball". Bolleke is pronounced boll-uh-kuh, which to an Englishman sounds awkwardly like a colloquialism for a testicle. Antwerpenaars have no such inhibitions, and know that - in their city, at least - this call will bring forth a man-sized glass of De Koninck (which translates as "The King"). When I asked in the fashionable London restaurant The Bank, "is it true that you have De Koninck?" the waiter silently responded by brandishing a Bolleke.

After years of renown as a brewery that made only one product, De Koninck in 1993 launched a second to celebrate Antwerp's year as Europe's City of Culture: a stronger ale, of 6.0w, 7.5v, called Cuvée Antwerpen 93. As a special edition, this was presented in a silk-screened bottle, and served in a new, small, goblet called Prinske. It quickly proved so popular that it has become a permanent offering. Cuvée Antwerpen is slightly darker and redder than the regular De Koninck, and has a distinctively rounded character, with a slight suggestion of lico-

When they begin the Begyn: Brewer Bernard Van den Bogaert pours a glass of the new beer for his colleague Hugo Smets.

rice. It embraces a powerful counterpoint of sweetness and hoppy bitterness, and has a warming touch of alcohol in the finish. Having made that leap, De Koninck seems to have been relishing its freedom. Since then there has been a golden counterpart, Antoon Blond: with a fresh, hoppy, yeasty, aroma; a firm, smooth, body; a vanilla maltiness; and a fruitiness reminiscent of gooseberry. This was launched for the 400th anniversary of Antoon Van Dyck. Yet more recent is an ale of 5.2w; 6.5v, darkened and smoothe-

ned with cane sugar "from the Spanish colonies", and hopped with blossoms. This is called Begyn. It is named after a beguinage at Hoogstraten, North of Antwerp.

'T PAKHUIS

"The Warehouse" is a new-generation brewpub, opened in 1996. As its name suggests, it is in a former warehouse - in a former quayside area that is becoming a centre for bars and restaurants. It is at 76 Vlaamse Kaai ("Flemish Quay").

With its brick interior, concrete pillars, basketwork chairs, open bar and highly-visible brewhouse, 't Pakhuis is clearly inspired by similar establishments in the U.S. The beers include the sweetish, perfumy, Blond; the malty, toasty, reddish, Antwerps Bruin (4.4w; 5.5v), broadly in the local style; and a very creamy, potent (7.6w; 9.5v) golden ale, well hopped with Saaz, called Nen Bangelijke. This expression, used by Antwerp's young, might translate as "Awesome". Specials have included a dark, chewy, spicy Foorkensbier for Antwerp's Whit Fair. The Pakhuis also offers dishes prepared with its beers.

Proud father Stan Sterkens shows the brewhouse at the Pakhuis.

A partner 't Pakhuis and a consultant to the Old Bailey is Stan Sterkens, whose family brewery is in the village of Meer, in the flat farmlands in the far north of the province of Antwerp, near the border with The Netherlands.

The Sterkens family records in Meer go back to 1654, and there is evidence of a brewery - on the same site - since 1731. At the brewery, I was shown the diary of the great-grandfather of the present principal. One entry, in 1868, read: "The Guild of Bowmen drank six and three-quarter barrels and eight pints. Price: 100 Belgian Francs and 98 cents."
Another recalled: "The doctor bought a quarter-barrel." A month later, the entry was repeated, and again in another four weeks. The doctor seemed to get through a quarter of a barrel each month. That works out at a litre a day, which does not sound excessive. The priest, on the other hand, bought half-barrels, though of a weaker beer, and seemed to have difficulty making them last a month. He paid at the end of the year.

In more modern times, the brewery for some years produced the copper-coloured, lightly fruity and malty, Ster Ale. This has gone, but there is a similar character to the bright amber, hoppier, St Paul Special (4.0w; 5.0v).

GODEFROY

A few miles west is the Moortgat brewery, at Breendonk. This brewery is best known for its Duvel (see Strong Golden Ales) and Maredsous (see Abbey Beers), but it also has an ale, called Godefroy. This has a rocky head, which is very well sustained, a soft body, and a very definite soft-fruit character in its palate. A suggestion of apricot, perhaps? It is a very complex ale, with a good hop character, and is bottle-conditioned.

THE ALES OF BRABANT

PALM

The biggest independent family brewery in Belgium has its origins in 1597, as a farmstead, called De Hoorn. at Steenhuffel, on the old road from the hop-growing town of Aalst to Mechelen, the regional capital. De Hoorn almost certainly made beer, though it is not documented as a brewery until 1747. A descendant of the owning family from that period, 84-year-old Alfred Van Roy, is chairman of the board. He travels round the brewery by golf cart. De Hoorn, largely rebuilt after World War I, made a darkish, top-fermenting, beer of low alcohol content until the late 1920s, when Pilsner-style lager was becoming popular. The brewery could not afford to re-equip for lager, so it was decided to produce a paler ale, of Pilsner strength. The family would have liked to adapt their name to create a brand. "Royale sounded good, but my uncle's brewery beat us to it," Mr Van Roy told me, still sounding wistful. The name Speciale Palm is popularly thought to celebrate victory in World War I, but Mr Van Roy told me it was suggested by a member of the family who was a priest. "The rest of the family weren't sure, but the Palm is a Christian symbol, and the word is the same in French and Flemish." In 1975, the brewery itself was re-named Palm. The brewery is still surrounded by a farm, with a stud for Brabant draught horses. The adjoining château of Diepensteyn, dating from the 1400s and once belonging to the Duke of Brabant, was

Patriarch Alfred Van Roy: „My uncle beat us to the name".

in the early 1990s restored to pristine condition as a guest-centre. The castle is moated, with ornamental ponds.

Palm's own wells provide brewing water high in calcium carbonate. Pale ale malt is used, with great attention to the fragrance and richness imparted in the gentle kilning (this chemical change is known to food scientists as the Maillard reaction, after the scientist who first explained it). The malt is tasted before being used, and can be rejected even if it is within its scientific specification. The most important hops are Kent Goldings and Fuggles.

An 1890s dome in still used on a 1930s vessel in one of two copper brewhouses. There is also a 1990s brewhouse, of traditional style but in stainless steel.

The brewery has very elaborate equipment for the propagation and handling of its three-strain Palm yeast, which to my palate imparts a distinctly orangey dryness (13.2 Plato, 1053, 4.1w 5.2v. A stronger version called Dobbel Palm (13.9, 1056, 4.4w, 5.5w) is produced for Christmas, and sold at the same price.

Curly hair and straight teeth seem to result from drinking Palm in this classic poster. „Top fermentation" is emphasised in two langauges.

OP-ALE

Palm's emblem is a Brabant horse, and the brewery breeds some beautiful examples at its property Diepensteyn Castle. Brewer and breeder Jan Toye is seen here taking part in the Palm Challenge Cup with his wife Carine.

The Brabant town of Opwijk gives its name to this ale, from its local brewery. There is also a pun in the name, as the word Op in Flemish means "up" (as in "drink up").

Op-Ale (4.0w; 5.0v) has a dense head and fine bead, leaving Brussels lace on the glass. It has a very soft body; a light, clean dry, palate, against a good malt background; a late fruitiness and orange-skin hoppiness (Styrians and Saaz; two gifts; generous), and a good clean hop bitterness in the finish.

The brewery traces its history to at least 1579. It was run by a family called De Smedt from 1832 for more than a century and a half. At one stage, there were 18 De Smedts with shares, a formula for dissent in any family. One was a bishop, and he wielded his crook with authority to keep the brewery on the true path. In addition to brewing its ales, it also makes beers for the Abbey of Affligem. In recent years, the brewery changed its name from De Smedt to Affligem. One of its assets is the yeast which imparts the distinctive fruitiness to its products. This culture was obtained from Scotland after World

A qu"et drink after work, „off duty", but the candid camera catches Vervloet appraising the bouquet.

War II by the grandfather of the current principal, Theo Vervloet. A highly skilled brewer, Mr Vervloet operates the brewery in partnership with Heineken.

GINDER ALE

Nothing to do with ginger ale. The brand derives from Van Ginderachter, family name of the brewer who created the beer, at Merchtem, in Brabant. The beer is still made in the province of Brabant, but in the city of Leuven, by Interbrew. The company claims that the specification of this beer, its spicier cousin Horse Ale and Vieux Temps (below) are still distinct, but there does seem to have been some convergence of character.

A distinct specification of pale ale malt was originally made for this beer Lublin and Styrian hops were used, with the original Ginder yeast (imparting a crisp, tart, fruitiness).

Ginder Ale has traditionally enjoyed a full amber colour and a distinctively fresh, assertively fruity (orange skins and tart apple) aroma. There has beenmore fruit, especially apple, in the palate and the dominant impression has been of dryness, despite a balancing nutty sweetness from the malt. Its alcohol is fractionally higher than that of the other Interbrew ales, at just over 4.0w; 5.0v.

VIEUX TEMPS

Another Brabant ale now made in Leuven by Interbrew, but facing south. Brabançonne, perhaps.It was originally made south of Leuven at Mont St Guibert, in the French-speaking part of Brabant. The brewery there, founded in 1858, was once known for a bottle-conditioned ale. When, in 1935 it tried to replicate that complexity of character in a filtered ale, it sought to sustain the sense of tradition with the brand-name Vieux Temps ("Old Times").

Perhaps fortuitously, the brewery had a yeast that provided very assertive, distinct, characteristics. The Vieux Temps yeast has a touch of phenol - a very light, fragrant, smokiness - with hints of sherbet and plummy flavours. Although the Mont St Guibert brewery has now gone, its yeast is still used. Together with a proportion of aromatic malt, it helps create a slightly syrupy, complex, pale-amber, ale of 4.0w; 5.0v.

THE ALES OF EAST FLANDERS

A good example of a Belgian ale, but with refermentation in the bottle, is the oddly-named Ever, from Van Steenberge, of Ertvelde, East Flanders. It is on the pale side for the style, but with plenty of creamy, fruity (apricot?) flavour.

Also from East Flanders: a soft, sweetish, amber ale (4.1w, 5.2v) called Artevelde and an extremely malty, nutty, chocolatey Grand Cru version (5.7w, 7.2), with refermentation in the bottle. The Artevelde brand-name belonged to a long-gone brewery, and was revived in recent years. Jacob, or James, van Artevelde was a Ghent farmer, brewer and merchant who was a central figure in the 14th-century wrangles between Flanders, France and Britain over trade (especially textiles) and political power. His statue dominates the Friday Market in Ghent.

These beers are now made by Huyghe, of Melle, near Ghent. There is said to have been a brewery on the site since at least 1654, and four generations of the Huyghe family have been involved. The beers are made in a handsome, well-kept, 1930s, brewhouse. For many years, the brewery was known only for its Pilsener-style beer, under the odd name Golden Kenia (this was a variety of barley, long vanished). In 1985, a new generation took charge and the brewery began to develop a wide range of speciality beers.

Southwest of Ghent, the small community of Gavere is known for cookies and bottled waters. Hidden behind what look like garage doors is a beautifully-maintained brewery, its mash-tin driven by pulleys, and its kettle in the old, bricked-in, style of Flanders. Here, the Contreras family produce a clean, delicate, lightly malty Pils and a delicious ale, called Tonneke. The ale is made with three malts: Pilsener, Caramunich and aromatic. It is hopped with Hallertau, Styrians and Goldings, as blossoms. Despite being an ale, it has two months of maturation, at 20-22°C. Tonneke has an orangey amber colour and a clean, malty palate. It is sweet at first, but develops a malty-fruity character in the finish. A Maarts Bier of 4.4w (5.0v) is similar in style but slightly sour. In the "March beer" tradition, this is laid down for the summer and sold in September/October.

When the Flemish entertainment and consumer magazine "Uit" ran a competitive blindfold tasting of ales, the winner was the little-known Speciale Stop, from De Brabandere, of Bavikhove, in West Flanders. This beer was complimented on its good bead, fruitiness, exemplary bitterness and length.

Despite this success, the ale was perhaps hampered by its curiously negative name. (Similarly, Guinness once had an ale terminally called Time).The non-arresting Stop, previously known with more mobility as Swing, has now settled for the name Petrus Speciale. It is to be hoped that matters rest there.

Petrus Speciale (4.4w; 5.5v) is made with "biscuit" and Vienna malts and spiced with coriander. It has a big, rocky, well-retained, head; a pale amber colour; a fruity-creamy aroma; a textured, dryish, malt background; and a zesty, rooty, rind-like, bitter finish.

The Facon brewery, of Bellegem, has a distinctive ale called Satchell (4.4w; 5.5v). The name refers to a person who pulls a canal barge. The ale is bronze in colour, creamy in body, with a slightly medicinal hop character in its late dryness. East Kent Goldings and Saaz hops are used.

The Strubbe brewery, of Ichtegem, has a robust ale called Dikke Mathile (4.8w; 6.0v), with a full, bright amber, colour; a grainy, syrupy, background (four malts are used) and a balancing dryness that seems peppery, with a suggestion of sour orange. Coriander is used in this ale, but no orange peel.

The Verhaege brewery, of Vichte, has a fresh, creamy, nutty, grassy, ale called Cambrinus (4.0w; 5.0v). There is also a bigger brother called Ezel ("Donkey", the self-deprecating emblem of nearby Kuurne). Ezel, at 5.6w, 7.0v, is smooth and malty, with a big hit of hop bitterness.

BRITISH-STYLE ALES

The Belgians are the most open-minded and cosmopolitan of beer-lovers. Despite having such a dazzling selection of their own brews, they have over the years found room for products from neighbouring countries, too.

In the course of two world wars, English and Scottish ales and Irish stout became well-known in Belgium. They were once very fashionable, and can still be found. Some are imported; others are made under licence; a few produced by Belgian brewers but given British-sounding names. The most famous importer was John Martin, an Englishman who settled in Belgium in 1909, and whose family still run the business. His imports included Pale Ales from Bass, and later Courage. From 1949, Courage brewed and marketed in Britain a fruity (warm-conditioned) strong Pale Ale of around 4.8w; 6.ov, called Bulldog that had been created for John Martin in Belgium. It was known as John Martin's Pale Ale in Belgium.

John Martin's is now made in Belgium by Palm, at a little over 4.6w; 5.8v. It is no longer identified as a Pale Ale, simply as a Speciale.

It pours with a rocky head, and has a Styrian hop aroma and flavour that is hard to match anywhere. It has a smooth, soft, lightly nutty, malt background, a hint of sweet orange, and a firm bitterness. The beer is heavily dry-hopped, with blossoms, and warm-conditioned in a circulating system.

After 90 years in the Belgian market, the John Martin's company added a celebratory neck-label to their ale. Apparently they could not wait ten more years for a round figure.

The average strength of beer is higher in Belgium than in Britain, and some English and Scottish products have more alcohol in their imported version than they would in their native countries. In some instances, a strong ale exclusively for the Belgian market, and with its own brand-name, is made by a British brewer.

The Belgians are especially fond of the most traditional type of Scotch Ale: strong, dark, and very malty. Extra-strong versions of these ales are also marketed as Christmas specials (although the Scots themselves traditionally preferred to celebrate New Year).

John Martin's imports from Scottish Courage's Edinburgh brewery a sweetly malty ale under the McEwan's label, at 5.8w; 7.2v. More famously, the same brewer and importer offer at over 6.4w; 8.0v the more rounded, deeper-tasting, drier Gordon's Highland Scotch Ale. Edinburgh may be in the Lowlands, but Gordon is a Highland name. A stronger version (7.0w; 8.8v) is offered under the name Gordon's Xmas. A sister product of no obvious Scottish antecedence, Gordon's Finest Gold, is a rather ale-ish strong (8.0w; 10.0v) lager.

The Gordon's range is marketed in France under the name Douglas. The Highland and Xmas are not readily available in Scotland. The producers apparently think they are too strong for the Scots.

Monastic beers

New breweries, holy and secular, at Belgian abbeys.

A new Trappist brewery in Belgium was big news in the beer world in 1999. It also meant that all six of the country's Trappist monasteries would now have breweries. Shortly afterwards, the only Trappist brewery outside Belgium - Schaapskooi, in The Netherlands, was sold, though it still operates, under private ownership. The Trappists have worked hard to emphasise that, in Belgium, they are the only Order to own breweries. Their task has not been made easier by the opening of a brewery within the Cistercian abbey of Val Dieu, though this is welcome news for beer-lovers. That brewery is not owned by the monks, but its beers are served in the restaurant at the abbey. A further new brewery has been opened at the site of the ruins of Abbaye D'Aulne.

These are far smaller than any of the breweries that have arrangements with abbeys of other orders to brew in their behalf. Or even those breweries that simply name a beer after a long-gone abbey.

Whether the brewery is in the abbey, owned by the monks, or financially benefitting the Order, the sum total of these possibilities links monks and brewing more strongly in Belgium than in any other country.

MONKS AND ALCOHOL

People, especially in Protestant countries, often express surprise when I mention beers made by monks. Surely the monastic life of self-denial cannot include beer? When I hear this question, I am surprised, for my part, that it should be asked. No one seems to consider it odd that Carthusian monks make the great liqueur Chartreuse or that the Benedictines are said to have provided the recipe for the lesser one that bears their name. A monk of the latter order, Dom Pérignon, was credited (dubiously) with having invented Champagne; there are well known vineyards owned by monks, and others that once were; in chilly Britain, the Benedictines of Buckfast make tonic wine. Why on earth should monks not make beer?

The opening of the Trappist brewery at Achel as recently 1998 was an historic moment. The Abbot looks proud, but leaves brewer Brother Thomas to raise a glass.

The links between monks and alcoholic drinks are several. In the days when the only travellers were pilgrims (or crusaders), the only hotels were abbeys. Naturally, the guests had to be offered a drink with their meals. In a southern European abbey, the drink would be wine, probably grown by the monks; in the north, it would be beer. In any great house, a brewery was as important as a bakery and a kitchen. Water was often unsafe, but no one was poisoned by drinking beer (nor is anyone today). Although it was not realised at the time, beer was safe because the brewing water is boiled.

In the days before universal education, the church was a central instrument of learning, and abbeys were havens of study, giving rise to the great universities. Oxford traces not only its oldest colleges but also its local brewery to monastic origins. In a more contemporary moment, a novice Trappist monk once excused himself from sharing another beer with me, because he had to complete an essay on Schopenhauer.

In earlier times, the pursuit of medicine, the growing of herbs, the study of fermentation and distillation, were all monastic activities. Several monks made important contributions to brewing science. In more recent times, the production of beer has been a means by which an abbey can support itself. There are famous abbeys that produce cheese, wine, bread, or sweets like nougat.

Self-sufficiency has been central to the calling since the first holy men retreated to caves, or hermitages, inspired by Christ's contemplation in the wilderness.

Modern monasticism began with St Benedict (480-547), and his rule "live from the work of your hands" is one of the foundations of every abbey. St Benedict's own community, at Monte Cassino, in southern Italy, no doubt served wine to its guests, but as monasticism spread, the abbeys that were established

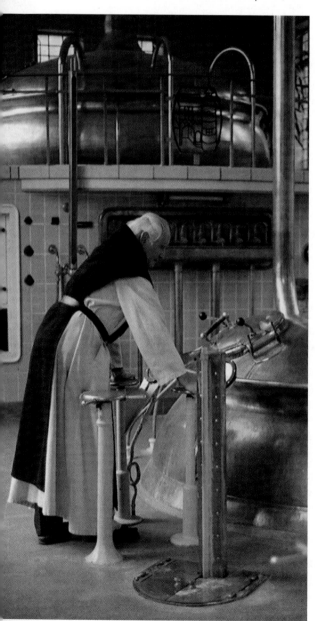

further north began to brew beer. The missionary monk St Columba mentions beer in his rule, which was drawn up in the early 600s. In the 800s, there were no fewer than three brewhouses in the important abbey of St Gallen, not far from Zurich. According to the preserved plan, one brewhouse made beer for the abbey community, another for guests, and a third for pilgrims. St Gallen today has more breweries than any other canton in Switzerland. Austria still has two abbey breweries. One is run by Norbertine (otherwise known as Premonstratensian) brothers; the other owned by Benedictine monks (though, confusingly, it is called the Augustiner brewery).

In the German-speaking world, an abbey is called a Stift (meaning "seminary" or "convent"), or a Kloster ("cloister"). One of these words on a label may indicate that the beer is still made in an abbey - or simply that it was in the past. The abbey breweries in the German-speaking world often have a strong, dark lager as a speciality, but there is no real sense there of a distinct monastic family of beers as there is in the Low Countries. In Germany itself, but all within the Catholic state of Bavaria, there are half a dozen abbey breweries still run by Augustine, Benedictine and Franciscan monks (or, in two cases, nuns) There are also in Bavaria several former abbey breweries that are no longer run by religious Orders.

Munich breweries like Augustiner, Spaten-Franziskaner and Paulaner bear testimony to their origins. The name Munich itself derives from the German word for "monks". The city's monastic history and its growth as a brewing centre are intertwined. A former Benedictine monastery at Weihenstephan provides the site for the world's oldest brewery and the best-known university faculty of brewing. Abbess Hildegarde of Bingen was the person to confirm beyond doubt the use of hops in beer. The German Jesuit brewer Benno Scharl, born in 1741, published a standard textbook on brewing as recently as 1814. There are similar stories throughout Europe, from Pilsen, in the Czech Republic; to Hoegaarden, in Belgium; to Faversham and Burton, in England; to Belhaven, in Scotland; and Kilkenny, in Ireland.

In Belgium, Orval was founded as a Benedictine abbey, restored once by the Cistercians, then by the Trappists. It probably brewed in its earliest times, and certainly in the 18th century, before the French Revolution. Several orders, notably including the Norbertines, brewed in Belgium in the past, and one or two until World War I.

There are said to have been five or six hundred abbey breweries in Europe over the centuries. Today there are a little more than a dozen, six run by the Trappists- though other orders in Belgium license their names to commercial brewers.

THE TRAPPISTS

In 1997, the six Trappist monastery breweries of Belgium started using a seal of authenticity on their labels. They wishedto make it clear that theirs is the only order in Belgium with its own breweries. They are Achel, Chimay, Orval, Rochefort, Westmalle and Westvleteren. There are also Trappistine convents, selling eggs, bread and other products.
I regard three or four of them as world classics. I would accord this soubriquet to Orval, Chimay Grande Réserve and Westmalle Triple, and others are in contention.
Orval has only one beer, albeit highly distinctive. The others each have a range of two or three, perhaps with the odd further special bottling. Taking into account these special bottlings, the six Trappist monasteries together have between a dozen and 20 different beers.

Rochefort dates from at least 1230, but originally as a convent. It certainly brewed in the 1500s, but none of the Trappist communities in Belgium was established until after Napoleon. Rochefort accommodated the Trappists in the 1880s.

Some are dry, like Orval's sole entrant and one of the Chimay range, but most are relatively sweet; most are dark; one or two are golden, such as Westmalle Tripel. For all their differences, they have certain features in common: All are, to varying degrees, strong; all are top-fermenting; all the bottled examples have a second, or third, fermentation; and all are fruity. Several,

Rochefort is gaining a connoisseur following, despite its own shyness. Chimay and Westmalle are much more widely known. Facing page: the Trappists now have a logo.

though not all, are made with a proportion of dark candy-sugar in the brew-kettle, and have the distinctively rummy taste that imparts. Some are spiced, though the monks are more reticent than most brewers on this subject. Most of the Trappist beers have the complexity deriving from yeasts that work at high temperatures and tolerate high levels of alcohol. They are distinctly different from the strong barley wines of the English-speaking world. In theory, any style of brew produced in one of these six monasteries could be called Trappist Beer. In practice, the Trappists have produced a recognisable family of beers. This is a major contribution to the world's pantheon of beers, but the Trappists hesitate to take credit for their achievement. Their worry is that, if Trappist Beer were regarded as a style, other breweries might feel free to use the term. ("This is our Pilsner, this is our ale, this is our Trappist-style beer..."). Some, in the U.S., have already dabbled in these holy waters. The beer-lover's worry is that the monks might self-defeatingly respond by launching a "Trappist Light". For the moment, they have preferred to resort to the courts to protect their identity.

It is perhaps because they are the strictest of Orders, and therefore the most enclosed, that the Trappists have so effectively retained their tradition of brewing. They are also the strictest adherents to the rule of living off their own land and resources, and these guidelines have no doubt helped to sustain their breweries where other orders have allowed the craft to die.

In some instances the breweries were established in order to fund the construction of the abbey as well as its subsequent upkeep; in others also to create employment locally; or to help start Trappist communities elsewhere (there are about 100, in 40 countries). It was not necessarily assumed that the monks themselves would work in the brewery. When Orval was rebuilt, no monks did, though several have done so since. Some of the monasteries were more self-sufficient in respect of their workforce. With the growth of national brewers, the monasteries have had to become more efficient if they are to compete. This has meant that the monks have over the years enlisted secular

workers in the breweries. With hourly calls to prayer or other observances, and a requirement to study, a monk cannot also run a brewery to modern working schedules. It is no longer a matter of fitting in the brewing of beer as though it were the occasional making of jam or pickles.

In every case, a monk still has overall responsibility for the brewery. In some abbeys, there is still a monk as head brewer. In others, monks or novices help on a part-time basis.

Some of the Trappist abbeys have a lower-strength beer, perhaps known as a "Single", so that those monks who wish may have a bottle with their meals. The stronger brews, sometimes known as Double and Triple (spellings vary, even within the French and Flemish languages) may be offered at religious holidays.

Although the Trappist order is silent, monks are allowed to speak when their work requires it. This is a far greater limitation than it may seem. "There is never any time when we can talk freely to one another," a monk once told me, taking advantage of his permission to speak to me as a guest. When I stayed in a monastery myself for a few days, I was conscious even of the rattle of the wire coat-hangers as I hung up my clothes at night. I felt as thought I was disturbing the whole community.

The outsider might imagine that such an atmosphere would discourage the recruitment of novices. Some of the monasteries take the opposite view. They feel that would-be novices are seeking tranquillity and may be put off by commercial images of abbey brewing and "jolly" monks.

These images are avoided by the Trappists themselves, but promoted by some of the secular brewers who have agreements with other orders to make "abbey" ales.

Trappist beers

After a walk, before dinner, with the cheese?
Choose your monastery.

ACHEL

The newest Trappist brewery, opened in 1998. It is also the world's only monastic brewpub, initially making only draught beer, for its own café. While the other Trappist abbeys have an inn nearby, the café at Achel is a part of the main buildings.

My first impression was of striking contrast. Inside, the brightly-lit bar-counter would not have been out of place in an airport hotel. Outside, the courtyard of the abbey had been turned into a terrace, filled with families sitting down to a beer. I had the sense of the abbey being the centre of its village community, as

such establishments must have been in medieval times. Every few minutes, customers wishing to contemplate the source would stroll in and press their noses against the glass wall of the brewhouse: lovers, hand-in-arm; a teenager in a Nike tee-shirt, three toddlers, who lingered, apparently hypnotised by the shining stainless steel vessels.

The nearest big city is Eindhoven in The Netherlands. From there, it is 20-odd miles south, skirting the town of Valkenswaard, to the barely-evident frontier with Belgium. The abbey's grounds are on the border, in the hamlet of Achel, near the village of Hamont.

Eindhoven, with big industries like Philips electronics, has made the whole area somewhat suburban. It was once an empty heathland on the route from Anwerp to Cologne. Cistercian monks did much to cultivate the area in the 12th century.

The abbey is dedicated to St Benedict, father of monasticism, but has always been of the Trappist order. The monastery was established in 1845, and had a brewery until the First World War. The Germans took away the kettles during the First World War, to use the copper in armaments and the monks have since earned their keep by running a farm, with vegetables, pigs and dairy cattle.

As the community of monks has grown older, and found difficulty in attracting younger brothers (though it has not stopped trying), the running of the farm has become a strain. The community began to wonder whether it might be time to bring back brewing. One of the monks, brother Titus, commented at the time that many readily-available Pils beers were "no better than a glass of water". He added: "Monastic life is about simplicity, quality and strength," so beer is the most suitable product for an abbey."

The gleaming stainless-steel brewhouse at Achel seems to fixate visitors, even though it is less handsome than some of its Trappist counterparts. Four of the other abbeys have their own inns nearby. Achel's is the only one to serve beer actually at the abbey. It is the world's only Trappist brewpub.

The brand-new brewhouse was fitted in a space that had formerly accommodated the dairy. The technical consultant was Brother Thomas, for years a famously opinionated head brewer at the Trappist abbey of Westmalle, near Antwerp. Since retiring from Westmalle, Brother Thomas had lived near Liège - in a convent. He assured me that his quarters were quite separate from those of the sisters. But why the opposite end of Belgium? "After 42 years as a brewer , I could not retire and live around the corner". He now had a 70-mile journey to Achel on brewing days, but talked airily of driving at more than 100mph.

The principal beer is identified as Achelse Blond 4, The number referring to the percentage of alcohol by volume. It is thus far lower in alcohol than any other regularly-available Trappist beer, but Brother Thomas explained that it was "for walkers and cyclists". It is a golden ale: with a beautifully delicate hop character, from its spicy aroma, through gently emerging, flowery, flavours, to a lingering but clean dryness.

It is brewed wholly from Pilsener malt, and the hops are Kent Golding, Hallertau-Hersbrucker and Saaz, but in five additions, to a respectable 33-37 units of bitterness. Brother Thomas said he was looking for "purity and subtletly", and added: "This is for drinkers, not tasters." He then put to me the argument so popular among brewers that the drinker must be able to enjoy "a few glasses", which is difficult if the beer is very complex in its maltiness, hoppiness, spiciness or yeast character.

While disagreeing with the premise (I think complex beers are more-ish), I asked whether the "few glasses" might cause drunkenness that would disturb the monks about their devotions.

"You can't get drunk on this beer!" he responded, thumping the table A stronger Achelse Blond, at 6.0 per cent, is decidedly creamier, with hints of vanilla in its maltiness, grapefruit in its hop character, and a hint of banana fruitiness. This one, he informed me, was "for tasters". A 5.0 per cent Achelse Bruine, with a touch of caramel, was lightly smooth and toasty on that occasion.

Brother Thomas explained that he had not yet found a dark malt that gave him quite the character he sought.

Shortly afterwards, the energetic Brother Thomas suffered a period of ill-health. His duties were taken over by Brother Antoine, who had in the meantime retired from Rochefort. I was able to obtain some draught beer for a dinner in Philadelphia, and began to wonder whe-

The one for tasters? *The benign-looking* *Brother Thomas...* *opinionated and* *emphatic on* *questions of beer.*

ther Achel would install a bottling line. It would then be able to produce beers with the added complexity imparted by bottle-conditioning, as the other Trappist monasteries do. No doubt beer-lovers would welcome such a move. The abbey café closes on Mondays. During the week, it opens at 11.0, closing at 6.0. At weekends, it remains open an hour later. (Tel 32-011-800-769).

CHIMAY

The best-known and biggest-selling Trappist beers are produced at the abbey of Notre-Dame on a hillside called Scourmont, near the hamlet of Forges, close to the town of Chimay, in the province of Hainaut. The monastery and its estate of farmland are in wooded countryside, at walking distance from the French border. The official name of the monastery is Abbaye de Scourmont, but the beers are labelled simply Chimay, and they are very widely marketed. Chimay sold its beer commercially from its early days, and was the first Belgian monastery to do so. It was also the first to use the appellation "Trappist Beer", between the two World Wars.

The town of Chimay once smelted glass, and is now a tourist centre for this part of the Ardennes. It has about 3,500 people, and the monastery's brewery, dairy co-operative and farm are important local employers. The brewery makes three beers, but they have for some time appeared in two different styles of bottle, and it could be argued that this influences their character.
One bottle is a standard size, with a crown top. The other is a

"wine" bottle, with a wired cork. The strongest beer has also been seen in a magnum. So are there three beers, or seven? Given that the beer is bottled with residual sugar and live yeast, it will continue to develop. The amounts of sugar, yeast and beer in the bottle; the surface areas of beer exposed to the "head space" in the bottle; the disturbance of the contents when the package is shipped, and even a slight porosity of cork, could all be influences. It could be argued that the smaller scale of events in the standard bottle would make for a slower maturation. A counter argument is that the CO_2 in the beer can expel any unwanted traces of oxygen because of porosity in the cork. Either way, there will be subtle differences in the development of the beer. These have not been proven scientifi-

The cloister at Chimay. The monks steadfastly protect their peace and privacy, despite the commercial success and international reputation of their brewery.

cally - and we are all susceptible to aesthetic influence - but I believe the beer in the large bottles has a softer, "fluffier" character. These differences will be most evident in the brewery's strongest beers.

One brewer I know (a monk at another abbey) believes that all beers with corks should be opened five or ten minutes before they are to be consumed, so that the CO2 that has been in contact with the cork can be vented. This might seem an excessive refinement, but Belgians are serious about beer. Equally, a beer as full of life as the Chimay products will still be plenty lively enough after ten minutes in the glass.

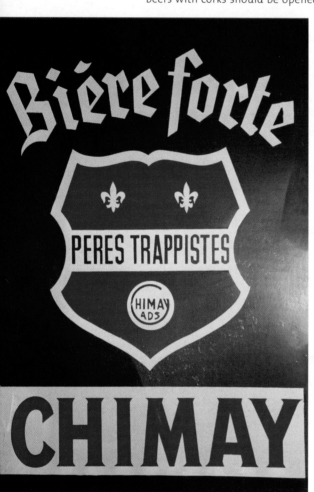

The style instantly associated with Trappist breweries is a yeastily-fruity, sweetish, strong ale; soft, full and deep in body, with a dark brown colour and perhaps a reddish tinge. Two of the Chimay beers fit into this style, and are its best-known manifestations. Both have a very emphatic Chimay "house character": a spiciness in which some tasters have found nutmeg and others juniper and thyme. I believe this aromatic tour-deforce arises from a very distinctive and extremely robust yeast, which permits unusually high fermentation temperature, of up to 30 °C, 86 °F. One of the two beers with the "house character" is the fruity (blackcurrant, ntumeg, vanilla?) Chimay Red. The colour refers to the crown-cork on the standard bottle, or seal on the larger type. This has a gravity of 15.5 Plato (1063) and an alcohol content of 5.5w; 7.0v. The larger bottling of this is also identified as Chimay La Première. Despite its considerable strength, this is the least potent in the range. Laying down is not essential, but I do feel that the flavours develop or round out for six to nine months.

Since the brewery was modernised in the early 1990s, with the open fermenters replaced by a closed system the beer has been

„Strong beer" was the simple advertising claim on this enamel, know decorating the wall of the tasting room at the brewery. The beer is still strong, but that is no longer the selling point.

"cleaner" but arguably less complex. Some of its complexities will emerge in bottle-aging. In the middle of the range comes a beer in a quite different style, Chimay White. This was developed in the late 1960s, when some cosumers seemed to be seeking drier strong ales. The White is fragrantly perfumy, much drier and hoppier, with a firmer body, slender for its gravity, and a quenching hint of acidity. It also has a paler colour,

more of an amber than a brown. Its gravity is 17.35 (1071), with an alcohol content of 6.3w; 8.0v. This beer was first put into a large bottle to mark the 500th anniversary of the town of Chimay, and was labelled Cinq Cents. Again, it does not demand to be laid down, but will become drier over a year.

A return to a more typical taste is represented by Chimay Blue, at 19.62 (1081), 7.1w; 9.0v. This appears in the large bottle as Chimay Grande Réserve. At this gravity and strength, it has a lot of character, especially in its spiciness (a hint of pepper and sandalwood?), though this has diminished slightly in recent years. It is the beer world's answer to a Zinfandel or Port. This beer definitely develops with some bottle age. The monastery considers two years sufficient, but I prefer it older than that. The beer is best stored at 15-18

°C (59-64 °F). In my view it's also best served at that sort of temperature. All three are most interesting beers. The White seems the most appropriate as an aperitif, and as an accompaniment to the vinegary spiced trout dish "escavèche", which has been popular in the area since the Spanish Netherlands. The monastery also makes a Trappist cheese, which is surely best accompanied by the Grande Réserve. Indeed, I am always happy to pit a Roquefort or Stilton against this beer. When I first compared it with Port, I was greeted with a raised eyebrow. Later, tests were carried out to monitor Chimay's development in the bottle over a period of several years. After five

The brew-kettle as street furniture... Chimay was a pioneer in what is becoming a Belgian custom.

years, aldehydes began to develop that were similar to those in Port. At the monastery, I have sampled a 25-year-old bottle that was positively "brut".

God clearly smiled on the monks of Chimay when they chose the site for their abbey in 1850. A dozen years later, they decided to establish a brewery, and discovered that the water under their land was perfect for the job. The water is remarkably low in dissolved solids of any kind, and it is clearly an influence in the softness of the beers. For the "husky" texture it gives to the beer, six-row winter barley, typically the variety Plaisant, is used. It is grown in the Champagne region and Gembloux, and malted in Belgium, to a high-enzyme specification. Cara-Munich malt, and wheat, are also used. The aroma hops are German but the bittering variety is American, and has been

since the 1960s; in recent years, it has been Galena. Primary fermentation temperatures are very high, up to 30°C (86°F).

The beers of Chimay in their present form owe much to the great Belgian brewing scientist Jean De Clerck. After the disruptions of World War II, he came as a consultant to help the monks put the brewery back on to its feet. His counsel proved invaluable to Father Théodore, who was charged with the job of being Brewmaster. When De Clerck died, in 1978, he was buried at the abbey. It is difficult to know who was the most honoured by this, De Clerck or the brewery.

I first met Father Théodore in the mid 1970s, when I was researching the first version of my book "The World Guide to Beer" I nervously asked if my photographer colleague could take a picture of him, standing in front of the gleaming, copper kettles (now replaced by a more modern, but less attractive, brewhouse). With great hesitation, Father Théodore agreed. The photographer took one shot and Father Théodore was striding away, glad that the ordeal was over. The photographer was dismayed: he had intended to take at least three exposures. Fortunately, the sole shot worked out well, and it has appeared widely since.

In the early 1980s, I arrived with another photographer, and Father Théodore was less shy. My assignment was to write an article about the monks' life for "Sphere" magazine. As Father Théodore led us round the abbey's farm and forest lands, he vaulted casually over a tree trunk, unencumbered by his flowing habit. I had to remind myself that he was in his 70s. I stayed in the abbey's guest quarters for a few days, and one evening Father Théodore gave me a tasting of some especially fine "vintages" I was acutely conscious that I was staggering

slightly, and banging against walls, as he soberly led me to my quarters. I was also aware that I had kept him up late, and that he would have to rise again for vigil prayers at some unearthly hour. That, anyway, is my recollection, but it seems that I may have consumed more than was good for my memory. I mentioned the incident in my writing, only to be told years later by Father Théodore that I had got it all wrong. "It wasn't me who saw you back to your quarters. It was Father Robert," he assured me.

A few years later, I heard that Father Théodore was no longer enjoying such good health. When I arrived in 1989, to make a film about the Trappists for my tv series "The Beer Hunter", I was concerned as to how I should find him. To my delight, he

Father Thomas, round, ruddy-cheeked and jovial, fit perfectly the image of the merry monk. He managed the brewery until his death in 2000, and is much missed.

was as spry as ever, and playing the organ in the abbey church. "I am delighted to see you so well," I remarked. "It's the Chimay beer," he laughed. I interviewed him for the film, and asked him about the early days, when he had spent long hours isolating the right yeast for the Chimay beers. He recalled: "I worked with Benedictine patience..."

ORVAL

The name derives from "Valley of Gold" Legend has it that a beautiful countess, from Tuscany, lost a golden ring in a lake in the valley and said that if God ever returned it to her, she would thank him by building a monastery. When a trout rose from the lake with a ring in its mouth, the princess was as good as her promise.

The abbey of Orval was founded in 1070 by Benedictines from Calabria, and re-established in the next century under the aegis of Cistercians from Champagne. It was variously damaged by fire and war, and finally sacked in the French Revolution. Louis XVI was believed to have been on his way to seek sanctuary at Orval when he was seized. The ruins of the old Orval can still be seen alongside the new Trappist abbey, built between 1929 and 1936. The finest craftsmen of the time worked on the abbey, the construction of which was seen to crown the centenary of the modern Kingdom of Belgium. The present abbey buildings, Romanesque and Burgundian in influence, have a dramatic purity of line. The visual impact of the buildings is, to beer-lovers, matched by the power of the goût d'Orval, and the two are held together in the elegant glass designed by the architect of the abbey, Henry Vaes.

The abbey's full name is Notre-Dame d'Orval, though that is seldom used. It stands alone in its valley in the Ardennes, on a bend in the road on the old route from Trier to Rheims, not far from the small town of Florenville, in the Belgian province of Luxembourg. The address is Villers-devant-Orval, but the hamlet comprises little more than the ruins and the present abbey, a baronial castle, a small hotel, an inn and a post-office.

The abbey's principal buildings overlook an ornamental, reflecting lake set among lawns and topiary. Occasionally, a robed figure will walk by...a monk in his own reflection. In its long history, Orval has been famous for its scholars, its study of pharmacy, surgery, and even of the forging of iron. (Wood from the Ardennes was once turned into charcoal to smelt iron and glass). One of the abbey's smaller structures, looking perhaps like a chapel, turns out to be the brewhouse. There is an hypnotic peace about the place, with its pristine mosaic stairs and beige tiled walls, the 1950s coppers set into decorative mustard-and-redbrick quarry tiles.

At each year's harvest, the secular brewer, Jean-Marie Rock, specifies the varieties of barley to be used by the maltsters. Samples are malted so that he can chew on the grains and make decisions. He is fond of Prisma, from Lower Franconia, but the final choice will depend upon each year's quality. Barley is bought from several countries, and malted in Belgium. A particular specification of crystal malt helps impart the distinctively orangey, sunny, colour of the finished beer (21-22 EBC). "I don't want the pale malt to be too soft," says brewer Rock. Let the softness come from the crystal. It's the way the two work together that gives me the beer I want to create. The crystal must not be too red. I want just the right colour, and I have to keep up the pressure on the maltsters to be sure of that.

Orval is one of the world's most distinctive beers, and the malt character is one element in that unforgettable personality. "Here, try some malt," Rock offers. I eat it as we look round the brewery. The pale is very firm and dry-tasting, the crystal sweeter, crunchy and nutty. Then he proffers some candy sugar, still made by the traditional method of crystallisation on strings. It looks like cracked ice.

The most elegant of the abbeys is Orval, its present buildings designed and constructed in the 1920s and 1930s.

The water, from the abbey's own well, is high in calcium carbonate. This no doubt heightens the firmness and bitterness of the beer, though that has diminished a little in recent years...

The gravity out of the kettle is 13.4-13.7 Plato. The brew has a conventional primary fermentation, at 14-21 °C(57-70°F), in

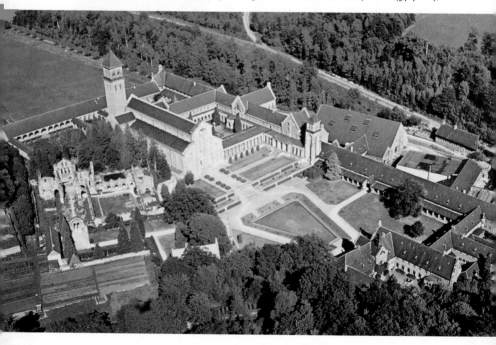

beautifully-kept, open, stainless-steel squares. The primary yeast is a flocculent, single-cell strain, low in esters, and it is skimmed by hand.

There is then a secondary fermentation, at around 15 °C (59 F°), in horizontal cylinders of stainless steel. The yeast used here is a symbiosis of as many as ten strains, which are cultivated together. These include Brettanomyces, which work over many months in the shaping of Orval. Not only do they promote the typical "hop-sack" and "fresh leather" aromas, they also consume sugars that conventional yeast cannot convert, making for a light, firm, body and more alcohol.

The use of Brettanomyces is not typical in this part of Belgium, or in Trappist beers. It may have been introduced by a brewer from East Flanders in the earliest days of Orval. He took refuge there when his own brewery closed. The first official brewer at Orval was a German, who would have been unlikely to propose such a method.

The secondary fermentation lasts for three weeks or more, and takes place on dry-hops. This is neither typically German nor Belgian (though the technique is popular in Britain. The dry hopping is a very important an infuence on the charatcer of Orval, especially on its aroma. The variety of hops used has changed over the years. Rock is especially fond of Styrian Goldings: "That flavour! I like it! That freshness, dry freshness." I remember his predecessor, Roger Schoonjans, rhapsodising about Kent Goldings "That indefinable special taste, that finishing touch." Without any centri-

Well equipped but traditional...Orval still uses open fermenters.

fuging or filtration, the beer is then bottled, with a dosage of the primary yeast and a priming of white candy-sugar. It then has a third fermentation in the bottle, at the brewery, for five to to nine weeks.

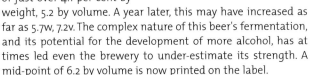

At this point, its alcohol content has reached a level of just over 4.1 per cent by weight, 5.2 by volume. A year later, this may have increased as far as 5.7w, 7.2v. The complex nature of this beer's fermentation, and its potential for the development of more alcohol, has at times led even the brewery to under-estimate its strength. A mid-point of 6.2 by volume is now printed on the label.

When the beer is not long out of the brewery, its hop aroma and flavour seems especially peppery and refreshing. At four to five months, the beer pours with a huge head. By six months, its combination of yeasts is beginning to impart some wild,

Brettanomyces and lactic, lemon-zest, characteristics. The present brewer likes the beer best at six months. His predecessor suggested one year, at which age I have found it to be very dry and perfumy, with a notably creamy head. Some drinkers like three years. At five years, the "best before" date settled upon to please the bureacrats, it will still be good, but

Like a coffee filter? Warm water runs through a bed of malted grain - though through a series of outlets. These are spaced round the vessel so the brewer can be sure that the flow is evenly distributed through the grain bed.

will have lost a lot, especially in its hop character. It should be stored upright, at a good cellar temperature of around 12 °C (53 °F), and poured gently so that the sediment remains in the bottle. It should not be kept in the refrigerator.

"People do not want our beer to taste exactly the same every time," Roger Schoonjans once observed to me. "They want the goût d'Orval, for sure, but they want to be able to chat about it: `I think this one is a little more hoppy yesterday's was rounder...' In that respect, they treat it like a wine." That is precisely my view about bottle-conditioned beers, but I rarely hear it from brewers. The goût d'Orval is a phrase often spoken among beer-lovers in Belgium. Goût translates as "taste", but the English seems inadequate. It is, anyway, as much aroma as taste. Some gastronomes detect sage, though no herbs or spices are used. Is it, in the end, the malt, the hops or the yeast? It takes all three to make the beer, but those unruly, earthy, yeast characteristics seem to me to be fundamental. It is beer with a devoted following. With its intense dryness, it is especially favoured as an aperitif. On another visit, the managing director at that time, Father Bruno, told me: "We like to see our sales rising, but we are not obliged to grow beyond our present capacity. We live simply. The monastery is very attractive, but that was just the style of the time."

As we strolled through the brewery yard, a truck was being loaded by a fork-lift. Father Bruno introduced me to the driver of the fork-lift: "This is Brother Dominic." The driver was visibly wearing his habit under his cover-alls. He smiled, and we shook hands. Father Bruno was succeeded by a secular managing director, Jacques Petre, an economist. He told me that there were only limited possibilities for expansion. "The monks want Orval to be an abbey, first, not a brewery."

When we took our stroll, we encountered the dynamic young abbot Dom Eric Dion, who was elected to his position on the day he was ordained. Before becoming a monk, he was a jurist. In the brewery one day, the abbot observed:

"You keep people happy and I will keep them holy." On summer weekends, people come from far and wide to have lunch of charcuterie at the auberge "A l'Ange Gardien" (tel. 061-31.18.86), an incongruously 1930s building on the site of the monastery's court of justice. They walk by the lake, visit the abbey ruins, and buy from the gift shop the beer, cheese, bread and honey candy made by the monks. Father Dominic now makes the honey candy. The more devout can buy religious books and the odd volume on beer.

Like a tea-bag? Perhaps a bouquet-garni is a more appropriate comparison? Hops have already been added in the brew-kettle, but now comes an extra „gift". This muslin bag, containing hops is placed in the maturation vessels. This adds the final touch of hop aroma and flavour.

It is not always easy to blend tradition, monastic or not, with the modern world. Years ago, I received a promotional document from Orval describing the monastery and its beer. The text said that the beer could not be exported because its content of living yeast made it insufficiently stable. A year or two later, I received the same material, but this paragraph had been crossed out. The truth is that bottle-conditioned beers can be exported, but must be handled with more care than is common. Meanwhile, production of Orval has increased considerably. The beer has become slightly more accessible and a little less austere, but it remains one of the world's most distinctive brews.

ROCHEFORT

Perhaps the least known of the Trappist breweries is Notre-Dame de Saint-Rémy, near the small town of Rochefort, once again in the Ardennes, in the province of Namur. Its Trappist beers are all of the dark, sweetish, style, and are very typical. I

Rochefort: there was a convent in 1230; the oldest builds are from the 1600s; and the Trappists have been there since the 1880s.

have always regarded them highly, and they seem to have been even better in recent years. In particular, they have a very good flavour development from the first taste to the finish.

In my travels over the years, I had visited every other Trappist brewery at least once before I finally managed to see Rochefort, as it is usually known. The problem was not geographical accessibility. From Brussels, it is an easy drive south-east even by the scenic route through the barley-and-malt town of Gembloux, down to the rocky gorge of the river Meuse at Namur and Dinant. Then east as the Meuse Valley rolls upward into the middle of Ardennes. As the roads wind into the hills, every bend has a sign offering farm produce: "oeufs frais, fromage de chèvre, lapin, foie gras…"

Like most towns in the Ardennes, Rochefort seems full of char-
cuteries, bakers and chocolatiers. A few more miles up a country road, with woods on one side and a vista of rolling hills on
the other - typical of the Ardennes - is the monastery. Some of
the Trappist breweries,
knowing that visitors to
the region will wish to
sample their beer, make
sure it is available in a
nearby inn, but Rochefort
has no such auberge.

All of the monasteries are
hesitant to admit visitors
to the cloister itself. Each
abbey has at times had
the name for being the
most private. The reputa-
tion may change in one
direction or the other with
the election of a new
abbot. Rochefort for many
years was known for its
shyness, but has in recent
years been much more
open, at least in respect of
its brewing.

When I finally arrived, I
was met by a grey-bear-
ded monk who seemed
unaware that I was expected.
He fetched Brother Antoine,
who was dressed for work
in a black sweat-shirt and
dark blue drill trousers.
Brother Antoine told me

Brother Antoine
(above) retired...
then moved to help
Achel. His successor at
Rochefort, Father
Pierre, admits to using
„a dash of coriander".

that Saint-Rémy dated from at least 1230, when it was a convent. In 1464, it became a monastery, and in 1595 it began to
brew. At that time, barley and hops were grown in the grounds.
The oldest parts of today's abbey date from the 1600s. After the
Napoleonic period, the abbey was restored in 1887, and the brewery in 1899. A plaque of St Arnold, with a mashing fork, overlooks the 1960s brewhouse. This is of a traditional design, in
copper, set into beige tiling. There are stained glass windows,
and potted plants add a further decorative touch.

Barley from as far away as Australia, Portugal and Poland has
contributed to the two Pilsener malts and one Munich type
used. There is also dark candy sugar in the kettle. The hops are
German Hallertaus and Styrian Goldings, added twice. Two

strains of yeast are used. The same two strains are used in primary fermentation and bottle-conditioning. White crystal sugar is used as a priming in the bottle. "Two of the pale malts, two of the sugars, two hop varieties, two yeast strains two of this and two of that we like to keep it simple," laughed Brother Antoine. Some fine beers seem to be made in a complicated

manner and others very simply. This is true beyond doubt, but cannot be explained analytically. Brewing is like cooking: there is no "best" way. The brewers who do it their own way do it best. Knowledge is essential whatever the approach, but a feel for beer, and a respect for it, make the best brewers.

Like many Belgian brewers, not only in monasteries, Brother Antoine had a crucifix watching over his kettles and another in his office. I could hardly avoid noticing that the shelves round his

Checking the wort-flow...Brother Antoine in younger days. Inside the vessel are rotating rakes that can stir the grain bed to clear any blockages. Sometimes there are problems: brewers refer to a „stuck mash".

office also accommodated about 400 beer-glasses, steins and bottles. He suggested that the Rochefort beers were best tasted at 12-14 °C (54-58 °F). Each is distinguished by its gravity in the old system of Belgian degrees, which is now falling out of use. Thus the beers are called simply six, eight and ten. This is handy, observed Brother Antoine, because they are ready to drink at six, eight and ten weeks. The brewery conditions them in the bottle so that they should reach the customer in an optimum condition. Some devotees like to lay down the strongest one for a month or two.

Rochefort 6 (which has 6.0 per cent alcohol by weight, 7.5 by volume) has a reddish "autumn leaves" colour; a soft body; and an earthy, herbal palate (a suggestion of Darjeeling tea?), developing to a deep fruitiness. Rochefort 8 (7.3w, 9.2v) has a tawnier colour, a more assertive palate, with an even richer fruitiness (a hint of figs?) and a dash more spicy, cakey dryness to balance the finish. Rochefort 10 (9.0w, 11.3v) has a deep red-brown colour; a dense head; a more viscous body; and a profoundly fruity palate (pears, bananas, decidedly rooty flavours), with notes of bitter chocolate developing in a late, warming, finish.

If the taste descriptions make some of these beers sound like a meal, that is appropriate enough. The notion of beer as "liquid bread" was apposite not only during Lent, Brother Antoine reminded me. It was absolutely necessary in order to balance the diet. "Trappists would have died without it." Traditionally, Trappists did not even eat cheese or fish. Those rules have been relaxed, but the Trappists still dub the Cistercians "meat-eaters". Today, the brothers at Rochefort do not in general drink the beer except on high days and holidays, though Brother Antoine said there was one member of the community who liked a glass at 10 in the morning. Such abstinence relieved him of the duty of making a weaker "table beer", which some of the monasteries have. Brother Antoine did not exactly say so, but I feel he is pleased not to have to make a table brew. I don't think he really saw that as beer.

He told me there were 25 monks at the abbey, and four of them had jobs in the brewery, along with five secular workers. For the monks, the important task is the putting in of a new brew each morning. All brewers start early, and those who are monks especially so. At Rochefort they rise at 3.15, and have the brew tidily under way before heading for High Mass at 7.00 in the morning.

WESTMALLE

The golden Tripel made by Westmalle has in recent years inspired countless imitators, though few match its complexity.
The abbey's full name is Our Lady of the Sacred Heart. It sits behind elm trees and high walls in neat, flat, countryside near the village of Westmalle, north of Antwerp. The monastery was founded in 1794, and is said to have been brewing beer for the brothers' own consumption since 1836, though the product was not sold until the 1870s, and initially only in the village.

Most of the present abbey edifice dates from around 1900. By the 1920s, the making of beer had become a commercial business, and the brewhouse building itself is strikingly 1930s in style. Inside, the vessels are copper, set into platforms tiled in a decorative pattern of blue, black, red and autumnal colours.

The brew-kettle is heated by direct gas flame, rather than steam, which is more common. This "fire-brewing", as it is sometimes known, produces hot spots in the kettle, and these very faintly caramelise the malt. This produces a hint of a toffee-ish, aromatic, quality that is a traditional feature in some Trappist beers.

The look of the brewhouse did not change dramatically in an upgrade in 1991/2, though a vessel was effectively gained by the addition of a mash-filter to replace a lauter-tun. There are now two brew-kettles, but the system of heating by (gas) direct flame has for the moment been retained. The brewery feels, rightly in my view, that this system may contribute to the malt character of its beers, but worries about the wear on the underside of the kettles. Experiments have been carried out with a steam system. The brewery produces three beers: "Single", "Double" and "Triple" beers. The single, actually known as Extra, is also a golden beer, delightfully delicate in character. It is very dry, and to my palate slightly salty. The brewery's water is quite hard, which suits the paler ales. The Extra is usually produced at a modest strength for the monks' own consumption, but it has been made in more than one version, and at a higher potency been marketed outside the abbey. Westmalle does produce the occasional experimental beer.

On the 150th anniversary of its brewery, the abbey issued a commemorative brochure which offered some interesting uses of the beer: "Against loss of appetite, have one glass of Tripel an hour before mealtime; against sleeplessness, drink one Trappist." I particularly liked the precision of the prescription against stress: "two glasses of Trappist will reduce stress by 50 per cent."

The golden colour, perhaps shading toward bronze was a novelty in a strong, top-fermenting, beer when the famous Tripel was launched. Here, the colour highlights the AW (Abbey of Westmalle) logo. The insignia has a 1930s look, like the brewhouse.

With the passage of only a few years, it is no longer possible to make such innocent suggestions. (In America, a brewer tried to present a fourteen-point analysis of his beer, including percentages of "negative" elements like sodium and "positive" ones such as protein and three B-vitamins, and was forbidden to do so).

All three of the regular beers contain summer malts from several sources, notably including Lower Franconia and Beauce-Gatinais (the regions south of Paris, in the direction of Orléans). The varieties will vary according to their performance each year. The Gatinais barley malts were especially favoured for their softness by Brother Thomas, when he was technical director at the brewery. In discussing a malt from elsewhere, widely used by other brewers, I asked whether he thought it was perhaps a trifle harsh. "It's brutal!" he replied, thumping the table. I first met Brother Thomas when he was 59 years old. I saw him again nearly ten years later, and he was still thumping the table, permitting himself a laugh at his own excitability. Soon afterwards, at the age of 70, he retired, handing over to his secular colleague of ten years Jan Adriaensens. The specifications of the beers do not seem to have changed.

The Dubbel, with a gravity of 15.7 Plato (1063) also has a dark malt and dark candy sugar. This beer has an alcohol content of 5.2 by weight, 6.5 by volume. It has a reddish dark brown colour;

a soft body; and a palate that is malty and coffeeish. with hints of anis and passion-fruit toward a dry finish. The Tripel has a gravity of 20 Plato (1080), and is made with pale candy sugar.

Its famously golden colour registers at 12-13 on the EBC scale. The beer has a dense, white, head that leaves very full lacework. It is very aromatic; creamy in body (almost shortbread-like); with a banana-like, orangey, fruitiness in its deep, complex, palate. When the beer is young, the banana can be too assertive. With a little bottle age, the interplay between malt, hop and fruit is superb. Throughout, there is in the background of the Tripel an appetising hop character. In a beer of such all-round power, 35-38 units of bitterness represent restraint rather than punch. The first time I visited the brewery, they were using English Fuggles, several German varieties, and Saaz from the Czech Republic. On a subsequent visit, Styrian Goldings, German Tettnangers and Saaz were emphasised, "along with others". All are aroma varieties, but Brother Thomas was shy of revealing his precise hop formulation. Later in our conversation, he mentioned three more varieties. He was also keen to emphasise that the brewery used blossoms rather than pellets. There are three additions, all in the kettle. The finished Tripel has an alcohol content of 7.2 by weight, 9.0 by volume.

Screened by trees, the monastery maintains its seclusion, despite the commercial success of the brewery on the site.

After primary fermentation, the beers have a long, slow, secondary of three weeks for the Dubbel and five for the Tripel, at 8-10 °C (46-50 °F). This is a very important part of the production procedure. The beers are then filtered, primed and re-yeasted. The same yeast is used at both stages. There then follows a warm conditioning in the bottle of two weeks for the Dubbel and three for the Tripel, at 21 °C (70 °F).

Brother Thomas told me he felt the beer hit a peak at three to six months. It then became more aromatic after two or three years, and he had greatly enjoyed a sample that had reached a decade.

"Keep some for five or six years, then use it to make a sabayon. It's perfect!" (Bangs table with glass. The vessel is a crystal goblet engraved with a flower pattern, but it doesn't seem to mind). I protested that I might not be able to restrain myself from opening it before then. "All right, drink it with asparagus. Westmalle Tripel is perfect with asparagus. What wine goes with asparagus? That's difficult, eh?!" (Another bang).

Food was on the menu, conversationally speaking. "Getting food right is an art. Just to get potatoes right is an art." (Bang). "Getting beer right is an art. When you can do that, you can call yourself an artisanal brewer. It is the brewer who makes good beer, not the equipment. You have to have a feeling for your beer know what you are smelling, what you are tasting." (Bang). "It's a question of being there."

"One of the existentialists said: `Know what you are thinking.' That's important. Sometimes in the modern world we know so much, that we don't know what we are thinking."

WESTVLETEREN

The launch in 1999 of Westvleteren Blond answered an obvious question: why would a famous brewery that overlooks hop gardens not emphasise the plant? This new golden beer, at 4.6w (5.8v) has a powerfully earthy, herbal, aroma; a light, firm, body; and an intensely appetising hop bitterness.

The abbey, properly called St Sixtus, is at Westvleteren, near Ieper (Ypres) and the hop-growing town of Poperinge, in West Flanders. It is easier to let the hop shine through in a golden beer than in a dark one. The malts required to make dark beers tend to have more dominant flavours.

The motive in creating the Blond was probably to have an entrant in what has in recent years become a popular category. Having welcomed it, I hope nonetheless that Westvleteren will not neglect its darker brews, which have their own earthy maltiness. A critic once dismissed Westvleteren's products as "farmers' beers". That is precisely their charm: they are robust, honest and wholesome.

The most elusive of the Trappist beers are those from Westvleteren. There is no distribution. Café-owners and shopkeepers have to collect their beer... and it is rationed.

The abbey dates from 1831, and brewing started eight years later. I remember visiting the monastery on one of those days when Flanders looks as though it has been painted in oils on canvas: iridescent light on flat fields dappled with brown cows and pantiled farm buildings. From the lane, the abbey appears the most rustic of the Trappist monasteries: a clutter of styles, with hints of country railway station at one moment and between-the-wars Italianate at another. The starkly modern church is not instantly apparent.

At the bottom of the brewery steps, a figure in cover-alls and green Wellington boots was waiting to greet me, waving enthusiastically to attract my attention. This was Brother Daniel, then the brewer.
"Let me change my battledress," he said. He was 33 at the time, a Bachelor of Philosophy who had previously taught French in Zaire. He talked of having felt a "fugitive" in Zaire of the sense of brotherhood in the monastery. He had been in the monastery ten years and had been concerned with the brewery for about seven. The previous brewer had taught him the job, and he had at first worked in the lab. Despite his familiarity with the place, he managed to bang his head on a pipe as he showed me round. He had just finished reassuring me that he was all right when I banged mine. "This place is a piece of industrial archaeology," he laughed, with a degree of pride and accuracy. He told me the brewhouse dated from 1900, though i think it might have been slightly later. The kettles, with saucer-shaped tops, were recessed into the brickwork. It was a typical design in old, artisanal breweries in Belgium.

In the monastery on that occasion, I was served a four-degree table beer with my lunch. The monks are expected to restrict themselves to one bottle a day. "Isn't that difficult?" I asked brother Daniel. His answer was simple enough: "Yes!" Then he told me that a student magazine had reported that Westvleteren's strongest beer was an aphrodisiac...

In 1997, I visited Westvleteren again, and met brothers Paul and Godfried, who seemed somewhat shyer. They showed me a stain-less-steel brewhouse, seven or eight years old, with two kettles.

The new brewhouse is in the former malt-barn, completely rebuilt in its original style of a hundred years ago, step-gabled and whitewashed. Arched windows overlook farmland, with a hop garden in the distance.

Malt is now filled into silos. Only pale malt is used, with white and dark sugar. The first runnings from the mash tun go to one kettle, to make a strong beer, the second runnings to the other for a lower-gravity brew, It is a very traditional method. Northern Brewer hops are used, and Westmalle yeast.

At no stage is the beer centrifuged or filtered. Protein and yeast are left to precipitate during maturation. The beer is then re-yeasted and bottle-conditioned. The brewery has held out against such refinements as labels, simply indicating the strength of its beers on the crown-top. With increasing regula-tion of packaging, such minimalism may no longer be possible in the near future. Meanwhile, the 8°, with a blue top, has a huge, rocky, head and a Burgundy colour. It is fruity and swee-tish, with suggestions plum brandy and chocolate(6.4w; 8.0v). The 12°, with a yellow top, has a creamy aroma; rich, raisiny, toffeeish, malty flavours; sa long finish; and a mahogany colour. This has 8.8w; 11.0v or more. I have seen analyses varying from 10.5 by volume to 11.5, but this is bound to happen with beers that are still "alive" in the bottle).

Westvleteren is the smallest of the Trappist breweries, and tradi-tionally it has produced "only what we need to live". The beer is not distributed. Shopkeepers, café owners and private individu-als queue at the abbey to buy it. Telephone callers (057-401057) hear a recorded message telling them which brew is currently available. If it is the 12°, lines of cars form long before the 10.00 opening. Each car is rationed to ten cases. Despite this, someone once assembled enough to ship it to the United States, add their own labels identifying the brewery (correctly, but without autho-risation) and put it on sale. Opposite the abbey is "De Vrede", ori-ginally a café but now referred to as a "meeting centre". The beer is, of course, served there by the glass.

Abbey beers

Raise a chalice in the refectory, or at the ruins.
Or drink to your patron saint.

Having their own breweries perhaps emboldens the Trappists to make some of Belgium's most individualistic beers, but it is no guarantee of greatness While the Trappists cherish their own mash-tuns and kettles, orders like the Benedictines and Norbertines have beers made on their behalf by secular brewers. These orders, which had their own breweries in the past, perhaps until the French Revolution, or in the odd case World War I, see their beers as a means of earning funds for their upkeep and work. Some of the abbeys have an inn nearby serving the beer. The abbeys' beers are typically strong, top-fermenting, ales: malty, fruity and well-rounded. Sometimes candy-sugar is used. Often, there is a dark "Double", a Blond and a stronger, golden or bronze, "Triple". Some, most often the latter, may be bottle-conditioned. The Blonde and Triple types have greatly gained in popularity during the current decade.

There are at least 70 abbeys, convents and beguinages in Belgium, and these divide in more or less equal numbers between those that are still inhabited, others that have been deconsecrated and put to different uses, and the remainder that survive as ruins.

Not all "abbey-style" beers are dedicated to extant communities. Many are named after deconsecrated abbeys, or ruins (some of which are local tourist attractions). Others simply celebrate local churches, shrines or saints.

AFFLIGEM

This Benedictine monastery, founded in 1074, played an important part in the religious, political and cultural history of Flanders, and in the hop trade. There are ruins from 1085; a 1665 farm, white-washed and standing round a cobbled courtyard; and 17th-century engravings showing hops and beer barrels.

The abbey once owned gardens in Kent, where the Flemish began the English hop industry. I visited Affligem in the mid 1980s, and photographed the abbey from a hop garden. It is the hop-growing region of Aalst, between Brussels and Ghent. Sad to say, cultivation in that region has greatly diminished in recent years. The present abbey is a mix of Renaissance and neo-Gothic. The main structures date only from 1928, though they express in modern building the Benedictine tradition. Brother Stephen took me into the 400-year-old cellars to taste his cherry wine. He told me he bought cherries in Brabant, at auctions, and made 10,000 litres of wine a year, aging it in Port pipes. He said it reached 15 per cent alcohol by volume.

The wine was offered in a Burgundy sampler. It had a deep, cherry, colour; an almost blackcurranty aroma; a soft, smooth, body; a sweetness offset by alcohol; and a hint of sharpness in the finish. When I commented that it perhaps had some Port character, from the wood, Brother Stephen disagreed. To prove his point, he fetched me a glass of Port as a comparison. Once, at another Belgian abbey - which I shall not mention here - a brother offered me a brandy that he had made on the premises though there was no evidence of any licence for a still. Affligem brewed beer until the First World War.

For some years, its beers have been produced by the De Smedt brewery, in nearby Opwijk. This brewery has now changed its name to Affligem. These beers have become noticeably sophisticated in character in recent years. They have a clean fruitiness, with notes of juicy sultana, orange and lemon; a smooth, dry maltiness; and a crisp, perfumy, finish.

The Blond (5.2-5.6w; 6.5-7.0v) is lemony, hoppy and almost talc-like. The Dubbel (5.6w-7.0v) has a reddish, tawny, colour; a spicy aroma and palate, with notes of orange and pear; and a clean, deep, dark-malt character. This beer is subtly spiced with caraway, aniseed and sweet orange. The Tripel (6.8w; 8.5v) has only the sweet orange. It pours with a dense, pillowy, head; has a fragrant aroma; a syrupy fruitiness of sultana, strawberry and pepper; and a whiskyish finish. A beautifully rounded combination of big flavours.

CORSENDONK

At the end of the 1300s, the Duke of Brabant's daughter Maria bequeathed her estate at Corsendonk, near Turnhout, to the Augustine Order. The estate became Corsendonk Priory, and gained an international reputation for its scriptorium and library. Erasmus went to the Priory to read the only Greek Bible in the Low Countries, but a few decades later the buildings were sacked during religious and political unrest.

Corsendonk Priory was restored in the 1600s, during which time it is known to have had a brewery. It finally closed in 1784, but the Priory buildings were restored again in 1969-75. They are now used for conferences of heads-of-state and captains of industry.

In the dining room, surrounded by original paintings by the pupils of Rubens, and tapestries from the 16th and 17th centuries, I sampled two beers, created in 1982, to which Corsendonk has licensed its name.

Corsendonk Pater Noster (identified in the English-speaking market as "Monk's Dark") has a Burgundy-brown colour; a yeasty, fruity, slightly smoky, bouquet; and suggestions of raisins and dark chocolate in its palate. It has an alcohol content of 5.6w; 7.0v. This beer is produced by the Bios brewery, in Ertvelde, East Flanders. The Pater Noster is available on draught at the astonishingly kitsch Corsendonks Hof, at the end of the lane that leads to the priory. Otherwise, both are bottle-conditioned beers.

Corsendonk Agnus Dei, is name meaning The Lamb of God, raised some eyebrows even in Belgium. In the English-speaking world, it is known as "Monk's Pale". This is a beer of the Tripel type. It has a clean, yeasty, bouquet; a surprisingly light, textured, body; and a great deal of finesse: beginning flowery and developing to a delicately dry finish. Its alcohol content is 6.5w; 8.1v. This beer is produced by Du Bocq.

The Corsendonk beers are the creation of Jef Keersmaekers, a member of a distinguished brewing family. His grandfather had a brewery making a dark, abbey-style, beer in the northern part of Flanders until 1953, and related families have in recent years been involved in three breweries, including Bios. Mr Keersmaekers, a

Corsendonk...from 1600s priory to 21st century conference centre.
De Keersmaekers family enjoys a beer meal at restaurant Vrouwenhuys,
next to the priory. (facing page)

tireless promoter of his products, makes a point that this has been certified in Germany under the terms of the Purity Law - the Reinheitsgebot - though sugar is used in the refermentation.

GRIMBERGEN

St Norbert (1080-1134) established his order in Prémontré, near Rheims and just north of what is now Champagne country. He also founded the abbey that towers above the cherry trees at the village of Grimbergen, now something of a northern suburb of Brussels. Grimbergen is thus one of the handful of abbeys in Europe that were established by the founders of their orders. The abbey has been sacked four times, and each time rose again. Its emblem is the Phoenix, and this appears on the labels of its beers.
In the Norbertine tradition, the abbey has a magnificent Flemish-baroque church, much of which was built during the 1600s. On my two visits, I have found the interior of the church so tall and narrow and rich in carved oak as to be stunning, almost intimidating.

No wonder the Norbertines inspire faith. I regained my composure when I noticed that the elaborate carvings in the choir stalls prominently included depictions of hops along with the grapes and cherries. The present cloister was rebuilt after the French Revolution and restored in the 1920s. Its vaulting and tiling are haughty enough, though they are softened by windows giving onto a garden of tulips. Nearby is a café called the Fenixhof.

Even among abbey beers, those bearing the Grimbergen phoenix tend to be on the sweet, liqueurish side. This sweetness is especially notable toward the finish.

Grimbergen Blond (5.6w, 7.0v) is a leafy gold in colour, lightly fruity, with a touch of dessert apples in the palate and aroma. Grimbergen Tripel (7.2w, 9.0v) is gold-to-bronze; more aromatic; with an orangey, winey fruitiness; and a warming finish.

Grimbergen Dubbel (5.2w, 6.5v), which has a Burgundy colour, is raisiny, and toffee-ish, with a finish that is brandy-like. While this version has the customary dosage of dark candy-sugar in the kettle, the stronger, deep amber, Optimo Bruno (8.0w, 10.0v) does not. The name recalls the notion that the finest beer in an abbey was the strong, brown brew traditionally consumed after Lent, at Easter. Optimo Bruno has a creamy, apple-cake, fruitiness, and again that warming, alcoholic finish.

All of these beers are produced for the monastery by Alken Maes. The Maes brewery is not far away, at Waarloos, but its top-fermenting beers are made in the company's charming old brewery Union, at Jumet, near Charleroi.

The Union brewery also produces the Ciney range of abbey-style beers, which have different specifications and their own yeast strain. Their house character is to start sweet, but finish drier, and to have a lighter, more expressive, palate. Ciney Blonde (6.8w, 8.5v) has a bright, golden, colour; a lightly sweet fruitiness; and a crisp finish. Ciney Brune, at the same strength, is soft but dryish, with a hint of cellar character. Ciney Speciale (7.2w, 9.0v) has a dark ruby colour; a "juicy", slightly oaky, palate; and a complex of spicy notes suggesting anis, coriander, cinnamon and even faint clove. In a somewhat esoteric beer-and-food combination, I once enjoyed this brew with sweetbreads and courgette flowers.

The Ciney beers are named after a small town, famous for agriculture and especially for beef cattle, in the province of Namur. Their label depicts the church of Ciney, and there is no link with an abbey. The brand-name is owned by a beer merchant.

LEFFE

A good example of a continuing community is Notre-Dame de Leffe. The abbey is close to the Meuse, where it is met by the smaller river Leffe, at Dinant. This is a town of great historic interest and a tourist centre, about 20 miles south of Namur and less than 50-odd from Brussels. The oldest part of the abbey is a garden dating from 1152, with herbaceous borders set round a fountain. Most of the buildings date from the mid 1700s. The valley of the river Leffe is noted for its herbal plants, and the Norbertine brothers still use these to make tisanes.

The abbey is believed to have had a brewery from the 1200s until the Napoleonic period, but emerged in the early part of this century without one. At the beginning of the 1950s, the Abbot was chatting to the local brewer and mentioned that the community was having financial difficulties. The brewer suggested that he make beer for the abbey, to be sold under their name as a commercial venture. There were other commercial breweries in Belgium making beers with ecclesiastical-sounding names at the time, but this is believed to have been the first such formal licensing arrangement. The local brewery was later taken over by another company, and then that was acquired by a larger concern, but the arrangement has survived and prospered, and the Leffe range are among the best known of the abbey beers.

In 1989, one of the brothers gave me a tour of the abbey. It is older, with smaller, and darker quarters than any I have seen elsewhere in Belgium, but it is the possessor of several very interesting antiques and works of art. Historically, the Norbertine tradition was to engage the most sought-after artists of the time to produce magnificent works that would inspire religious zeal. The brothers follow the Rule of St Augustine. It is not a closed Order but one that preaches and does pastoral work.

Leffe...gardens are still an imprtant part of the abbey,s life.

After my tour, I was seated at an old oak table and offered a tasting of the Leffe beers. In general, these are very rounded beers, with an aromatic malt character and a firm fruitiness. Leffe Blonde (5.5w;

6.6v) has a sunny colour; a fragrant, faint, clovey-ness of aroma; a restrained orangey fruitiness in the palate; and a cedary dryness. Leffe Brune is a deep, autumnal brown. It has a hint of dessert apples in the aroma, a suggestion of brown sugar in the palate, and an oaky, sappy, dryness in the finish (5.2w; 6.5v). I have been served both of these beers chilled and found them rather thin. At the abbey of Leffe, they were presented from the cellar, and had more flavour. There are also two stronger counterparts.

Leffe Triple is the most delicate and complex beer in the range. It has a rich, golden colour; a clean, light, cedary, appetising, aroma; a fluffy, medium-to-full, body; a winey, oaky, palate; and rosewater in the finish. A lovely, fresh, apéritif beer. Alcohol: 6.7w, 8.4v.

The Leffe beers were for many years made at the Mont St Guibert, using the Vieux Temps yeast. Because this brewery did not have facilities for bottle-conditioning, the one beer with that treatment, the Triple, has always been brewed elsewhere. It is made at Hoegaarden, using the Vieux Temps yeast in primary fermentation and the Hoegaarden strain in bottle-conditioning. The other Leffe beers are now made in Leuven.

Leffe Radieuse (the name referring to the halo that radiates round the head of a saint) is an extra-strong dark (actually, claret-coloured) beer. This has an earthy, slightly smoky, aroma; a slightly syrupy body; and a whole range of flavours: cherry-like fruitiness, chocolate, roasty notes, balancing bitterness. It is a very rounded beer, preferably with a book at bedtime (6.8w; 8.5v).

MAREDSOUS

This is a Benedictine abbey, at Denée, south of Namur. It
began as a community of Bavarian monks, on land donated
by a Belgian ecclesiastical printer, and became an abbey
in 1878. The buildings are a good example of the neo-
Gothic architecture that flourished in Belgium and
France during that period. The Maredsous beers have
long been favourites of mine, and I was delighted
when they performed outstandingly in a blindfold
tasting organised by Bier Passion magazine in
1999. They have in general a delicate, complex,
flowery-fruity character and a very fine,
Champagne-like, bead. They are each identified
by numbers in the Belgian degrees system.
Maredsous 6 has a spritzy fruitiness in the
aroma; a very good, soft, clean, malt character;
and a lighty dry, perfumy, finish (4.8w; 6.0v).
There is no Maredsous 7. The next beer in the
range is Maredsous 8, with a deep, tawny, colour;
a body that is light for the strength of the beer
(just over 6.4w; 8.0v); a sweeter palate; and hints
of chocolate and coffee towards the finish. There
was at one stage a Maredsous 9, but that has
been dropped. Maredsous 10 has an amber colour; a
soft, creamy, well-rounded, body; a beautiful balance of malt and
fruit; and a long, warming, finish (just over 7.6w; 9.5v). The last is
an especially delicious beer. These beers are made by the Moortgat
brewery, in Breendonk, in the province of Antwerp. This brewery is
best known for its Duvel (see Strong Golden Ales).

ST FEUILLIEN

The Friart family brewery... restored by Dominique and her brother Benoit.

The name derives from the Irish missionary monk St Faelan, or Foillan (c 655) is said to have founded the settlement that is now the town of Le Roeulx, The town had an abbey until the French Revolution. The family Friart established a brewery in the town in 1860. Later, they expanded into an 1890s brewery nearby, and ran it until 1980. After the brewery closed the family remained in the beer business by running a drinks market, and had their beer produced under contract by the Du Bocq brewery.

Then, in 1988, a new generation re-opened the family's own Friart brewery. "When I was five or six years old, I had to work in the brewery during school holidays, and after it closed, I missed it," Benoit Friart

told me. "It was our family brewery, and I wanted us to make beer here. I put it to my sister Dominique, and she agreed." I asked Dominique if she now worked in the brewery, and she replied: "Sure! Perhaps not so hard ... but I work there. I had it in me. I didn't know but it was there."

Behind handsome iron gates, brightly painted in blue, the brewery yard is set round a magnolia tree. The former maltings and the brewery are chunky, red-brick buildings, their line softened by smartly-painted woodwork, hop vines (for decorative purposes only) and window-boxes of geraniums. It is a tower brewery, still using its original, wood-clad mash tun, the hood of which is raised by chains and pulleys. St Feuillien beer is produced at 7.5v by Du Bocq and 8.5v by the Friart brewery. Both make pale and dark (blonde and brune) versions. Friart also has a 9.0 per cent version (Cuvée de Noël) for Christmas. The Friart-brewed Blonde is very aromatic, with a fresh, fruity, peachy aroma; a pillowy head; a pinkish-bronze, colour; a creamy, distinctly orangey, palate; distinctly hoppy and dry, with a hint of juniper in the long finish: an almost gin-like aperitif. The Brune has a head like Café Liègeoise; an attractive, deep reddish-brown, colour; a much softer, smoother, toffeeish, body; and a tasty, bitter-chocolate, palate: a perfect dessert beer or digestif. The latter role might be fulfilled even better by the Cuvée de Nöel, which tasted like a rich Viennese coffee laced with Italian Sambuca.

The Friart versions are in corked bottles, not only 75-centilitres but also Magnums (1.5 litres); Rehoboams (4.5); Methuselahs (6.0); Salmanazars (9.0); and occasionally Balthazars (12.0) and Nebuchadnezzars (15.0). One private customer in Virginia buys the biggest, and brings his bottle back personally twice a year for a refill.

VAL-DIEU

Apart from the six Trappist monasteries, this is the only abbey in Belgium to accommodate a working brewery. The Cistercian abbey of Val-Dieu is near the village of Aubel, in the region known for Herve cheese, between Liège, the Dutch city of Maastricht and the German city of Aachen (Aix-la-Chapelle).
In 1993, the abbey turned its stables into a tavern called the Casse-croûte, serving onion soup, local cheeses and charcuterie and a range of beers under the name Val-Dieu. The beers were made at a recently-revived

family brewery, in Aubel. Unfortunately, the revived brewery quickly ran into difficulties. The idea of making the beer in the abbey itself came from tow outsiders: Alain Pinekaers, a drinks wholesaler in the areas; and brewer Benoît Humblet, formerly with Kronenbourg, who had just returned from a period of working overseas. Brasserie de l'abbaye du Val-Dieu was established at the end of 1996.

Like most monasteries, Val-Dieu is in a somewhat hidden, tranquil, spot. It stands on a winding, oak-fringed, country road, in the steep

Hops grow wild in the area, but those climbing outside the brewery were planted as decoration. Many brewers do this as a symbolic gesture to the magic blossom.

valley of a small river. The abbey was founded in the 1200s and restored in the late 1700s and mid 1800s. It had a brewery in the distant past, probably until the French Revolution, and there are still hops growing wild in the ground.

The first time I visited the abbey, I was enthusiastically guided by Father Joseph: "Those Cistercian capitals date from 1260; that door is a fine example of Liège Baroque; there are the guest quarters where the Empress of Austria stayed..."

On a more recent visit, there was the brewery to tour, in farm buildings with the odd flourish of Moselle Renaissance architecture.
One building has been decorated wth a trellis training hops. The beers are made from Belgian malts, the soft well-water from the village supply of nearby Charneux, German and Czech hops (of the Hallertau-Hersbrucker and Saaz varieties) and yeast from Louvain-la-Neuve. They are re-fermented in the bottle.

I tasted them in the Casse-croûte, with its cobbled floors, tables covered in oilcloth with rustic designs, and open beams. Abbaye du Val-Dieu Blonde, at 4.8w (6.0v), was crisp and clean, with an interplay of nutty malitness, hoppy bitterness, and earthy, yeasty (faintly lemony?) aci-dity. A Triple, at 7.2w (9.0v), had the colour of golden plums, yet more nutty malt-iness, and a drying finish. A Brune, at 6.4w (8.0v), had a garnet colour, aromas and flavours of bitter chocolate, nougat, and raisins.

The only beer to be spiced is a Christmas brew, which I was tasting at seven months old. This deep amber brew was oily, very spicy and dry. Benoît asked whether I could guess the spice. I might have said juni-per, but this seems unlikely, as the brewery already has a further beer using that spice, produced for the Rademacher distillery, of Raeren. The Christmas spice will have to remain a secret.

TONGERLO

The abbey of Tongerlo towers over the flat heathland known as the Kempen, in border country close to The Netherlands. It was once a powerful abbey and still has many valuable artefacts.

The Dubbel Bruin (5.6w; 7.0v) has a dark, russet colour, a syrupy smoothness and a toffee-licorice palate, with some balancing rooty, dryness in the finish. The Dubbel Blond (4.8w; 6.0v) is again toffeeish, with lemony, sherbety, notes, and beautifully balanced. The Tripel (6.4w; 8.0v) starts with honeydew melon and finishes spicy and peppery. The Norbertine abbey of Tongerlo, about half way between Antwerp and Hasselt, dates from the 1130s, and had a brewery at its foundation, growing its own barley and wheat. The abbey today makes bread and spicy pastries, Coincidentally, a notably spicy yeast is used to ferment the beer, at the Haacht brewery, in Boortmeerbeek, nearer to Mechelen.

FURTHER ABBEY BEERS, WITH TASTING NOTES

The brew-kettle on the lawn is surely a sign of passion for beer. Jean-Pierre Eloir and his wife started brewing commercially in 1979. This picture was taken around that time.

Abbaye des Rocs: New-generation brewery named after a farm that was once a monastery, near Montignies-sur-Roc, in Hainaut. Its principal product is an abbey-style beer bearing simply the name of the brewery. This has a soft, fruity, spicy, character and 7.2w; 9.0v. The brewery was started as weekends-only operation, in his garage, by a civil servant and beer enthusiast. When he started marketing his beer commercially, I asked him whether there were any difficulties with legal requirements, taxes, and so forth. "I know all about that," he told me. "It's my week-day job."

AUGUSTIJN

Dedicated to the order of the same name, but not an individual abbey. The full gold Augustijn (6.4w; 8.0v) is hoppier, both in its spicy, earthy, grassy, vanilla-like, aroma and dryish flavours, than most abbey beers. It also has a good, creamy, malt background. It is additionally unusual in being available with re-fermentation in the keg. Augustijn Grand Cru is slightly stronger (7.2w; 9.0v), paler and drier. These beers are made by the Van Steenberge brewery, of Ertvelde, East Flanders.

BORNEM

Also from Van Steenberge, a garnet-coloured Dubbel, with hints of apple, cinnamon and coffee. Named for a one-time Dominican abbey.

BRUNEHAUT

An interesting revival. After the local brewery closed, the copper hoods from its kettles were acquired by friends. They were trained brewers, a married couple, working overseas. When they returned, they used the hoods in a smart, new, purpose-built brewery. The stylish structure looks incongruous in a no-man's land on the French border. It is at Rogny, South of Tournai, in the province of Hainaut. Brunehaut Villages Blonde, at 5.2w (6.5v) is bright gold, with a a perfumy (almost talcum-powder) aroma; a light, firm, body; a fruity (sweet limes?) palate; and a grainy, dry, finish.

Brunehaut Tradition Ambrée, at the same strength, has an attractively reddish colour; a slightly fruitier aroma; a touch of sweet, licorice-like, maltiness in the palate; and a rooty, dry, finish. Bière du Mont Saint-Aubert (6.4w; 8.0v) is made with the old brewery's yeast, and has a distinctly creamy, vanilla-like, character. Abbaye de St Amand (5.6w; 7.0v) is a flowery-tasting brew with a hnt of jenever-like junper.

DENDERMONDE TRIPEL

A lightly hoppy, dryish, crisp, beer of 6.4w; 8.0v, named for a long-gone Carmelite abbey. The beer is from De Block, of Peizegem, near Merchtem, in Flemish Brabant. The family De Block have been in brewing since perhaps the 1500s. Their premises, with a coke-fired kettle, is something of a museum early industrial brewing.

ENAME

Well-made, tasty, beers dedicated to the St Salvator Benedictine abbey (founded 1063), the ruins of which are a tourist attraction at Ename, near Oudenaarde. These include a chocolatey, minty, leafy, oaky, garnet-brown, Dubbel (5.2w; 6.5v); a fragrant, lightly fruity, Blond at the same strength; and a firm Tripel (7.2w; 9.0v) with a big, dryish fruitiness (orange marmalade, pineapple, banana?).

FLOREFFE

The Double (5.2w; 6.5v) offers a big pop of the cork, the aroma of star anise, and a lemony, sweetish, but lively, beer. The Blonde, at the same strength, is creamy, tart and clovey.
The Triple (6.0w; 7.5v) is bittersweet, lemony and cedary. La Meilleure ("Best"), is a mahogany-coloured brew with a very rich malt character, cedary, aromatic and soothing (6.4w; 8.0v). These beers, made by Lefèbvre, of Quenast, help support the seminary of Floreffe, between Namur and Philippeville. The seminary has its origins in the Norbertine abbey of Floreffe, which brewed from its foundation, in 1121.Lefèbvre also dedicates beer to the seminary of

Bonne Espérance, at Vellereille-les-Brayeux, near Binche, in Hainaut. This also was a Norbertine abbey, which brewed in the early part of this century.

PATER LIEVEN

The Blond (5.2w; 6.5v) has a fresh, creamy, aroma; a firm, crisp, palate; and a dry, faintly salty, very appetising, palate. The Bruin, at the same strength, is very dark, and yet creamier, with a very good malt character and rich, long, flavours. These beers take their name from their home village of St Lievens Esse, between Ninove and Oudenaarde, in the "Flemish Ardennes". They are made at the brewery Van den Bossche, currently in the third generation of that family. It began as a farm brewery in 1897, near the town square and church of the patron saint Livinus. There are touches of Art Nouveau about the brewery facade, but the interior has a more agricultural feel, with malt still delivered in sacks, and spices ground in a mill that looks like a kitchen mincer.

Ignace Van den Bossche demonstrated by grinding coriander into a bowl like a saucepan lid. "I use one of these, full, per brew," he told me. "What is the weight," I asked. "I don't know," he replied. Coriander and Curaçao have been well featured in the beers for at least 30 years, according to the brewhouse logs. The brewery has a spicy, medicinal, dark ale called Buffalo, something between an Oudenaarde brown and a sweet stout. Allegedly, a lone brewer accidentally created it by allowing the mash to scorch while the rest of the staff had the day off for Buffalo Bill's circus in 1907. A

very fruity (blood oranges?),nutty, gingery, Tripel (6.4w; 8v), with a bronze colour, is named Lamoral after a patriotic count who was beheaded during the period of Spanish rule.

PETRUS

Just one abbey-style beer in this range from Bavik. It is a deliciously drinkable Triple, at 6.0; 7.5. Spicy aroma; malty and creamy palate; notes of fresh apple, lemon and coriander. A bottle-conditioned development from an earlier beer called Cuvée St Amand.

ST ARNOLDUS

A Triple of 6.0w; 7.5v, with a very fresh hop aroma; lightly nutty malt character; and elegantly rounded late dryness. Dedicated to the brewers' saint and made by Riva.

ST BERNARDUS

A secular brewery that has past connections with the Trappists (see P268). The brewery, at Watou, West Flanders, is in an imposing, 1930s, former cheese dairy, masked by lime trees. The whitewashed brewhouse has handsome copper vessels bought second-hand in 1946. An arbor of chestnut trees leads to an office with a billiard table and oriental antiques, collected by partner Guy Claus. There are four St Bernardus beers. Pater 6 (5.4w; 6.7v), chestnut in colour, is very fruity, with notes of melon and very fresh banana; Prior 8 (6.4w; 8.0v), ruby to purple, has a richness of texture that is almost oily, and a malt-fruit complex reminiscent of coconut. Abt 12 (8.0w; 10.0v or more) is almost ebony in colour, even bigger and more assertive, like a warming coconut brandy. The lighter, more flowery, Tripel (6.0w; 7.5v) has a pale amber colour, the aroma of rosewater, and the orangey-grassy flavours of Styrian hops. All have re-fermentation in the bottle, but the Tripel with a different yeast.

ST HERMES

A creamy (white chocolate?), fruity (lemon rind?), abbey-style from the Clarysse brewery, of Oudenaarde. Hermes is parish saint of the nearby town of Ronse (in French, Renaix). "My husband also liked the name," I was told by Novella Clarysse. "He had a good friend called Hermes who was always full of joie-de-vivre."

ST IDESBALD

A very aromatic Dubbel (5.4w; 6.7v), with flavours reminiscent of prunes in ice-cream, and a leafy, dry finish (a good dessert beer); a fluffy, sherbety, lime-like, Blond (5.2w; 6.5v); and a sweet, raspberry-ish, perfumy (garden mint?) Tripel (7.2w; 9.0v). Dedicated to a long-gone Cistercian abbey, and brewed by Huyghe, of Melle, near Ghent.

TER DOLEN ABDIJBIER

This clean, sweet, nutty blond of 4.9w; 6.1v, was the first product from a new brewpub at Helchteren, north of Hasselt, Limburg. The brewery is in the stables, and the pub in the farmhouse, of a château, "De Dool", which has its origins in 1107. The present buildings, dating from 1634, were once used as a refuge for the monks of St Truiden. A former sales manager at the brewery Riva, of Dentergem, is one of the principals at De Dool (Eikendreef, Helchteren, tel 011-522999; fax 521318).

VILLERS-LA-VILLE

Cistercian Abbey that brewed at its foundation in 1215. The ruins are a tourist attraction, 25 miles south-east of Brussels, past Waterloo and Genappe. Villers Triple (6.8w; 8.5v) has a hazy, gold-to bronze colour, with creamy but dryish suggestions of pepper and apricot. Made by Huyghe.

WITKAP

The name clearly alludes to the white cowls of the Cistercians, but without identifying an abbey. The individualistically-crafted Witkap beers are produced by the Slaghmuylder brewery of Ninove, in East Flanders. Among them, Stimulo is a golden brew with a heavy yeast sediment; a talc-like aroma; a dense, pillowy, head; sherbety on the tongue; and a palate that develops from peachy fruitiness to lemony, salty, hoppy, dryness (4.8w; 6v). At the other end of the range, Witkap Tripel is fruity, honeyish, winey, and more assertive (6.1w; 7.6v). These beers were inherited from the long-gone brewery of Brasschaat, in the province of Antwerp, and I believe this was the first golden Tripel, before the style was taken up by Westmalle.

THE TERM TRIPEL

In the days before widespread literacy, breweries would brand their casks with crosses, diamond shapes, triangles, or other simple marks to distinguish between different strengths, colours or lengths of maturation. Beers marked, for example, "x", "xx" and "xxx" would certainly have contained ascending levels of alcohol. I am not sure the number of x's would always have represented a multiplier, but I have heard it said that in Belgium the words Single, Double and Triple typically indicated three degrees, six and nine. These were the old Belgian degrees of gravity, but the figures for alcohol by volume would have been similar, perhaps fractionally less.

Today, the term Single is rarely used, but Double and Triple are popular designations in Belgium. A Double is usually a dark brew of 6.0-plus per cent alcohol by volume, and a Tripel often (but by no means always) a pale one of 7.0-plus to 9.5 or more. This is especially true in the case of abbey beers (where the designations are perhaps inspired by the success of the Westmalle Trappist products). Elsewhere, a Triple may just indicate a top-of-the line product.

Historically, the term Tripel seems to have been especially widely used by the many brewers that once existed in the Bruges area. This tradition has been strongly maintained by the former 't Hamerken ("Little Hammer") brewery, now known as Gouden Boom ("Golden Tree").

On a site that was once at the edge of town but is now quite central, this establishment dates from the 1500s, and has been variously a tavern, brewery and distillery. It has been in the Bruges brewing family Vanneste since the 1870s. In 1983, the brewery was threatened when one branch of the family did not wish to continue, and at that time it was re-constituted as De Gouden Boom. The name "Golden Tree" is an allusion to a trophy traditionally given to jousters in Bruges. It is now run by Paul Vanneste, with partners who include Rodenbach. In its new life, De Gouden Boom has become best known as a specialist brewer of white beer, but it is also very proud of its abbey-style products, including two Triples.

For the abbey of Steenbrugge, with its links to St Arnold, the brewery makes two beers. The amber-brown Steenbrugge Dubbel (5.2w; 6.5v) is full of flavour, with an outstanding malt character and a dry

ANNO 1439

Brugse Tripel

LEVEND BIER MET NAGISTING IN DE FLES.
BIÈRE VIVANTE REFERMENTÉE EN BOUTEILLE.

sappiness in the finish (like biting into a toffee apple). The very pale, greeny-gold, Steenbrugge Tripel (6.8w; 8.5v) has a fruit character more reminiscent of peaches-in-brandy, and lovely citric overlay of Styrian hops. The brewery's own Brugse Tripel is fuller in its golden colour and creamy maltiness, with warming alcohol, a perfumy hop character, and a honeyish complexity of flavours (7.2w; 9.0v).

Behind a façade of 16th-century gabled buildings, through an arch in which the keystone bears a statue of the Virgin Mary, De Gouden Boom still has its 1902 maltings, though they have not worked since 1976, and the top ten metres (the kiln tower) blew off in a storm in 1986. The 1964 block brewhouse, the first of its kind in Belgium, is softened by the Vanneste family crest and an oak carving of Madonna and Child. In the tiling is a depiction of St Arnold.

Belgium's tallest beer-maker, Paul Vanneste, stoops to check the filtration of the mash. His family have been brewers since at least the 1870s.

Whenever I visit the brewery, I am reminded that the present, 58th, abbot of the former Oudenburg and now Steenbrugge monastery is the living successor to the brewers' saint. De Gouden Boom (47 Langestraat) also has an excellent museum of Bruges breweries past and present, which is open from Thursday to Sunday during the summer, or by appointment (tel. 050-33.06.99; fax 050-33.46.44).

Golden ales

Reticent but stylish... beautifully judged.

Reticent but stylish... beautifully judged brews for a quiet moment or an aperitif Amid the more assertive, bigger-bodied or more colourful brews that help make up Belgium's rainbow coalition of beer, it is easy for a golden ale of relatively conventional strength (4.0-6.5v) to go unnoticed. The designation "golden ale" is not commonly used in Belgium, but there are a growing number of beers that fit this description. At first, they can seem unassuming, but several have a beautifully-judged interplay of malt background, hop aroma and restrained fruitiness. They are quietly stylish beers.

The use of the typically Belgian aromatic malts, sometimes candy-sugar, estery yeasts and warmer fermentation and maturation temperatures, distinguish these beers from some other styles of golden ale: for example, the famous but more delicate Kölschbier of Cologne, Germany. Equally, they tend to be fuller in body than the golden ales traditional in Canada and the North-East of the United States.

DE RYCK

The much-admired brewer Anne De Ryck makes an example, which she says has been golden since at least the days of her great-uncle. Mrs De Ryck runs the brewery that bears her family name, in endive-growing country near the hop town of Aalst, in East Flanders.

Her great-grandfather started it as a farm brewery in 1886, and the original buildings still stand, with additions from the 1930s and 40s. He went to Germany to study brewing, as did Anne, before gradually taking over the running of the family business from the late 1970s onwards.

De Ryck is unusual in that it sticks to the German Purity Law, disdaining sugar, an influential ingredient in many Belgian beers. Its De Ryck Special (spelled the English way after Anne's father spent some time with a Newcastle brewery) has a golden colour with a tinge of bronze; a soft, notably clean, lightly sweet, malt accent; and a delicate hop character. It is brewed from Pils and aromatic malts, with three additions of Belgian Hallertau and Saaz hops and a further gift of Styrians during its four-week maturation (3.4 w, 4.2v). The brewery also has a stronger (4.3w, 5.4v), cherry-red, fruity-malty, ale called Rochus, after the parish saint. There is also an aromatic Christmas Pale Ale.

Opposite a 12th century castle keep, through a wooden arch, the brewery is set round a cobbled yard. After the Germans confiscated brewing vessels in the two World Ward, second-hand equipment was installed in 1949. The brewhouse, now something of an antique, is well fitted and impeccably clean and tidy. I asked Anne if she had a cleaning day each week, and she reproachfully told me that the place was cleaned after every batch: "Brew-and-clean brew-and-clean."

Brewster De Ryck...
„always watch
and listen".

Anne's father installed a malt silo, and an auger to move the grain, so that she would not have to heft 160-pound sacks, but she has been known to shovel out the 1800-pound mash-tun. Across the courtyard, the brewery's shop sells the beers, which can be ordered gift-wrapped in baskets and cellophane. The bottled versions are unfiltered.

Anne, her husband Omer, and their children, live on the premises. "You can never leave a brewery all alone," she told me. "You must always watch and listen."

It is hard to imagine such pure, clean, beers giving anyone a headache but, should that happen, aspirin is at hand. Anne's husband is a pharmacist, and he runs his shop in the brewery's former stables.

DE HALVE MAAN / STRAFFE HENDRIK

The "Half Moon" brewpub is hidden in a cobbled yard next to the beguinage of Bruges. It stands on a canal marking the inner limit of Bruges harbour in the days when the city was one of Europe's greatest trading ports.

De Halve Maan has since 1856 been in the hands of, a family called Maes (not connected with the Pils brewers of the same name). The male Maes have all been called Henri or Hendrik. The fifth Hendrik currently works in the brewery. His sister Véronique is the manager. She married into the Vanneste family, , of the city's Goudenboom brewery. Veronique's son Xavier is a sixth generation in the Halve Maan brewery. He studied brewing in Ghent and economics in Antwerp, and is a keen propagandist for the family's business.

In 1981/2, a "blonde" ale was created to be served at a reception to celebrate a new statue of St Arnold in the city. At 7.5v, it was slightly stronger than the brewery's regular beer, and came to be known as the Straffe ("Strong") Hendrik. This was later toned down to 6.0v (4.8w), in which form it became the brewery's flagship beer.

Straffe Hendrik Blonde has an earthy-fruity hop aroma (East Kent Goldings); a creamy, fresh-tasting, start; and a clean, crisp, very dry, finish. This beer fills a gap between golden ales of conventional strength and the strong type such as Duvel (P282). The success of Straffe Hendrik gave rise to a bigger, darker, brother brew, though less emphasis is given to this beer. Straffe Hendrik Bruin (6.8w; 8.5v) has a rich, deep, flavour-packed, malt character, with notes of rum and pears.

Beer brewed at the Halve Maan is bottled by the Riva brewery, in Dentergem, West Flanders. Riva also on occasion brews Straffe Hendrik, especially for export, and owns the trademark. Admirers of Straffe Hendrik Bruin might also enjoy a Riva beer with notes of coriander and aniseed, named for the Dutch poet and dramatist Vondel.

LOUWAEGE / FLANDRIEN

The name speaks of regional pride, and Flandrien (4.0w; 5.0v) deserves to be better known. It is smooth, clean, well attenuated and flowery, with full, hoppy flavours. Flandrien is from the Louwaege family brewery, in the brick-making town of Kortemark, south of Bruges.

The beautiful step-gabled brewery house overlooks the town market place. Flandrien is brewed from Pilsner and Munich malts, providing a colour somewhere between gold and bronze; hopped with Hallertau-Hersbrucker and Saaz; and fermented with a yeast said to have been obtained in Britain by the grandfather of Jan-Baptist Louwaege, the present principal. Already, a further generation of the family is being acclimatised to brewery life. Last time I visited, I was greeted by Mr Louwaege's children Sebastian, aged seven, and Benjamin, five.

The brewery was founded in 1887, and once specialised in a Flemish Old Brown. The characteristically curved, chimney-like, vent of the original maltings still stands, albeit in retirement. So do the original kettles, which were heated by a fire, A cartoon mural shows the kettles exhaling steam; maturation tanks "sleeping"; and casks "laughing". The illustration fills the wall behind the present-day brew-house, which dates from the 1950s. By now, it has become a period-piece, with a muscular counterweight to lift the hatch on the kettle. The brewery is behind the original family house, handsomely step-gabled, on the town square.

MALHEUR

"Would you mind climbing on to the roof? Good! Now, look across the fields to the church spire. Just to the left, you can see a derelict brewery. My grandfather's grandfather established that place."

Emanuel De Landtsheer was in a reverie. "See those fields over there? My grandfather grew his own barley, and malted it himself." We wandered over to the maltings, in buildings set round a farm-style courtyard that looked to have changed little since the earliest days. The malting floor still had the typical Gothic arches, but now converted into an informal bar for guests. So far as I could see, there seemed to be three bars for guests in different parts of the brewery.

"Manu" De Landtsheer was warming to his theme. "My grand-father was also called Emmanuel. He was the son of a brewer. His wife was the daughter of a brewer. Emmanuel's brother was a brewer, too, in St Amands.

"My grandfather was very keen on blending. He said you must always mix barleys and malts to iron out inconsistencies. Same with hops. He thought you should blend two harvests. Our family continued to grow hops for a long time, in that field over there."

The brewery closed just before World War II, but the family continued to grow hops until the 1970s. Manu, then in his late teens, remembers rushing home from school on his bike to help with the picking, and recalls the aroma in the oast as they were dried.

"As I grew up, we all talked about re-opening our own brewery one day. When my father died in 1991, I decided I must make this dream true. As he reminisced, he showed me photographs of his forbears. In one black-and-white print, a group of stern-looking men stood behind several children. One very small child was a boy in a smock. "That was my father." Manu's eyes clouded as he spoke.

The mansarded house of the family, still occupied by Manu's mother Monique and one of his sisters, Martine, is now linked by an entrance to a new, building. The latter, in a similar architectural style, houses mash-tun, kettles and fermenters. The new brewery has one of those typically Belgian self-mocking names: Maheur, which roughly translates as "Misfortune".

(right, with on the left his brewmaster Luc Verhaegen) Manu De Landtsheer... „see those fields over there?" Malheur began with just one beer, of 5.3v; 4.3w. This is a golden ale, made from three varieties of French barley (remember what grandad said?), malted in Belgium. These are all Pilsner malts. A fourth, speciality, malt is also used. This has variously been Caravienne, Munich and Aromatic, as the brewer has experimented in developing the product. No sugar or adjuncts are used in the brewhouse.

The hops are Saaz, Styrians and Hallertau-Hersbruck, all as blossoms, in three additions. "Having grown and picked hops, we could hardly use pellets."

The yeast is from the nearby Affligem brewery. The bottled Malheur is re-fermented. When I first tasted the beer in this form, in my office in London, I was particularly struck by the Saaz hop accent. I also noticed a spiciness. Perhaps this was due to the citric, perfumy, yeast, though the culture has been re-cropped at Malheur, and has gained its own character. At the brewery, I found the bottled product very aromatic, rose-like and slightly oily. The draught had a more obviously orangey flavour and a big, fresh Saaz character.

This being Belgium, I was also asked to taste several vintages. At two months, the beer still had some yeasty sourness. At four, it was very assertive, with an almost stony, flinty, grassy, Saaz character. At eight, the oily, rosy characteristics were coming to the fore, and Manu thought he detected nuts and honey. I was not sure, but definitely found honey in flowery version of only 40 days that had been filled into a 75-centilitre bottle with a cork.

Soon afterwards, Malheur 6 was launched, at 5.8v (4.6w). This is hoppier, fruitier and spicier, with a very good, cleansing, acidity. Then came Malheur 10, launched as a Millennium brew. This contrives to see light (despite an alcohol content of 10v), but is also creamy, with a powerful fruity bitterness reminiscent of gooseberries. I tasted this at a time when Manu was planning to bottle-condition it in a Champagne cellar, with remuage and degorgement, in Epernay. It was not clear at the time whether this experiment would work. Were it to work, it would be a remarkable new speciality. I also sampled Malheur 12, which is a dark interpretation. The

colour is a dark chestnut, the flavours nutty and fruity, and the texture syrupy. I was reminded of Belgian waffles, fruit breads, and the apple syrup of Liège.

Are these "wicked" brews the
"white alcohols" of the beer world?

A beer as pale as a Pilsener lager, but twice as potent (7.5-11.0v), and with the fruitiness imparted by a top-fermenting ale yeast. It strongly resembles a Trappist or Abbey Tripel, but it may be yet paler, lighter-bodied, and perhaps crisper and drier.

Just as most golden abbey Tripels were inspired by Westmalle's example, so the Devil's beer fired up countless rivals to make demonic brews.The original, Duvel, is distinguished by the use of sugars that boost alcohol but not body, and by a long and complex sequence of warm and cold fermentation and maturation.

DUVEL

With its pillowy, white, head; its innocent golden colour; its fine, sustained, bead; its slender, satin-smooth body; its delicately flowery-fruity dryness; and the lingering perfuminess of its finish, this is a deceptively elegant brew: it packs a mighty 8.5 per cent alcohol by volume (6.8w). "The devil of a beer," a brewery worker is said to have observed when a test batch was sampled. Hence the name, which is a corruption - suitably evil word - of Duvel (Flemish for "Devil"). The beer's name is pronounced

(more or less) Doov'l. It is not a French-speaking beer, so the stress on the second syllable, often applied by people in other countries, is inappropriate.

Duvel is typically served as an aperitif, though I like it as a digestif, a beery counterpart to a Poire Williams.

Even by Belgian standards, the serving of this beer is something of a ritual. The Duvel glass resembles an over-sized Burgundy sampler. The beer is served with a huge head, and poured bright. Most top-fermented ales taste best at cellar temperature, or only lightly chilled, but Duvel is often presented in a glass that has been kept in the refrigerator.

Perhaps this is what prompted the thought of Poire Williams. Brandies are customarily served warm, but the "white" eaux-de-vie of Alsace are more often presented chilled, sometimes in a glass that has been treated in the same way. Not only does Duvel resemble an Alsatian eau-de-vie in presentation, it also has a distinct suggestion of Poire Williams in its bouquet and palate.

Some individual brandies and wines are legends, and the same is true of a handful of beers. This one has a remarkable story. At the height of the fashion for Scotch Ales in Belgium, between the two World Wars, a bottle of McEwans was "taken apart" under a microscope by the great brewing scientist Jean De Clerck. It is a scientist's job to study and investigate, and that is what he was doing. Perhaps he was especially interested in flavour characteristics that seemed to derive from McEwans' yeast, which turned out to be a mix of between ten and twenty strains. In those days, McEwans' Scotch Ale was bottle-conditioned, and therefore contained living yeast.

De Clerck did the work together with the local brewery owned by the Moortgat family, in Breendonk, north of Brussels and not far from Mechelen. At the time, Moortgat made dark top-fermenting brews.

With cultures isolated from the McEwans yeast, the Moortgat brewery introduced a new dark strong ale. After the Second World War, golden beers of the Pilsener type began to gain ground in Belgium, and this set Moortgat to some more experimentation. In 1970, they unveiled a golden version to replace the dark Duvel. Once again, De Clerck was involved. Even using a Pilsener-style malt, it is hard to produce a truly golden strong ale. The problem is that the density of the malt needed to make such a strong brew inevitably makes for a ful-

ler colour. Why did the brewery want such a pale colour? In part, for cosmetic reasons. They wished to produce something that responded to the fashion for paler beers, but did so with its own distinctive flourish. By making the beer with an unusually pale malt, they also gave it a distinctively clean body. They could equally have gone the opposite way, sought a fuller maltiness in the palate, and made a beer that was delicious in that style, but it was not what they were seeking.

The ability to turn barley into malt of a particular colour or natural taste is both and art and a science (like brewing itself). The development of the science has over the centuries had a major influence on the introduction of new styles of beer. The Moortgat brewery was originally able to achieve just the right character because it had its own maltings, at the brewery. This was a floor maltings, and it ceased to operate into the 1980s. By then, free-standing maltings were able to match Moortgat's own, the company felt, and the success of Duvel meant that the space was needed for maturation warehouses. I would swear that the Moortgat maltings gave Duvel an extra refinement, but such memories cannot be proven any more than we can say whether Joe Louis would have beaten Muhammed Ali.

Whether the brewers admit it or not, all beers evolve over the years. Even if nothing else changes, the character of each year's malt is different, and sometimes one variety becomes unavailable and has to be replaced by another. The same is true of hops. Different raw materials will also vary in their inter-action with the yeast, causing it to adapt. Some brewers introduce changes to respond to these circumstances, others to render their lives easier or make their beers less challenging to the consumer. Over the years, Moortgat has refined the yeast in the bottle to make it precipitate and compact better. Brewers of greatly-loved beers have to be careful with such changes: the devotees, quite properly, watch them with eagle eyes.

Two-row summer barley is malted in France and Belgium to a colour of between 2.5 and 3.5 EBC for the production of Duvel, and the finished beer has between 7.0 and 8.0, or 9.0 at the absolute maximum. Pilsener-style beers as a finished product generally vary from 5.0 to 7.5.

The original gravity is 14 Plato (1056). An infusion mash is used, and in the boil hops are added three times. The varieties are Saaz and a particular type of Styrian Goldings. (Final EBU is 29-31).

Bel Pils is quite clear about its style. It is a Pilsener. Clean, dry and well-hopped. Passendaele (below) is a strong-ish ale, but not as potent as Duvel. All these hoppy, golden, products are from the Moortgat brewery.

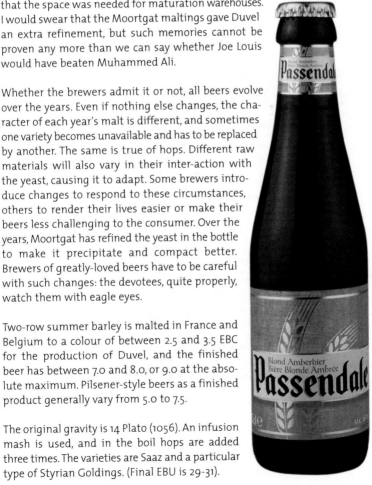

A proportion of dextrose is added before primary fermentation, to boost alcohol and further attenuation. This effectively upgrades the original gravity to 15.5 Plato (1066).

Primary fermentation is at between 16 °C (60 °F) and 28 °C (82.4), and the brew stays in the vessels for five or six days. It is then transferred to cold maturation vessels, where it has a secondary fermentation for three days, during which the temperature is dropped to minus one degree Celsius (30.2 °F). It is then held for a minumum of three to four weeks' cold maturation before being dropped to minus three (26.6 °F) to complete the precipitation and compacting of the yeast. (The outside walls of the lagering cellars, with inspection ports, make a visually dramatic pattern round the brewery yard. Moortgat is a very modern brewery, but its equipment is all stylishly designed and assembled). After cold maturation, the brew is filtered and given a priming of dextrose and a dosage of the original yeast. The original gravity has at this point been effectively boosted to the equivalent of 17.0 or 17.2 (1073-4).

Such step-by-step increases in original gravity are, of course, not unique to Duvel, and take place in the production of a good many other Belgian beers, but I have set them out

Original Meura equipment from 1973.

here because this regime of fermentation and maturation is one of the most elaborate. With the priming and dosage, the brew is bottled, and spends eight to 14 days at 22 °C (71.6 °F) undergoing its third and final fermentation. This takes place in two huge sheds, each about 50 metres long, which together house 175,000 cases at any one time. The sheds have temperature control systems in both the floors and ceilings. These buildings are visible from the main road, and are painted with the legend: "Ssst ... hier rijpt den Duvel". The word "rijpt" means "ripens", and the rest hardly needs translating.

Finally, the beer is stabilised in cold storage at 4-5 °C (39-41 °F) for two three months before being released. Some customers then store the beer for a further three to four months, in a cool, dark, place, before serving it. In Belgium, when Duvel is served chilled, it is usually at 7-8 °C (45-46 °F). It also expresses its flavour well at a natural cellar temperature in the range of 12-13 °C (53-55 °F). Duvel is by far the biggest-selling product ofMoortga.In 2000, the brewery launched a beer called Passendale. Some

Peaceful Passendale... Michel and Philippe Moortgat, whose brewery is famous for Duvel.

consumers were mystified as to why a beer would be named after a tragic battlefield. More pleasant connotations are intended. It is meant to accompany the Belgian cheese of the same name. This strong ale (6.0 per cent alcohol by volume), golden to pale amber, has a leafy (nettles?) hop aroma; a surprisingly light body, drying on the tongue; and a spritzy acidity in the finish. Perhaps I am being suggestible, but it does seem to have a slightly apple-like fruitiness and tartness. The latter could derive from the grist: wheat is used, in addition to crystal (a very small proportion of that, I would guess), pale ale and Pilsner malts. The hops are all Saaz (hence that "fresh" note?), but there are no herbs or spices. The beer has an unusual regime of fermentation. It begins with a lager yeast (for a fuller attenuation) but at an ale temperature (for those apple esters). It is then bottle-conditioned with a top yeast.

Moortgat additionally makes the Maredsous range (see Abbey Beers), Godefroy (Ales) and the hoppy BelPils.

FURTHER "WICKED BREWS" WITH TASTING NOTES

Brigand: A slightly darker (bronze to copper) variation on the theme). Brigand has a very good, flowery hop aroma; a soft body, with an insistent bead (it can be very lively); some yeast "bite"; a nutty, fruity, rounded, palate; and an earthy, dry, finish. It starts with a gravity of 20 Plato (1080), is made with Pilsener and pale ale malts, and a touch of wheat; and hopped with Saaz. It is also dry-hopped with the same variety. The final alco-

hol content is 7.2w; 9.0v. The month and year of bottling are printed in the cork. Brigand expresses its flavour most fully at three to six months after bottling. It should be stored at a natural cellar temperature, and served without excessive chilling.

Delirium Tremens: The flippant name was deemed unacceptable in the United States, where the beer was dubbed Mateen, after an early Flemish brewer in Americas. Delirium Tremens is very bright, despite its being bottle-conditioned. It has a dense head; a very fruity (greengage? gooseberry) bouquet; a sweetish palate; and a lot of warming alcohol in a rather abrupt finish (7.2w, 9.0v). The hops used include not only Saaz but also Styrians, and its fermentation demands three different yeast cultures. These are employed consecutively in a two-stage primary fermentation and in the bottle-conditioning. In 1999, a dark-brown brother brew called Delirium Nocturnum was launched. That beer, made with five malts, is smooth, rich and perfumy.

Deugniet ("Rascal"): Yeasty bouquet; light but firm, textured, body; beginning flowery and developing to a hoppy, finish. From Du Bocq, from Purnode, in Namur.

Hapkin: A fine example from the Louwaege brewery, of Kortemark, south of Bruges. The name of the beer derives from Boudewijn Hapkin, a 12th-century Count of Flanders, whose deterrent wielding of an axe is said to have brought peace to his land. Or did he simply use it to cut trees? The region between Bruges and Kortrijk is known as "the Woodland" but trees are today not especially evident. Either way, there is an axe on the label of the beer. Hapkin (6.5w; 8.5v) has a very good, fresh, flowery, Saaz hop aroma; a very big, creamy, head; a soft malt character; and a spritzy, perfumy, fruitiness, drying toward the finish. It is made with a decoction mash, has no fewer than four hop additions, and has a two-stage primary fermentation. Hapkin was launched in 1982. Other products from Louwaege include Flandrien, introduced in 1987 (see P 278), and the long-established Akila ("Eagle") Pilsener.

Delirium Tremens is quite an agresssive brew. The newer Nocturnum (left) is rounder. A yet newer Delirium Christmas (10v) has a tawny colour , with both fruity and spicy flavours, reminiscent of dried orange peels.

*Sitting with Satan...
Paul Saerens,
of De Block*

Judas: Big, assertive, fruity, reminiscent of sweet oranges in syrup. With earthy, fresh, complex hop aromas.(6.8w; 8.5v). From Alken-Maes.

Julius: Perfumy aroma; very white head; firm, grainy texture; syrupy flavours, becoming winey and then drier (7.0w; 8.8v). From Interbrew.

Piraat: A hoppy interpretation, with a lot of Saaz character, from Van Steenberge, of Ertvelde, East Flanders. Piraat has a gold to bronze colour, a spicy hop aroma, creamy, nutty (almondy?) palate, and a fruity dryness in the warming finish. (8.4-8.8w; 10.5-11v).

Satan: A malty, slightly sticky, Gold (6.4w; 8.0v), and a fractionally stronger, caramelly, Red (labelled in English), from De Block, of Peizegem, Brabant.

Sloeber ("Joker"): Attractive, enticing, pale amber colour. In the aroma, spiciness and malt. In the palate, sweet maltiness balanced by the drier, lively, "orange-zest", flavours of Styrian hops. A complex, teasing, appetising, beer, at 6.0w; 7.5v. From Roman, of Oudenaarde.

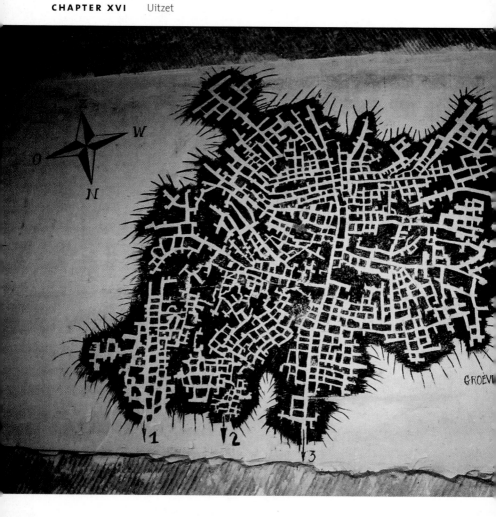

Selected specialities

The idiosyncratic, the regional... the beers that defy categorisation In much the way that France has two or three hundred cheeses, each representing its own locality, so all the brewing nations once had countless beers, each associated with one brewery, village, town or province. Belgium still has some beers that are hard to categorise but that have their own integrity. Better yet, their numbers are increasing as small breweries try to distinguish themselves by developing their own specialities. Below are some examples, identified by brewery or beer, according to which is best known. Some are very traditional, but not all.

BINCHOISE

The 14th-century town of Binche is known to connoisseurs for its pre-Lenten carnival, its own traditional mask for the occasion, and a museum that explores these themes. Binche, in a loop on the river Samme, was once a frontier between France and the Low Countries. In the modern world, it can be found equidistant from Mons and Charleroi.

Opposite the medieval ramparts, a maltings and brewery, using river water, operated for two or three centuries. The brewery closed in the 1920s, but the maltings continued until World War II. The maltings buildings were then given a new life in the late 1980s as a revivalist brewery, this time using town water.

I had tasted the beers elsewhere in Belgium, and even in Canada, but did not have the opportunity to visit the brewery until 1997. When I did, I was sur-

André Graux...
"my wife brought
some rigour"

prised to greeted by a reception committee of a dozen or 20 townspeople, including politicians and the director of the museum. Every town with a good brewery should appreciate that, but I had never seen quite such a display of civic pride. I later learned that 20 local restaurants offer a menu à la bière Binchoise.

The man behind it all is André Graux, a photographer, who was out of work: "My father used to brew at home, so I thought I would try it professionally. A year later, I married, and that was my salvation. I had been behaving like an artist, but Françoise brought some rigour to the business."

At the time of my visit, the beers were being brewed in a soup-kettle which previously saw service with the National Guard. Such vessels are often use by new small breweries, especially in America. The Binchoise beers, like many from small breweries in Wallonia, are hard to categorise. All have re-fermentation in the bottle.

La Binchoise Blonde (5.2w, 6.5v), has honey in the bouquet; a touch of Curaçao in the spicing; and a peppery, dry, very appetising, finish. Flora, a spring beer (5.6w; 7v), has a champagne-like pop, a vanilla flavor and a nutty malt accent. La Binchoise Brune

(6.8w; 8.5v) is aromatic, with a dusty spice character (star anise is used), rich and warming. Bière des Ours (6.8w; 8.5) is a richly honeyed, but beautifully balanced beer. Honey is added after the primary fermentation Speciale Nöel (7.2w; 9v) has a chewy maltiness and a hint of cinnamon.

After I had sampled the range, André presented me with his own personal mask.

BOELENS

A familiar story with a surprise twist: the Germans removed the coppers during World War I; the old-established family brewery was reduced to acting as a wholesaler (which it still does, selling a very wide range of beers, glasses and cheese). The twist: a member of the current generation, Kris Boelens, took a vacation in Germany and was inspired by a brewer there to restart production, in 1993. The vacation was in Baden-Baden and the inspiration came in nearby Karlsruhe, where a notably assertive range of lagers is produced by Rudi Vogel, one of Germany's more colourful new-generation brewpub-owners.

The Boelens family had stayed with products employing grain, water and yeast; they had been manufacturing cookies. Kris returned them to their original faith by taking vessels from the cookie bakery and using them to build a brewhouse.

Beer with a twist...brewer Boelens restores the family tradition.

One of the vessels had been employed to mix honey, and Boelens uses the same ingredient in one of his evolving range of specialities. This brew, Bieken (punningly named for the bee), is based on Pilsner malt and hopped with Styrians (three times). Curaçao orange peels are used to give a fruity edge to balance the sweetness of the honey, which is added at the end of the boil. At 6.0w (8.5v), it is intended to be a big beer, with just a touch of honey. Bieken is gold to bronze in colour; flowery in the middle; with an appetising dryness in the finish.

The brewery, is in what looks at a glance like a suburban house, just off the village square of Belsele (7 Kerkstr, tel 03-772-32-00; fax 03-722-09-92; guest bar closed Sun and Mon), near St Niklaas, West of Antwerp. This sliver of countryside, between the river Schelde and the border with The Netherlands, is known as the Waas ("Haze"). The mists allegedly part on occasion to reveal a wandering wolf. This tends to happen when the media are short of news. Waase Wolf (5.2w; 6.5v) is a beer with a full orange colour and a fruity, spicy, palate. Curaçao and coriander are added, along with Brewer's Gold hops, and 20 per cent of the grist is wheat.

A richer brew celebrates two men named Pauw and Gijsling, who in 1898 modelled for a statue marking an earlier revolt by Flemish farmers against their French rulers. Pa-Gijs (6.0w; 8.5v) is hopped with Styrians and contains some roasted malt. It has a dark walnut colour, and some cookie-like, chocolatey, notes. "We all have one to close the working day at the brewery," Kris told me.

BUSH

A new name for the classic Bush Beer. The alliteration, modest simplicity and oddly English spelling have been sacrificed for Bush Ambrée. Meanwhile, there have in recent years been several additional variations.

The estate Domaine de Guyssegnies gave birth to this brewery, which later crossed a main road and established itself independently on its present site in 1769, but still as part of a farm, with barley prominent among its crops. It has been in the Dubuisson family since at least the 1890s. The brewery still has something of the appearance of a small château: in a handsome, whitewashed building, in part original, well-maintained, with pantiled roof and green shutters, among oaks, poplars and ash trees. It is one of two breweries in the village of Pipaix, and three in the community of Leuze, north of Tournai (in Flemish, Doornik) and Mons.

A century ago, the Dubuissons made several products, including a strong Saison. At the end of the First World War, the brewery was liberated by a

Millennium moment... British battalion, and the family wanted to commemorate
Hugues and Vincent this. The family name refers to Buisson, meaning Bush.
Dubuisson celebrate Between the two world wars, the English word was adopted;
with a magnum. so was the English spelling of Beer. When, in 1933, the family decided to stop farming, and concentrate on brewing, Bush Beer became its principal product.

The Beer also has an English accent in its style: it is reminiscent of some Barley Wines. Since the 1950s, the beer has been filtered, but it is not pasteurised. In 1981, the brewery decided to concentrate all of its efforts on Bush Beer, and drop its other products.

Later, it began to export in a small way. One of its markets is the United States, home of Anheuser-Busch, the world's biggest brewer. A-B has a beer called Busch (as well as Budweiser, allegedly "The King of Beers"). The question arose: Despite the

small difference between the spellings, and the huge differen-ce between the beers, could the consumer be confused? Lest that happen, Bush Beer has been marketed there as Scaldis, the Latin name for the river Schelde. The river is not especially near, but is as important to Belgium as the Rhine to Germany or the Mississippi to the U.S.

Bush Beer is made to an original gravity of 24.5 Plato (1098), from winter and spring Pilsner malts, and crystal. It is hopped three times, twice with Kent Goldings and once with Styrians. Some sugar is added in the kettle, and there is considerable eva-poration in the boil.

Dubuisson has a well-kept, 1950s, copper brew-house, and its traditionalism has also been evident as it has upgraded its fermen-tation vessels: retaining the same geometry in the new stainless-steel. After top-fermentation at 24-25 °C (75-77 °F), with a com-plex, estery, yeast, the brew is skimmed by hand. It is then warm-conditioned for four weeks, and finis-hed cold. Bush Beer has a deep golden-amber colour; a pillowy head; a soft, creamy-fruity aroma; and a clean, soft, beautifully rounded, palate, chewy and nutty; with a superb balance of clean, dry, long, spicy hoppi-ness in the finish (32 EBU).

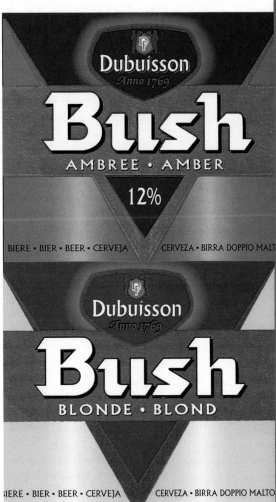

Among products added in the 1990s is a Christmas beer, Bush de Noël. This is made with more crystal malt, hopped slightly less in the kettle, but given an extra dosage of Saaz in the maturation tank. It has an amber-red colour; a delicately leafy,

earthy, aroma; a lighter hop character in the palate (27 EBU); and a beautiful balance of malt and fruit. Both the regular Bush and the Noël have 9.6w, 12.0v. In 1996/7, the Noël was introduced also in a re-fermented version, in a 1.5 litre bottle. This has a fresher, fruitier (peachy?) aroma, an oilier texture, and rosewater notes in the finish. Its alcohol content may creep up to 10.4w; 13v in the bottle.

At the end of that decade came Bush Blonde, at 8.0w (10.5v). This has a bright gold colour; fresh, fruity, hop aromas; a smooth, firm, malty, palate; and dryish suggestions of vanilla, lemon-grass and hoppy acidity in the finish. For drinkers who find all of these products just too strong, a modest concession is offered in a version at 6.0w; 7.5v, called 7°. Why the old Belgian degree sign on a new beer? "Bush Sept" is said to sound like "Bouchette", implying a small one. This beer is flowery (violets?), lemony, peppery and drily spicy. It does contain a touch of coriander, and makes a terrific aperitif. In North America, it could with justification have been labelled Bush Light. Instead, is called Clovis, after the King of the Franks. So as not to embarrass "The King of Beers"?

CARACOLE

In addition to its "White" wheat beer Troublette (P135), this remarkable revival, at Falmignoul, near Dinant, has a colourful range of well-made specialities. One echoes Dinant-born

Adolphe Sax, a clarinet player and son of a maker of musical instruments. From the bass clarinet, Sax developed in the 1840s the instrument that helped shape jazz. Those who think this the Devil's music may point to a Duvel-like beer called Saxo: with a seductively fresh fruitiness reminiscent of bananas and cherries in cream; smoothly seductive but penetrating and strong (6.4w; 8.0v). This beer is brewed from Pilsener and Munich malts, and hopped three tmes, entirely with Saaz. It also has just a hint, the very lightest touch, of Curaçao orange peels, At the same strength, Caracole Ambrée is lean, elegant and long, with lingering Styrian hop and orange-zest flavours. The yet-stronger (7.6w; 9.5v) Nostradamus, with a distinct influence of aromatic malts, tastes like chocolate pralines filled with port wine, with a colour to match. The brewery is open to visitors, seven days a week in summer, and Mon-Fri year-round. A wood-fired brewery is not to be missed (tel 082-74-40-80; fax 74-52-38).

St Arnold watches over the wood fire as the brewing water is heated at Caracole.

DE DOLLE BROUWERS (THE MAD BREWERS)

La brasserie "Dolle Brouwers" vaut bien une visite. Elle produit quelques-unes des spécialtités les plus colorées et les plus délicieuses de Belgique.

The name is a typically Flemish shrug. The 1840s brewery at Esen, near Diksmuide (and not far from Ostend), in West Flanders, seemed doomed to close, because the owner had become ill. Instead, it was acquired by a family of professional people (an architect, a doctor ...) who were keen home-brewers. They used the brewery at weekends only, and developed a range of speciality beers for commercial sale. They called themselves The Mad Brewers (De Dolle Brouwers), and their antique, working, brewery is open for tours at weekends (tel 051-502781). De Dolle Brouwers has, among several items of historical interest, a remarkable collection of bottles from Flemish breweries of the past. The principal Madman, architect Kris Herteleer, is also noted for his published drawings of breweries and cafés.

I once took a tour, with Kris's mother as a guide. In no other brewery have I met a guide with such knowledge or passion: "Malt, hops and yeast are medicines! We must capture the vivid elements of the hop!! We must be careful of the savage yeasts!!!" The latter was surely a too-direct translation from the French. The Dolle Brouwers' beers, all bottle-conditioned, have rightly won a great deal of acclaim.

The first product was Oerbier (meaning "original beer"; Oer is the Flemish counterpart to the German Ur). This is a slightly Scottish-accented, strong (6.0w; 7.5v), very dark ale, made from six malts, candy sugar, and three hop varieties. It has a fruity aroma; a remarkably smooth, creamy, texture; and a sweetish palate with winey undertones. The original version is sub-titled Donker (dark). Oerbier Licht (Light) is very similar to Arabier, the brewery's paler product. The name Arabier represents an impossibly convoluted joke, but the brew is serious enough. It is a very well attenuated strong beer

(6.4w; 8.ov), notable for its dry-hop bouquet of Kent Goldings. Boskeun ("Easter Bunny"), at the same strength, is - as its name suggests - a seasonal beer. It has a brassy colour; a yeasty body; and an interesting balance between sweetness and dryness. It has some cane sugar in the kettle, and is primed with honey for the bottle-conditioning. Different vintages of this beer have varying degrees of honey in the aroma, but all have hints of Sauternes sweetness. Oeral is a summer beer of 5.6w; 7.ov, similar to Arabier but not dry-hopped. This brew is available re-fermented on draught. Dulle Teve is a gold-to-bronze beer of 8.ow; 10.ov available most of the year. Stille Nacht ("Silent Night")

Mad Brewer Kris Herteleer (far right) entertains guests with his wife (middle) mother (far left)

finally is a Christmas beer. It is stronger still: 7.2w; 9.ov, with a claret colour; a fruity, apple-like aroma; some dry spiciness (Darjeeling tea?) in the palate; and a sweeter finish. Problems were posed in 2000, when Rodenbach, which had supplied the yeast, ceased to do so. It is understood that arrangements have now been made to ensure a supply by re-culturing.

DE RANKE

An ale with an intensity of aroma and lingering bitterness more typical of Washington State or Oregon, but an English-sounding name, XX Bitter, has won much admiration. It has 5.0w (6.2v) and is made entirely from Pilsner malt, but its golden colour seems to

have a greeny tinge. Suggested perhaps by the resiny hop flavours? The brewers feel that a very high hopping rate (65 units of bitterness) is mitigated by the gentleness of the two varieties: Brewer's Gold (which can have a sweetish flavour) and Hallertau. There are two additions, but no dry-hopping. The beer is enjoyed by some devotees who feel disappointed by the softening of Orval - but XX was inspired by Verdraagzaam, from the Steedje brewery, which has now closed.

„I dreamed of this beer"...Nino (middle) and Guido (left)

Nino Bacelle, whose family had soft-drinks company, went to brewing school, and helped at Brasserie à Vapeur, before starting De Ranke in 1994. The name refers to a frond of hops. "I dreamed of this beer, and my brewing partner created it," says Nino, referring to Guido Devos. The latter was an amateur wine-maker before an interest in Lambics drew him into beer. Both have "day" jobs: Bacelle sells cooling systems, often to breweries. Devos is a topographer. Their wives help them running the business, which is operated from Nino's home in Wevelgem, West Flanders. The beers are produced in the same province by the Deca brewery, of Woesten, near Vleteren. Other beers from De Ranke include a Kriek (5.6w; 7.0v) based a sour-ish ale, but with a hint of the Girardin character; the intensely flowery Guldenberg Tripel (6.8w; 8.5v); and a Christmas beer, Père Noël (5.6w; 7.0v), with suggestions of orange and anis.

DUYSTERS

Revived brewery in the town of Diest, in the far East of Flemish Brabant, near the border with the province of Limburg. Diest, centre for a region called Hageland ("Hedge Country") once had 20

or so breweries. The original Duysters ceased production in the early 1970s, becoming a distributor for, among others, local rival Cerckel. That brewery then closed in 1978/9. The buildings of both, in the town centre, survived. Duysters was re-started in 1995 by Marc Beirens. Initially, he used only part of the buildings, and installed a 4.5hl kettle I myself had seen some years earlier at a brewpub in Paris. In 2001, he began to move into the main buildings, with a 25-30hl brewhouse that had been silent for 15 years.

Why take on a such an ambitious project? "My family have brewed for 350 years. It's in my genes," Beirens told me. His family had owned a brewery not far away in the province of Antwerp, then at Zichem, near Diest. When they acquired the latter, it had already ceased production and become a distribution depot. That had led him to acquire Duysters. The brewery also has a tasting room (013-32-36-28), open on the first Saturday of the month, from 4.0 in the afternoon. One of my contemporaries

was somewhat dismissive of the principal product, a golden-bronze ale called Lotberbol (after a charac-ter in local folkore). I was surprised, as I found it startlingly floral and hoppy. Beirens had an interesting explanation for this: "The big brewers make their beer less hoppy every year. I make mine more hoppy every year. Perhaps your colleague tasted it some time ago." Loterbol has 5.2w (6.5v) on draught, but is stronger ((5.6w; 7.0v to 6.0w; 7.5v) in the bottle, thanks to secondary fermentation. It has two additions of Goldings in the kettle and is dry-hopped with Styrians. A Christmas beer, Kerstbol (6.0w; 7.5v) has a chestnut colour, with toasty, brown-sugar, and cherry-pie flavours, followed by a peppery hit of alcohol. The town of Diest was once known for very sweet dark beers, but Beirens regards that style as "part of the past".

GROTTENBIER

This "Grotto" or "Cave" beer was created by the endlessly enterprising brewer Pierre Celis, founder of Hoegaarden. He was the first to have the dream of maturing a beer by the Champagne method, and in the 1980s took me to see natural caves where he had arranged to do this. Before he could put his plan into action, he suffered a fire at the Hoegaarden brewery; re-financed

it; sold it to Interbrew; set up a brewery in Texas; sold that; and experienced various other adventures. Fifteen years later, he took me to another set of caves, in the valley of the river Jeker, which flows into the Maas (the Meuse, in French). The entrance is at the village of Kanne, in the municipality of Riemst, in Belgium, just across the border from Maastricht, the Dutch city where the two rivers meet.

The caves at Kanne are so large that a car can comfortably explore them. Indeed, they are so extensive that a car is essential - and a guide. A map shows more than 10 miles of tunnels, with a layout that could be the street system of a sizable medieval town. From the outside, I felt we were driving into a huge garage cut into a hillside. Inside, the tunnels are neither arched nor rough-sided. They are trapezoidal, and sometimes as high as 20 metres. They were man-made, by the extraction of stone as a building material. This left square cut-marks where each huge block was removed. These lines create the illusion that the tunnel walls are constructed from blocks of stone, as though it were the inside of an Egyptian pyramid.

Fossils far older than a pyramid: sea shells, a shark's tooth, a dinosaur, have been found.

We drove up hills and round corners, and eventually came to a cellar containing 5,000 bottles of Grottenbier, in Champagne racks ("riddles" or pupitres, in which the bottles can be tilted and turned to precipitate the yeast). This method is being used, though Pierre has abandoned the idea of freezing the bottles and removing the icy sediment.

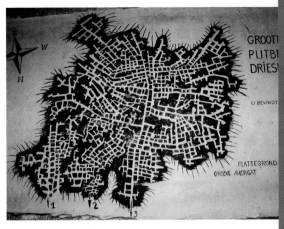

He is interested to see what influence the turning might have, and whether more subtle flavours are created in the caves, with a natural, constant temperature (12°C; 53-54F) and 95 per cent moisture, than would develop in drier, refrigerated cellars at a brewery. A more significant dimension might be the adaptation of the yeast to these temperatures. As it habituates, it will surely produce different flavours.

Grottenbier is brewed at Affligem. It is a strong (5.2w; 6.5v) ale, in which small quantities of "exotic" spices create a gentle, balancing dryness and crispness. The beer has a chestnut colour; a huge, meringue-like head (marron glacé?); and big aromas reminiscent of oloroso sherry. It is dry at the front of the tongue, developing a medium to full body, with layers of maltiness. The flavours are drily toffeeish and honeyish. The finish is slightly medicinal, resiny, and very long. When I tasted an early batch, I named it my Beer of the Year. When I tasted it in the cave, the aroma seemed fruitier and the palate more res-

iny and herbal, with a suggestion of licorice. Does beer taste different 40-odd metres below the earth's surface? An odd place to drink. All the odder, we were in a somewhat modernistic bar down there. The publican appears only be arrangement, but he does cater for subterranean private parties (tel 012-45-53-55; fax 45-44-79).

Ready to riddle? Pierre Celis in his caves...racked full of Grottenbier

HET ANKER (GOUDEN CAROLUS)

Lovely old brewery that seems finally to be gaining new life under a new generation of the owning family, after brief collaborations with other companies. "The Anchor" is a common name for a brewery. It may refer in this instance to barge transport, but is more likely to be a Biblical allusion: "Hope anchor of the soul" (Hebrews vi, 19). Het Anker, which has documents dating to 1369, may originally have been the brewery for the archbishop's palace in his home town of Mechelen (Malines, in French).

The brewery has its offices in a step-gabled building that was part of a beguinage dating from the 1400s. It is said claimed that sisters from the beguinage founded the Hospices de Beaune, during the Burgundian period. Gouden Carolus is the brewery's speciality.

The name means Golden Charles. It could refer to Charlemagne, who ruled Europe from Aix-la-Chapelle, which is not far away. Or, more likely, to Charles V (1500-58), who grew up in Mechelen and extended the influence in the Low Countries of the Holy Roman Empire. In the 1870s, the brewery passed into secular hands of the family who still run it. Het Anker brims with evidence of its history. Its imposing 1909 maltings was one of the first concrete buildings in Belgium. Its 1950s brewhouse is a classic of that period. The brewery's most unusual feature is its open cooler, which is effectively a copper trough covering the entire roof. Around the edges are a dozen pillars supporting a canopy, which forms a second roof. Apart from railings, the sides are open. It affords a magnificent view of Mechelen. I first visited Het Anker in the 1970s, and have been at least five times since. On the first

A cityscape framed in an open cooler... Mechelen,s Het Anker.

two occasions, I was entertained so assiduously by the then-principal of the company, Michel Van Breedam, that we somehow failed to make the usual tour. This has not happened at any other brewery in the world. On my third visit, I finally got the tour, topped by the remarkable cooler, the like of which I have not seen anywhere else in the world. At this point, Mr Van Breedam told me that the system was now being replaced by a modern paraflow.

When the original device was in use, the wort was run indoors before it was sufficiently cool to embrace wild yeasts. Inside, a Baudelot cooler finished the job. Was there really no spontaneous fermentation? Mr Van Breedam thought not, saying that the house yeast was such a mixture, and so habituated, that it was dominant.

Today, the café at the brewery, and some local bars, offers a very pleasantly hoppy, clean, crisp (but top-fermenting) "Pils" called Blusser ("Extinguisher"). In a twist on a universal folk tale, the people of Mechelen are said to thought the canal was on fire when it reflected the moon.

Mechelse Bruyne, at 5.2w (6.5v) is a less strong, more soothing and relaxing version of Gouden Carolus. The golden-bronze Toison d'Or Triple, at 6.0w (7.5v) is flowery and lemony.
Gouden Carolus begins with a gravity of 19 Plato (1076) and emerges with 6.8w; 8.5v). It is made from one pale and two dark malts, imparting a claret colour. The body has in recent

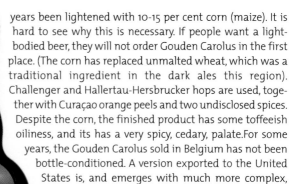

years been lightened with 10-15 per cent corn (maize). It is hard to see why this is necessary. If people want a light-bodied beer, they will not order Gouden Carolus in the first place. (The corn has replaced unmalted wheat, which was a traditional ingredient in the dark ales this region). Challenger and Hallertau-Hersbrucker hops are used, together with Curaçao orange peels and two undisclosed spices. Despite the corn, the finished product has some toffeeish oiliness, and its has a very spicy, cedary, palate.For some years, the Gouden Carolus sold in Belgium has not been bottle-conditioned. A version exported to the United States is, and emerges with much more complex, chocolatey, flavours.

Since 1999, Het Anker has had annual open day at which brewing can be seen. A beer made of this day is a higher-gravity version of Gouden Carolus, at 22-23 Plato (1088-92), with more dark crystal. It has a tawnier colour, a hint of port, and an alcohol content of 7.2w; 9.0v to 7.6w; 9.5v).This brew is called Cuvée van de Keizer.

KARMELIET / KWAK

The Carmelites of Dendermonde, in East Flanders, apparently brewed a three-grain beer in the 1600s. This information, from a book on local brewing history, was discovered coincidentally after the Bosteels brewery, of nearby Buggenhout, had decided on "three grains" as its next, highly-distinctive, speciality. Karmeliet was my first "Beer of the Year". That was just a spontaneous response. The thought has since occurred to me in respect of other beers, fortunately not more than once a year.

Karmeliet is a Tripel (6.4w; 8.0v) but made from barley, wheat and oats. As each of these grains is used in both raw and malted forms, it could at a pinch be called a six-grain beer. Indeed, it was inspired by the fashion for multi-grain breads.

It is a golden-to-bronze brew, with huge, creamy, head. Karmeliet has great finesse and complexity. These characteristics derive not only from the grains but also from a restrained hopping with Styrians, a generous spicing, and the fruity, bananas-and-vanilla, character of the house yeast. The vanilla blends with the orangey hop aroma; there is a wheaty lightness and crispness, yet also an oaty creaminess; and a spicy, lemony, almost quinine, dryness.

The brew is presented in one of Belgium's most elegant beer glasses, decorated with a stylised fleur-de-lys.

The glass was designed by Antoine Bosteels, one of the principals of the brewery. The fleur-de-lys is intended simply as a traditional decorative motif, and not a French symbol. The Bosteels' interest in antiques and decorative arts is reflected in the furnishing of the house that guards their little "château" brewery. Whitewashed, and set round a courtyard, the brewery dates from 1791, and has been in the family for six or seven generations.

In 2001, the family invited me to lunch at a restaurant that is by happy coincidence called Karmeliet. The restaurant, in Bruges. Was originally next door to a former Carmelite abbey. The meal centred on rabbit, braised in Karmeliet, then rolled and stuffed with goose liver, shallots and spinach, seasoned with laurel and thyme. This was, naturally, accompanied by Karmeliet. The other three courses were enjoyed with the brewery's hoppy Pils, Prosit Premium; a flowery, malty, bronze ale at 4,8w (6.0v), called 't Zelfde ("Same again"); and the long-established speciality Kwak.

There was once an innkeeper called Pauwel Kwak. The first name means Paul and the second is a nickname for someone expansive. Pauwel Kwak brewed his own beer, which was dark and strong. He had a coaching inn on the road from Mechelen to Ghent, and his customers included horsemen who had stopped to water their charges. Kwak would hand them a beer in a glass that they could rest in their stirrup.

Pauwel Kwak's type of beer became a district beer in East Flanders, until it died out with the passage of time. Some years ago, it was revived by Bosteels. The brewery popularised the beer by serving it in a "stirrup cup" rather like a yard of ale. As this has a rounded base, it has to be placed on the bar counter or cafe table in a supporting bracket. The presentation of such an elaborate device leaves no one in doubt as to which beer is being served.

Kwak is a deep amber beer, with an earthy aroma; a licorice-like maltiness; a nougat chewiness; and a warm, finish reminiscent of caramelised bananas. It is made from three malts, including some wheat, and white candy sugar is added in the kettle (6.4w; 8.0v).

Having dubbed the glass "a trifle showy", I got my come-uppance on the day of the lunch. "Bring a heavy coat." they had said. "Why?" I asked. "You'll see," they replied, enigmatically. It turned out that we were to ride there and back by horse-drawn mail coach. I was seated atop the vehicle, with the driver. On a February day, I was glad to be warmed by the strong beer in my stirrup cup.

Haute Bière...the beer has secret spices, the rabbit dish laurel and thyme. Restaurant Karmeliet, Bruges. (facing page)

Outside their family home, the brewing Bosteels...Antoinse (left) and father Ivo (right).

KASTEEL

Maison bourgeoise... One of Belgium's most colourful brewers, Luc Van Honsebrouck, *avec les caves pour* known for beers like Brigand, joined with some family members *être un château* in the 1980s to buy Ingelmunster Castle. This is a 1736 mansion, *à bière.* protected by a moat, on a strategic site once occupied by the Duke of Flanders. In the 1400s, the castle is said to have had a brewery noted for its dark beer. Now it has a model brewery as part of an exhibit for visitors. An earlier castle was built in 1075, and there was said to have been an abbey there in 640. The extensive cellars of the present castle are now being used to mature beers from the Van Honsebrouck brewery.

For the castle, Van Honsebrouck created a highly distinctive, very serious, malt-accented strong ale. It is called simply Kasteelbier. To the world outside Flanders, Château Beer might more immediately strike a chord.

This is an immensely rich brew, of 25 Plato (1100), 9.6w (11v). The grist includes two dark malts and some dark sugar. Kent Goldings are added twice, and the brew is also dry-hopped. It has at least two yeastings, with its own culture, a second fermentation of two to three weeks at the brewery, at least three months cold maturation in tanks, followed by six to 12 weeks in the castle cellars.

In colour, viscosity and even palate (especially finish) it resembles a dark Port. There are also aromas and flavours of a malty dark bread with dried fruits and spices. These complex flavours emerge without any further bottle-age.

Luc Van Honsebrouck, the most colourful brewer of Belgium.

The first brew was in 1989. Since then, Luc Van Honsebrouck has on several occasions invited me to taste and compare vintages. On a day when I was visiting eight breweries, and tasting anything from six to a dozen or more beers at each, he seemed to want me to appraise every age of Kasteel in his cellar. When I retired after three, he implied that I was shirking my duties - and that I probably would not turn up at his funeral, either.

When the first vintage was ten years old, he led a group of devotees to what he called "The Tabernacle", unlocked a portcullis, and removed a few bottles. I expected the beer to have become drier, but the more obvious change was Maderisation. It seemed initially sweeter and more toffee-like, with raisiny notes, and a touch of smoky dryness in the finish (Brettanomyces?).

After some years, golden counterpart was introduced at the same strength. Kasteel Gouden Tripel is soft, creamy, nutty, and rounded, with a vanilla note and some spiciness.

The castle has a park, tea-room and tavern, and the beer is served there, with Belgian cheeses and hams. It may also be bought to take home. Ingelmunster Castle is at 3 Station Straat (tel. 056-353491 or 051-300385).

KERKOM / BINK

Revived farmhouse brewery amid cherry orchards at St Truiden, in Limburg. The whitewashed but weathered buildings, set round a cobbled courtyard, surely pre-date 1878 when the original brewery is said to have been founded. It closed in 1968,

Some cases of Kerkom...in the extended family. and was re-started 20 years later by Jean Claerinx, grandson of the founder. Claerinx retired in 1999, and the business is now being run by a couple, Marc Limet and Marina Siongers, usually with no further assistance. Marc worked at the now-defunct Villers brewery. Marina's parents had a café.

Many Belgian breweries might be regarded as working museums. In this one, pieces of original equipment survive, some retired, others still functioning, while newer items work among them. It is like an extended family of machinery.

This being down-to-earth Limburg, the beers have an unpretentious name: Bink, which the British might translate as
"Bloke" and Americans as "Guy". Bink Blond (4.4w; 5.5v) is refreshing,
with a firmy fruity sweetness in the middle and resiny hop flavours drying into a cleansing finish. A more sophisticated
name might befit such a Martini-like beer. A Bruin at the same
strength is creamy and toasty.

A more specialised product is launched during the area's blossom season in mid-to-late April, but available all summer.
Bloesem Bink (5.7w; 7.1v), made with honey and local pear
syrup, is delicate, dryish and spritzy. Later in the year,
Winterkoninkske (6.6w; 8.3v) is brewed from six types of malt,
including rye, and crystal sugar. It combines freshness on the
tongue with rich, dark flavours, like treacle-toffee flavoured
with mint. When I visited the brewery in 2001, I was surprised
that it has not produced a beer using the most local of fruits.
Marc offered me an experimental brew that was refreshingly
dry, with a perfumy but restrained cherry character. I enjoyed
it, but he felt that it was "still missing a bit".

I tasted the products in the brewery's café, which still has the
original bar counter, a decorative tiled floor, family photographs round the walls, and an anaglypta ceiling. It was like
having a beer in someone's front room

LA CHOUFFE

The most successful new-generation small brewery in
Belgium, with a big following in several other countries, from
The Netherlands to Quebec. The name comes from the hamlet
of Achouffe, in a spectacular valley in the Ardennes, near the
small town of Houffalize, just north of Bastogne, in the Belgian
province of Luxembourg. Is there, though, such a thing as a

Chouffe? Yes, the Chouffe is the bearded gnome, wearing a red hood, who is the emblem of the brewery. An 1805 farmhouse became the first home of the brewery D'Achouffe, in 1982. Soon afterwards, I made the first of several visits. Set into the building is a statue of St Joseph, the parish saint. The founders of the brewery added a painting of their Chouffe on the gable end of the whitewashed building. The founders are brothers-in-law. One was a food engineer in an ice-cream factory and the other was a computer engineer. They brewed at home before setting up in business.

An early grist mill was a machine formerly used to mash beets at a farm, and a temperature gauge was salvaged from a steam locomotive. Their first kettle, which could brew two hectolitres, was made from a wash-copper found in an antique shop. (This is not as eccentric as it may sound: the first Carlsberg lager and Ind Coope Pale Ale were brewed in similar vessels). A couple of years later, a seven-hecto kettle was built, then the size went up to 22. Finally, or probably not, the brewery moved across the farm track, on the same site, and increased in size to 70 hectos, in a purpose-built, chalet-style structure.

The beers are brewed from piney Ardennes spring water, Pilsener and crystal malts, candy sugar in white and dark forms, Styrian and Saaz hops, and coriander. Bog myrtle was used for a time, but the brewery says it has moved away from some such elaborations. There are two principal products, both with a clean, soft, lightly malty fruitiness and considerable subtlety and complexity.

La Chouffe (19 Plato; 1076; 6.4w; 8.0v) has a golden-to-peachy colour and a sweet, fruity, aroma and palate, with citric notes, becoming tarter, winey and more complex with bottle-age. It is intended to be a refreshing strong brew, but not to accord with any classic style.

While La Chouffe has become slightly paler over the years, the darker McChouffe has gained a little in colour. This beer was inspired by a Scottish friend of one of the partners.

McChouffe is yet more aromatic, with a dense head, and is more robust in both its sweetness and winey dryness, with a touch of warming alcohol in the finish. Other specialities are produced on occasion.

After fermentation, the beers have a period of cool maturation in tank before being filled into Champagne bottles, dated on the cork, and conditioned at the brewery. There is also a magnum, called Big Chouffe (the English word is used). Customers are recommended to lay down the bottles for three months to a year. A farmer in the Ardennes makes a crusty, semi-soft cheese flavoured with La Chouffe, and a charcutier produces a pork and beef sausage seasoned with coriander and the beer.

Honoured by the Confrerie de la Chouffe...members must believe in Chouffes, and be passionate about beer.

Overlooking the brewhouse is a dining room serving dishes prepared with the beers. Adjoining this is a less formal tavern. The brewery also has a gift shop (tel. 061-28-81-47). There are now 6,000 visitors a year. The beers have a considerable following in Canada, where they are brewed under licence by Le Cheval Blanc, of Montreal.

In 1996, D'Achouffe acquired the brewery of Aubel, near the cheese town of Herve, between Liège and Aix-la-Chapelle (in German, Aachen). This brewery makes ales flavoured with local apples, and yet more elaborate projects are now under way.

POORTER

This name has nothing to do with the English term Porter, which indicates a beer in a similar style to Stout. In Belgium, Poorter is the brand name of a speciality made by the Sterkens brewery, and dedicated to the community of Hoogstraten, in the province of Antwerp.

The brewery's home village, Meer, is in the municipality of Hoogstraten. The name Poorter, derived from the word for a gate, means "Freeman of the Borough". This beer, which comes in a pottery crock, was first marketed in 1985, to mark the 775th anniversary of Hoogstraten.

Poorter is a top-fermenting, dark, strong beer of 5.2-5.5w; 6.5-6.9v that is soft, fruit-sweet and very easily drinkable. It is perfumy in aroma; slightly syrupy in body; malty in palate; with a lightly dry finish. A similar beer is marketed as St Sebastiaan Dark. The brewery was originally named after St Sebastiaan. There is also a slightly more conditioned version of this beer,

called St Paul Double, marketed in a striking, bell-shaped, coloured-glass, bottle.

The same brewery has another speciality that is in my view more distinctive, Bokrijks Kruikenbier. Bokrijk, near Genk, in Limburg, is a town with an open-air museum of agricultural life, including a brewhouse (formerly at Hoegaarden). The beer is available there (Kruik means "crock"). This is a top-fermenting golden strong beer of 5.76-6.0w; 7.2-7.6v, that is very firm-bodied, fruity-dry and assertive. It has a slightly earthy hop aroma and a splendid aperitif bitterness in palate and finish. It is dry-hopped, with German varieties. Bokrijks Kruikenbier has a secondary fermentation in the bottle. A similar beer in filtered form is available as St Sebastiaan Grand Cru, and in some markets as St Denise. A less hoppy derivative is called St Paul Tripel, and in some markets St Laurent.

UITZET

"Out Set" was a style of beer said originally to have been made in Wetteren, near Ghent, in the late 1700s. It seems to have been popular throughout the 1800s, and perhaps into the 1900s, then vanished. The name remains familiar to lovers of Belgian beer, but accounts vary as to what it was. An educated guess suggests that it might have involved removing part of

Once a bakery... its new occupation is proudly and simply proclaimed.

André Paeleman...
„save the beer!"

the mash, or the boiled wort, to combine with another batch, perhaps as part of a deliberate souring. Now, the name at least has been revived. "Oh, you want the Uytzet brewery," responded a mailman at Wetteren when I said I was looking for André Paeleman. Wetteren is his home village. When I found him, André explained that, as a teenager, he had been told by his parents that he could not got to brewing school. "They thought it would be all drinking." After a career as a nurse, he did study brewing, and now follows the profession that was his first choice. "Why did you want to be a brewer?" I asked. "I'm a Belgian," was initially his sole response. "I like cooking. Brewing is cooking," he eventually added. He acquired the premises of a former bakery, dug his own well, and uses vessels that previously saw service with a dairy, a jam company, a cola bottler and various breweries.

　　THE GREAT BEERS OF BELGIUM

What is his story on "Out Set"? André has a romantic tale about casks of beer hastily being set outside when a brewery caught fire in 1730 . "Save the beer!" does sound an authentically Belgian cry. Based on a 1790 document prescribing Uitzet against cholera, he believes that the style employed oats and ginger. His Uitzet (5.4-5.6w to 6.8-7.0v) also uses coriander. It has an opalescent bronze colour; a fruity background flavour reminiscent of Seville orange, though no citrus is used; and a spicy, bitter, finish.

The Uitzet is also the base for a Kriek with a very good cherry character and he has a suitably winey, tannic, slightly sour Druiven (grape) beer. This employs the red Dornfelder grape, picked in October, as though for an Auslese.

Lam Gods (5.0w; 6.2v) has an almost olivey brown colour, and is brewed from crystal and black malts. It is very lightly hopped, but spiced with star anise. Its spicy flavours also suggest pepper and passion-fruit. The beer commemorates a man from Wetteren who confessed, while dying of a heart attack, that he masterminded the theft of a panel from Van Eyck's altar piece in the cathedral of Ghent. The panel has never been found.

Pils

How the Czechs inspired the everyday beers of Belgium... and the world.

Once, all beer was either dark or cloudy and yeast-sedimented, and many classic styles still are. Only when techniques of temperature control made it possible to kiln a very pale malt, and yeasts could be bred and trained to precipitate in an orderly fashion, with the help of artificial refrigeration, could a golden, clear, beer reliably be produced.

The world's first such beer was a pale lager produced in the town of Pilsen, in Bohemia (then a province of the Austrian Empire, now one of the two components, with Moravia, of the Czech Republic) in 1842.

At the time, Bohemia's language of government and trade was German. In German, a town of origin becomes adjectival when the suffix -er is added. The new style of beer was identified as "Pilsener". Sometimes this is spelled "Pilsner", with only one "e". Or abbreviated to "Pils".

This Pilsener type of beer was not better than other styles, but it was different, and visibly so. Its brightness was a dramatic asset at a time when mass-produced glass was taking over from stoneware or pewter drinking-vessels. Other styles of golden lager (the malty Munich type; the slightly bigger, firmer, Dortmunder Export; the strong Maibock) emerged later, but have never become as widespread. Neither have the older styles of lager such as the amber Vienna or the darker Munich types.

The beer made in Pilsen was very good, thanks to the sweetness of Moravian barley and the extraordinary delicacy of Bohemian hops, not to mention the skills of the brewers there. It could be made in large quantities, because steam-power was enabling breweries to work on a larger scale. By the middle of the century, steam railways were beginning to revolutionise distribution. The Austrian Empire was a single, German-speaking market, soon to be joined in a trading bloc by Bavaria and Prussia.

That first golden lager at Pilsen had actually been made by a Bavarian brewmaster. A Bavarian yeast, taken to Denmark in 1845, set Carlsberg on its way.

In 1883, at the Carlsberg brewery, the first pure culture, single-cell, lager yeast was isolated, making for a much more reliable production of clear, golden, lagers. In 1886, Heineken, of Amsterdam, began to use a pure culture yeast. These two breweries - in small, maritime nations, keen to export - did much to popularise "Pilsener-style" beers worldwide.

Meanwhile, Europeans who emigrated to the New World in the middle of the last century opened up Middle America and established the new brewing technique there. With their central position, and the spread of the railways, they soon had national brands, with the names of Czech cities like Pilsen and Budweis on their labels.

The brewery in Bohemia that made the first Pilsener beer is still operating. Its beer is called Pilsner Urquell ("Original Source"), and is still a fine product, though less characterful in recent years. The town of Pilsen has a second brewery, next door to Urquell, and making a very similar but very slightly less elegant beer. This is known as Gambrinus, though most Czechs are probably unaware that the name has Belgian origins.

It all started in Pilsen in 1842... this is how the bottle looks today.

The Czechs argue that only Urquell and Gambrinus can be regarded as Pilsener beers. They are the only two made in Pilsen, after all, though the Czech Republic has many other breweries producing similar beers. Based on the original, a classic Pilsener has a gravity ofaround 12 Plato (1048); a golden colour; a delicately flowery hop bouquet and an "elegant" hoppy dryness, or bitterness, in the finish. Alcohol content is around 4.0 per cent by weight, 5.0 by volume (though this may vary by a few decimal points to either side).

Outside the Czech Republic, the closest interpretations of the Pilsener style are in general those made in Germany, followed by the slightly less hoppy, lighter, examples from Belgium. The Dutch and Danish examples are usually milder, and they have influenced the international interpretation. Britain's golden lagers are generally lacking in character, and the mass-market examples from North America very light in both palate and body.

Like the Czechs, the Germans make all-malt Pilseners, at least for their domestic market, though some export versions are lightened with corn, rice or other fermentable sugars. German Pilseners' hop character is reflected in units of bitterness ranging from the lower 20s to around 40. Belgian Pilseners are usually 70-100 per cent malt, and units of bitterness are customarily in the range of 20s to 30s. Many of the international Pilsener types have similar levels of malt, and bitterness in the lower 20s. Some North American examples have 60 per cent malt and 12-15 units of bitterness.

Continental Europeans in traditional brewing nations tend to mature their Pilsener-type beers for between one and (in rare cases) the classic three months. Those elsewhere often mature their pale lagers for a maximum of three weeks.

Such comparisons cannot tell the whole story, but they provide some measurable indications of a beer's likely character. Because most other Belgian styles are more distinctive to their home country, only the Pils beers easily be compared with those from other nations. Belgium's four biggest Pils breweries are reviewed here in alphabetical order. There then follow tasting notes on Pilseners from smaller producers.

CRISTAL ALKEN / MAES

Having spread from Central Europe and Germany, the Pilsener style entered Belgium in the East. Not far from the German border is the village of Alken, in the North-East of Belgian Limburg, The Alken brewery was established to cater for the robust tastes of the coal-mining industry that grew up in Limburg during the 1920s and 1930's.

Another of Belgium,s persistent copper brew-kettles...standing guard at Alken.

The distinctive yeast from the well-known German Pils brewery König, of Duisburg, was obtained to set Cristal Alken on the road. It was the first Belgian beer consciously to present itself as a Pilsner, giving a great emphasis to aroma hops, especially the Saaz variety. The brewer who introduced it is remembered in a stained-glass window at today's modern brewery.

Cristal pours with a very creamy head, leaving excellent lacing. It has very firm hop flavours and a cleansing, dry, lingering bitterness. Although it has lost some hop character in recent years, it is still one of the more bitter examples of the style in Belgium.

Alken and its northerly rival Maes linked up some years ago, but retained separate breweries. In 2001, it was confirmed that the Maes brewery, at Waarloos, between Antwerp and Mechelen, would close.

327

Waarloos is believed to have had a brewery since the 1300s, and in the 1800s a brick-maker who had too many sons to absorb into his own business saw one of them turn to making beer.

The oldest building today is the handsome 1935s brewhouse (one of two) visible from the main road. After the Second World War, the company became especially known for its Pils.

In its heyday, Maes was known for contracting a Czech maltings; for employing the classic double decoction method of mashing; and for using Saaz hops throughout; allowing the brew to cool naturally in an open vessel in a room known in the brewery as "The Chapel"; following a classically cold (5.5-8.6 °C, 41-47 °F), slow (12-day), two-stage, procedure of fermentation; and maturing the beer for two months. The result was a Pils with a distinctively flowery, "Chardonnay" bouquet and palate and a light, firm, body.

Over the years, Alken-Maes has been part of the Kronenbourg group, and is now owned by Scottish and Newcastle. It remains to be seen how these two Pilsners will evolve as they share a brewery.

HAACHT

Sizable lager brewery, near the village of Haacht, between Leuven, Brussels and Mechelen. Its Pils is identified as Primus. This beer. starts lightly sweet; moves to a light but firm maltiness; and finishes quenchingly with a fruity touch of hop flavour. The malts are from The Netherlands and France. Saaz hops are used for aroma, and American Galena for bitterness.

Haacht also makes a golden lager intended to be in the Dortmunder style, though it is half way to a Maibock. With a nod to the German eagle, it is called Adler. This is very clean, smooth and malty, with a sweetish palate and a balancing dryness in the finish. Adler has a gravity of 15.5 Plato (1062), 5.3w; 6.6v.

Its other products include, discussed elsewhere in this book, include a "White" wheat beer, a very distinctive regional speciality called Gildenbier and the Tongerlo abbey beers. Haacht also sells a mineral water from its own wells.

The company began in the 1800s, as a dairy. The Belgians drink a lot of milk, but perhaps prefer beer, so a brewhouse was added in 1898. A maltings from that period still stands, though it is now used as a warehouse. The present principal buildings date from a major expansion in 1923. The following year, this was the subject of a royal visit that is still remembered in prominently-displayed photographs. The gathering of moustachioed men in greatcoats looks over a handsome brewhouse with a hint of Art Nouveau.

That brewhouse is now mothballed, but still usable. The 1920s brewhouse has been replaced with one that looks as though it dates from the 1930s. The working copper hoods on the vessels are, indeed, restored 1930s equipment, and they are mounted on brick skirts as intended, but the invisible structure beneath is 1990s stainless steel. It is a beautiful brewhouse and a remarkable gesture to tradition.

Opposite the brewery, the Brouwershof pub, in a Victorian house, with a conservatory, is open to the public seven days a week. It offers cuisine à la bière, and the range of Haacht brews. The Pils is served unfiltered, as Primus Met Gist. People tend to order this with affectionate abbreviations: "Two Mets". Three Gisties". The beer is soft and smooth, with the yeasty smell of sourdough bread. The brewery is close to woodlands, near the village of Boortmeerbeek. Across the main road is the village of Haacht itself.

JUPILER

The biggest-selling Pilsener in Belgium. This beer takes its name from Jupille, once a village but now an industrial suburb of Liège. This city, steeply set into the valey of the river Meuse, was historically important in the development of coal-mining and steel-making. A company there manufacturing boilers for breweries turned its hand in 1853 to the making of beer. It seems an odd transition. Were the brewery perhaps a working showpiece for their equipment?

The founding family was called Piedboeuf, and that was the name of the company for many years. Freely translating as "Calf's Foot", it does not necessarily suggest beer, but still appears proudly in a 1930s typeface on the tower of the old brewery building, a landmark in Jupille. Piedboeuf, which had a big business in table beers, did not make a Pils until around 1960, when the style was growing fast in Belgium. This was cal-

It may lack the romance of copper, but stainless steel can be smart...Jupiler,s three brewing lines can make four million hectolitres a year.

led Extra Pils, but seems to have been a token gesture to the style. Then, in the mid 1960s, test brews were made to develop a more serious Pils. The fifth batch was deemed suitable, and launched in 1966. Initially, it was labelled as Jupiler "5". Despite being a late-comer to the Pils market, the beer established a strong foothold (enough to drop the corporate name Piedboeuf in favour of Jupiler). Its success was helped by a rigorous and sustaied training of bar staff in the care, dispense and presentation of the beer.

Jupiler is 90 per cent malt, the remaining ten per cent being corn. It has 23-25 units of bitterness, and the aroma hops are Saaz. A double fermentation system is used. It has a fresh, lightly nutty, aroma and a slightly maltier palate than its immediate competitors. It is now made in a handsome modern brewery, towering alongside the old one.

The new brewery followed the merger of Jupiler with Artois, of Leuven, to form Interbrew, in the late 1980s. The two companies already had cross-shareholdings. Interbrew has several well-known Belgian specialities, which are discussed elsewhere in this book.

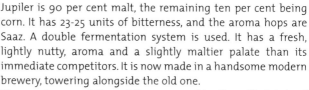

After Anheuser-Bush, of the United States, Interbrew is now the world's second-largest brewer.. In 2000-2001, it sought to pursue the acquisition of Bass, in the United Kingdom, where it already controlled Whitbread. It owns the major Canadian brewing group Labatt, the U.S.brewery Rolling Rock, and others in about a dozen countries, from the Dominican Republic to Romania.

STELLA ARTOIS

Becoming a bigger name in ever more countries as its parent company grows. Interbrew sees Stella as its international "premium" product. Even before its recent advances, Stella was well known outside its home country, and for many years the bestseller in Belgium. It is no longer market-leader there, but still a consderable presence. Stella is made in Leuven, a city conveniently placed near the middle of the country and the border between Flanders and Wallonia. The brewery traces its histo-

With this premium packaging Stella Artois wants to conquer the world.

ry to at least 1366. At that time, the existence of a brewpub called Den Horen was noted in local records. The inn's sign was a hunting horn. Nearby was forest land in which wild boar and deer were hunted. In 1425, Leuven became a university town, after which its importance grew. A century later, it had 42 breweries. In 1708, Sebastien Artois, who had been an apprentice at Den Horen, graduated as a

The new brewhouse at haaght

master brewer there. Less than ten years later, he had bought the business. Through siblings, marriages and inheritances, Artois remained in the family for more than 100 years, and its shares are still privately held.

In 1892, Artois began making a golden lager, called Bock. In Germany, the term Bock indicates a strong beer. In Belgium and France, it was in the past widely used for a golden lager weaker than a Pilsner (perhaps because such a beer could be consumed in the larger mugs favoured by the Germans?). In 1926, the brewery introduced a Christmas beer which was a golden lager of a typical Pilsner strength, with a spicy hop character. Taking the Christmas sign as its symbol, this was called Stella (Latin for "star").

Stella Artois became Belgium's best-known beer, both inside and outside the country. Artois grew into Belgium's biggest brewing company and bought not only local competitors but also brewers in The Netherlands and France.

Barley from France, the British Isles and Denmark is used in Leuven. The French barley is bought by barge. Leuven is an inland port on a canal, linked in the other direction through Mechelen to the Schelde and the sea. At the canalside, the various Artois buildings dominate a section of the town.

Stella has a Czech hop character in its aroma, and a faint hint of new-mown hay; a light, dry, maltness in the middle middle; and a nice touch of hop in the finish. In recent years, it has become very slightly more aromatic and malty, and fractionally less dry.

Artois also has a stronger (4.6w; 5.7v), maltier, sweeter, creamier, golden lager called Loburg, which is actually intended to compete with some "super-premium" entrants from Denmark. Loburg has its own yeast culture. The company also produces Pils under several local labels, including Wiel's and Safir. These were originally breweries in Brussels and Aalst.

FURTHER PILSENERS, WITH TASTING NOTES

As Pils became the everyday beer of Belgium, especially after World War II, in the 1950s and 60s, almost every brewery tried to make one. Some of the smaller breweries, equipped only to make top-fermenting beers, used that technique to produce approximations of the lager style. Toward the end of the 1970s, there was a rediscovery of top-fermenting specialities, and some local brewers stopped emphasising Pils. The reviews here are based on recent tasting notes.

AKILA

The name means "Eagle". In the days before literacy, such heraldic images were used on inn signs. As inns brewed their own beer, the images transferred to breweries. "Lion" breweries are especially common worldwide, but "Wolf" and "Eagle" are also typical. Louwaege's "Eagle Brewery", in West Flanders, makes Akila Pils. This has a light, herbal, aroma; not much hop bitterness; but a very clean, quenching, dryness. Reminiscent of Cristal Alken in its heyday.

BAVIK PREMIUM PILS

From De Brabandere, of Bavikhove, West Flanders. This Pils seems to have gained in herbal, lemony, hop character, and become crisper, recently. Four or five years ago, my tasting notes consistently emphasised malty sweetness.

BOCKOR PILS

The name, confusing two beer styles, dates back to 1930, when lagers from Germany and Czechoslovakia were first being imitated in Belgium. Bockor Pils has a brilliant clarity; a light, dry, aroma; a crisp body; and a slightly sharp, but appetising, finish. From Vander Ghinste, of Bellegem, West Flanders.

GOLDEN KENIA

The name derived from a variety of barley that was popular in Belgium when this Pils was launched. It has a fresh, minty, hop aroma and a firm, smooth, malty, body, but falls away somewhat in the finish. It is made at Melle, near Ghent, East Flanders, by Huyghe. Golden Kenia was once the brewery's principal product, but Huyghe now has a colourful range of specialities, including the strong Delirium Tremens (P208).

MARTENS PILSENER

This family concern is the Belgian brewery closest to the German border. It is in a village called Bocholt, which has a namesake not far away in Germany. If anyone can sell a Belgian Pils to the Germans, this Limburg brewery can, and does. In a Belgian perspective, its hoppy Martens Pils could almost be regarded as a regional speciality.

It has a brilliant, full gold, colour; a fresh, camomile-like, slightly medicinal, aroma; a bigger body than most Belgian Pils; and a hoppy dryness that is sustained all the way thrugh to its long, firm, finish. (Saaz hops; two gifts; 27 units of bitterness).

PAX PILS

Why give a beer the Latin name for peace? Perhaps the period of its origin, and the brewery's location near the German border, give a clue. Pax has a flowery bouquet; a clean, light maltiness; and a firm, crisp, finish. It has a high malt proportion: 94 per cent, with the remainder maize. The brew is hopped three times, with Northern Brewer, Hallertau and Saaz, and the flowers are chopped in a mill (an unusual, though by no means unique, process, intended to get the most out of the hops). The maturation is for four to five weeks. This beer is from the St Jozef brewery, in the village of Oppiter, near Bree, in Limburg.

The present brewhouse dates from the 1930s, and overlooks the parish church. The company is in the fourth generation of the same family. The brewery also makes a fuller-tasting golden

lager with the misleading name Ops-Ale. This is not to be confused with Op-Ale, from Brabant. There is also an amber, maltier lager, in the Vienna style, called Bokkereyer, after the brigands that once roamed Limburg.

PROSIT PILS

Perhaps the German name implies a reasonably robust hopping (26 units of bitterness; Hallertau-Hersbrucker and Saaz). This is a very herbal, flowery (violets?), aromatic, Pils. From the Bosteels brewery, of Buggenhout, East Flanders. The brewery is better known for its Kwak and Karmeliet (P308).

ROMY

From the brewery of the family Roman, near Oudenaarde, East Flanders. This Pils has a "green fruit" hop aroma; a clean, light, refreshing, palate; and a late, appetising, dryness.

SAS PILS

The name refers to a canal lock of historical importance near the Leroy brewery, in Boezinge, West Flanders. The beer pours with a very white head, and good lace. It has a very slightly malty aroma and palate; a light, "spring water" mouth-feel; and a gently emerging dryness in the finish. This beer is 95 per cent malt. The remaining 5.0 per cent (scarcely worth the trouble?) is rice, to lighten the colour. A similar name, Sasbräu, is applied to a Dortmunder-style lager of 5.0w (6.3v). This is all-malt, firm and perfumy, with a very good hop aroma.

CHAPTER XVIII

Drinking Belgian Beer

The elegant experience.

No other country has elegant beer cafés quite like those of Belgium, especially Brussels. This is where to enjoy the art of the Belgian brewer in its grandest surroundings. It is a part of the ritual of Brussels. Perhaps there should be a winter visit to admire the decorative arts and a summer one to sit on the terrace and watch the pavement life.

The expansive visitor should probably stay (and the less extravagant merely pop in for a drink) at the Hotel Métropole, built in 1895 on the Place de Broucquères. Its bar is a chandelie-red extravaganza of the Belle Epoque, within which you may be offered the speciality of the house, a Campari-based cocktail called an Italiano. Nice drink, but wrong place. When in Brussels, do as the Bruxellois do: at the tables around you, people will be drinking a Duvel here, a Radieuse there, a Hoegaarden White across the room. This is by no means a speciality beer café, but nonetheless it has about 20 brews on its list, most of them Belgian. Even one of the decorative glass panels depicts beer being decanted from a cask into stoneware jugs.

If you prefer somewhere plainer, pop over the road to the 1884 Brasserie Vossegat 54 Boulevard Adolphe Max), which restricts itself to stuffed animals in glass cases and dominating waitresses in white aprons. They sit by the bar with the look of tricoteuses, but turn out to be quite friendly.

Along the main thoroughfare, the Boulevard Anspach, stand and face the Stock Exchange (in French, Bourse). Down each side is a small street, and on each is a classic period café.

"On the left side, Rue de la Bourse has Taverne Cirio also from the Belle Epoque (it was built in 1886), with panels - outside and in - advertising Vermouth Bellardi, of Torino, Champagne Jacot, of Epernay, Ferroidas Royal Port, of Oporto and London, and McEwan's Scotch Ale on Draught. The customers are drinking Palm ale and Hapkin (a spicy, fruity, sweetish, strong beer somewhat fuller in colour than Duvel). Again, it is not a beer bar, but it offers about 45 from which to choose. The old lady nursing a Bush beer looks as though she should be drinking absinthe. An elaborately carved back bar has five shelves of glasses gleaming expectantly. There are three rooms, partially divided by carved wooden screens and swirly mirrors into half a dozen chambers. In an inner chamber, 50 medals, awarded to Francesco Cirio for services to the drinker, are displayed in a frame.

On the other side of the Bourse, in the Rue Henri Maus, is the most famous Art Nouveau café, Falstaff. This is in two houses built in 1883 by Baron Allard, with 1903 interiors by a designer who worked for Victor Horta, the best-known architect in Belgium's Art Nouveau movement. The tavern is very large, and again partially divided into chambers, with fretwork arches, lampshades in the shape of flowers, lots of bevelled mirrors, stained glass and leaded panels depicting Falstaff drinking beer, claret-coloured walls, and a couple of recessed corner areas at the back for those intent upon a tête-à-tête.

Memories of the Belle Epoque at the Métropole.

I had always simply used the Stock Exchange as a landmark to find Falstaff, and when I finally took the trouble to note the street name, a thought stuck me. Was Henri Maus not the man who coined the term Art Nouveau? No, I had apprehended the wrong mouse. It was Octave Maus who, with Edmond Picard, also a Belgian, founded the magazine "L'Art Moderne", in 1881. Their publication is credited with having first used the expression. The term later established itself in Paris, too, with the opening of a shop there called Art Nouveau in 1895. When we talk of Art Nouveau, we should probably think of Belgian cafés rather than Paris Metro stations. In fact, some of us do.

The movement argued that a man who designs buildings, decorations or furniture can be an artist. It recognized the craftsman - the artisan - for his cultural contribution, and that has passed into Belgian consciousness. It is no accident that "artisanal" is the word with which so many small brewers choose to describe themselves.

Belgium's tradition of handicrafts and technical skills goes back to the hermitages and abbeys in the forest of the Ardennes, the charcoal-burners, iron-melters and makers of glass, and to the tapestry-weavers of Flanders. When the Industrial Revolution came, and the brief colonial era, Belgium's privileged enjoyed a period of great prosperity and creativity. It was the "Belle Epoque", the good times before the First World War. It was during that period that a group of middle-class and wealthy intellectuals developed "the art of the people" as a design theory. It is still there for us to enjoy when we have beer.

Follow Henri Maus, and keep walking until you reach the Grand' Place. Everyone visiting Brussels goes to the magnificent Grand' Place, with its 17th-century Guild Halls (among which the only one used for its original purpose is the Maison des Brasseurs, the Brewers' House). At numbers 24-25, you can take the weight off your legs and have a beer at La Chaloupe d'Or, dating from 1900.

Not every historic café in Brussels is fin-de-siècle, and a good few are older. There are several hidden off the streets around Grand' Place:

"La Bécasse" (up an alley at 11 Rue de Tabora) serves sweetened Lambic from stoneware pitchers, but also has a drier bottled brew from Cantillon. Sausage and cheese platters are offered. It has wooden benches and an architectural style that blends Flemish kitchen with a hint of Moorish influence from the days of the Spanish Empire. If there are no free tables, look upstairs. Au Bon Vieux Temps (12 Rue duMarché aux Herbes) offers the beer of the same name and has a stained-glass window depicting the Virgin Mary and St Michael). This café dates to 1695.
If you would like a beer in a café where Max Ernst once exhibited, and René Magritte was a customer, look for La Fleur en Papier Dor (55 Rue des Alexiens). Two tiny rooms, linked by a few stairs, endless clutter and friendly atmosphere.

One of Brussels' favourite cafés is Mort Subite ("Sudden Death"), at number 7 Rue Montagne aux Herbes Potagères. This was established in the 1800s and remodelled in 1926, but has very much that turn-of-the-century ambience. With its bench seats against the cream-painted walls, its ceiling-high mirrors, and the row of tables in the middle, it has something of the feel of a railway station brasserie. Mort Subite was the setting of a ballet of that name by Maurice Béjart. (see Lambic).

Still in the city-centre, but more of a stretch of the legs (and well worth the effort) is the Ultieme Hallucinatie (316 Rue Royale), built in 1850 and restored in 1904. This has a classic Art Nouveau interior, with its marble staircase, brass peacocks and bench seats worthy of a train. One part of the Ultieme Hallucinatie is a student café, which serves snack meals, and the other is a very good restaurant, with prices to match (tel. 02-217-0614).

All of these cafés are interesting for their interiors, and each has what anyone but a Belgian would probably regard as a wide range of beers. With the possible exception of the Ultieme Hallucinatie, none would regard themselves as specialising in having a large selection.

The true specialist beer café was pioneered by the Belgians and Dutch, and it is not possible in a book such as this to do much more than give a list of some well-established favourites.

While most of the cafés discussed elsewhere in this book are featured for their ambience or the availability of a particular beer, there are many establishments that have a more extensive selection. Since first I wrote about Belgian beers, over 25 years ago, other writers and enthusiasts have been inspired to document the places in which they might be found.
A Selective Guide to Belgian Bars, is a newsletter published by Stephen D'Arcy of the country's branch of Britain's Campaign for Real Ale, Postbox 5, 67 Rue des Atrébates, 1040 Brussels, Belgium. E-mail: Stephen.D'Arcy@cec.eu.int. Essential reading - and regularly updated.
CAMRA in Britain also publishes a paperback by Tim Webb Good Beer Guide to Belgium and Holland (230 Hatfield Rd, St Albans AL1 4LW, England, U.K. Fax 01727-867670). The Beers of Wallonia by John Woods and Keith Wrigley (Artisan Press, Bristol, England) provides a detailed list of breweries. I am indebted to those writers for their additions to my own list of favourites. Opening hours change, businesses move or close: please call ahead before making travel plans.

IN BELGIUM

Festivals
There are at least a dozen several local festivals (check Stephen D'Arcy's Selective Guide, above), but the following are national.

Late June: **"Beer Passion Night"** is a commercially-run new festival, organised by the magazine of the same name, in Antwerp (E-mail: desk@greatbelgianbeers.com).
Early September: **"The Weekend of Beer"** is held by the Belgian Confederation of Brewers (CBB), on the Grand' Place, in Brussels (www.beerparadise.be)
Mid September: Every three years, a **hop pageant and beer festival** is held in Poperinge (Tourist Office, 1 Stadhuis Markt, Poperinge, B-8970. Tel 057-33-40-81). See also chapter on hops, and section on Trappist abbey of Westvleteren, and references below to Poperinge and Ypres.
Mid October: the 24-hour Festival is held by the consumerist movement **the Objective Beer Tasters**, in Antwerp. (Tel 03-332-45-38)

VISITING BREWERIES

Most breweries accept visitors, but an e-mail, fax or letter in advance is often appreciated. The Trappist abbeys do not offer public brewery tours. At Achel, the beer can be enjoyed on the premises. With the exception of Rochefort, each of the others has an inn close to the brewery.

MUSEUMS

Many Belgian breweries regard themselves as working museums. Brussels has the classic example, the Cantillon brewery. The city also has a small museum, open to the public, in the beautiful Guild House of the CBB, at 10 Grand' Place. A third museum in Brussels is at Schaerbeek (33 Ave Louis Bertrand). This has bottles, glasses and advertising materials, but opens only Wed and Sat (2.0-6.00 pm). See also entries for cities.

LAMBIC

Base yourself in Brussels. Make sure to visit: Beersel: See entries for Drie Fonteinen and Oud Beersel (in Lambic chapter). Drie Bronnen is a café producing its own Kriek, based on the Lambic of Girardin. It also has Faro and a big selection of Abbey beers. Closed Tuesday. 13 Hoogstr. Tel 02-332-0720. Giradin Gueuze is also also available at the Oude Pruim. Closed Wed, Thurs. 87 Steenweg op Ukkel. Tel 02-331-0559.

Antwerp
There is a remarkable selection of pubs in this port city. See also section on De Koninck for notes on **Den Engel** and **Quinten Matsijs.**
Aux Armes de Tirlemont. Tiny, 400-year-old, café, offering Gueuze from a well-filled cellar.
No sign, just a statue of the Virgin Mary. On, a main shopping street (29 Eiermarkt), opposite the Hilton.
De Gouden Ecu. Beer cuisine, often featuring game, in large portions, at modest prices. Evenings only, closed Sundays. 11 St Michielsstr. Reservations advised, especially at weekends, Tel 03-232-7125. Fax 03-213-07-04.
De Groote Witte Arend. Has its own chapel, sometimes live chamber music in the courtyard, and about 25 beers. Opens 11.00. Tel 03-226-31-90. 18 Reyndersstr. In the same street, at number 33, jazz and blues fans would prefer De Herk. At number 21, De Vagant specialises in Belgian gin. At number 2 is a shop: Belgium Beers. Tel. 03-226-68-53. Closed Tuesday.

De Loteling. Beer cuisine. Bar-restaurant in a thatched building dating from 1741. Turnhoutsebaan 112, Schilde (10-15 miles E of the city). Tel.03-3542700, Fax 03-226-85-32.

Het Elfde Gebod (the 11th Commandment). Astonishing collection of religious statues and icons, with about 30 beers, both ecclesiastical and sinful. Good Flemish snack foods. Opens 10.00. Tel 03-232-36-11. 10 Torfbrug, just behind the cathedral.

Kulminator. Famous speciality beer bar, which has bottle-conditioned beers cellared for many years, including some no longer made. Flemish emphasis. Monday, evenings only (opens 8.0). Other weekdays, from 11.0.. Saturday, from 5.0. Closed Sunday. Tel 03-232-45-38. (32 Vleminckveld).

't Waagstuk. Several small rooms - and tables on a cobbled courtyard. Off a small square near St Ignatius University. Good selection, well chosen. Some beer dishes. Open weekdays at 10.0. Weekends at 2.00.Tel 03-225-0219.(20 Stadswaag).

Bruges
In chapter on Golden Ales, see also Goudenboom and Halve Maan (both of which regard themselves as working museums)

't Brugse Beertje. In a narrow alley near Simon Stevinplein. World-renowned beer bar with knowledgeable owners. More than 200 brews, and beer seminars by arrangement. Opens at 4.00 Closed Wednesdays. 5 Kemelstraat, Tel 050 33 96 16. A couple of doors away, at No. 9, is the beer-and-gin bar 't Dreupelhuisje, Tel. 050-34 24-21

De Brugse BierKaai, Newish, comfortable, brewpub, with Flemish dishes. Opened in 2000 (9 Nieuwstraat). Beers include a clean, firm, malty Blonde; a smooth, rich, raisiny Dubbel; and a fruity, peppery, Tripel. Established by brewer Stan Sterkens, with Jan De Bruyne, of 't Brugs Beertje (above). Opens 11.30 daily. Tel. 050-34-38-00

Den Dyver, at No. 5 in the street of the same name: Beer cuisine. Admired by beer-lovers and gourmets alike. Opens 11.00, closes Wednesdays. Tel 050-33-60-69.

Hotel-Brasserie Erasmus, beer cuisine all day, café, terrace . Open from 11.00, closed Mondays. 35 WolleStraat. Tel 050-33-58-71. Email: info@hotelerasmus.com

Staminee de Garre. Conveniently near the tourist office. Beer café, Classical music. Open from 12 noon weekdays, 11.00 weekends, 1 de Garre Passage, Tel. 050-34-10 \-29.

Brussels - City centre
A La Bécasse. An institution (See introduction to Drinking Belgian Beer). 11 rue de Tabora/Str, just off Grand' Place. Open daily from 10.00. Tel. 02-511-00-06

A La Mort Subite. (see introduction). From Grand' Place, walk through the Galeries Royal St Hubert arcade. 7 Rue Montagne aux Herbes Potagères/Warmoesberg Str. Open daily from 10.00 (12.00 on Saundays) Tel. 02-513-13-18

Le Bier Circus. Rare beers from Wallonia. Innermost bar celebrates Belgian cartoon art. Closes weekday afternoons, and Sundays, unless there is a concert next door at the Cirque Royale. Tel 02-218-00-34. , (89 Rue de l'Enseignement/Ondwerwijs Str),

L'Etoile d'Or. High quality beer cuisine. 30 rue des Foulons (Voldersstraat 30) Open 12.00- 3.00 and 7.00-12.00 weekdays, Saturday evenings only, closed Sundays. Tel. 02-502 60 48

In 't Spinnekopke ("Little Spider"). Best known spot for beer cuisine. Unpretentious restaurant, with terrace. Spanish-born owner Juan Rodriguez is author of Cuisine Facile à la Bière. 1 Bloemenhofplaats/Place Jardin aux Fleurs, in St Catherine's restaurant area. Open from 11.00 (Kitchen: 11.0-3.0 and 6.00-11.00). Closed Saturday lunchtime and all day Sunday. Tel. 02-511-86-95.

Estaminet Le Zageman. Specialises in gueuze, kriek and faro. 116 rue de Laeken/Lakense Str. Weekdays 10.00 am - 10.00 pm, closed weekends. (Late opening first Friday of each month) Tel. 02-219 50 65

Shop: **De Bier Tempel,** newish beer shop selling around one hundred beers, glasses T-shirts etc. 56 Marché-aux-Herbes (Grasmarkt 56)

BRUSSELS - DISTRICTS

Elsene/Ixelles
L'Atelier. Near the University. Good beers at modest prices. Can be smoky. 77 rue Elise/Elizastr. 4.00 pm weekdays, 6.00 pm weekends. Tel. 02-649 19 53

Les Brassins. Brews and blues. Poster collection. 36 Rue Keyenveld/Keienveldstr. Weekdays from 5.00pm; closed weekends. Tel. 02-512 69 99.

Le Châtelain, Steaks and "folk foods". Opens 10.30. 17 Place du Châtelain/Kasteleinsplein. Weekends: from 7.00pm. Tel. 02-538 67 94. Market on the square on Wednesdays.

Au Stoemelings. Cosy bar. 7 Place du Londres/Londenplein. 11.00 am weekdays, 5.00 pm weekends. Tel. 02 512 43 74

L'Ultime Atome, Well-chosen beers. Hearty, inexpensive, food. 14 Rue St Boniface/Sint Bonifaasstraat. Opens 11.00. Tel 02-5111367.

Shop: **S.B.S** (Special Beer Service; formerly called Drink Market Delépine). Still notable for its cellared selection of 100 artisanal beers. Also glasses, accessories, condiments, books. 13 Rue Eugène Cattoir/Cattoirstraat. Opens Tues-Fri 10.00 am -12.30 pm, and 1.00 pm - 6.30 pm. Tel. 02-640 45 64

Shop: **400 Bières Artisanales.** Approximately 400 beers. Glasses, shirts etc. 174 Chausé de Wavre/Waversesteenweg.11.00 am 7.00 pm. Tel. 02-512 17 88
www.users.skynet.be/beermania

Zuidstation / Gare du Midi
Cantillon Brewery and "museum". Essential visit. (see Lambic chapter)
Au Laboureur. Basic bar with spectacular murals and stained glass. 3 Place de la Constitution/Grondwetplaats. Open daily from 9.00 am, closed Saturdays. Tel. 02-520 18 59

St Gillis / St Gilles
La Porteuse d'Eau. Art Nouveau bar. 48A Avenue Jean Volderslaan.
Open daily from 8.00 am Tel. 02-538 83 54

Jette
De Gele Poraa (The Yellow Leek). Boon beers in a good range. Music can be loud. 27 Rue J. Lahaye/Lahayestraat 27. Opens 4.00 (6.00 weekends) Tel 02-426-5836.

Marolles/Marollem
La Fleur en Papier Dorée. (see introducttion to Drinking Belgian Beer). 55 Rue des Alexiens/Cellebroersstraat 55. Daily from 10.30 am. Tel. 02-577 76 59
Ploegmans. Basic bar with local character. 148A rue Haute/Hoogstraat. Daily from 10.00am. Tel. 02-514 28 84
Het Warm Water. Traditional Bruxellois food. 19 rue des Renards/Vossenstr. 8.00 am - 7.00 pm daily except Thurs. Tel. 02-513 91 59

Schaarbeek / Schaerbeek
't Narrenschip. Art school café with about 30 beers and modest prices. Rogierstraat 185. Open 10.00 am daily, closes Sat, and during July-August college vacations. Tel. 02-218 33 00
De Ultieme Hallucinatie. Impressive Art Nouveau style bar. 316 rue Royale (Koningsstraat 316). Open from 11.00 am weekdays and from 4.00 pm. Tel. 02-217 06 14
Musée Schaerbeekois de la Bière (Schaarbeeks Biermuseum). See above.
For eclectic drinkers: **Distillerie Fovel.** Brussels's oldest Genever distillery. Owned by the same family since 1864. 69 rue Thiéfry/Thiéfrystr Open 10.00 am - 5.00 pm weekdays. Tel. 02-215 58 15

Ukkel / Uccle
Au Vieux Spijtigen Duivel. Oud Beersel Gueuze and unsweetened Kriek, in a 16th-century building. 621 Chausée d'Alsembergse Steenweg. Opens noon. Closed Sundays, and for a vacation in Aug/Sept. Tel. 02-344 44 55.

Denderleeuw/Liederkercke
Well worth the detour, **De Heeren van Liederkercke.** Comprehensive selection of Gueuze and 200-300 other beers, including rare vintages. - plus beer cuisine of a remarkably high order in an unpretentious bar-restaurant run by young brothers. (33 Kasteelstr). Monday-Saturday from 11.30am. Sunday from 1.00 pm. Tel. 053-68-08-88. Denderleeuw is 10km (6 1/4 miles) from the malt-and-hop town of Aalst, and 50km (30 miles) from Brussels.

Ghent
De Hopduvel, 10 Rokerelstraat. Famous café, with good selection of vintage brews and spontaneously-fermenting beers. 150-200 beers in all. Hot food (not Tuesdays) and Belgian cheeses. Garden. Open every day. Tel. 091-253729.
Ghent has a good selection of beer cafés. After De Hopduvel, the two best known are: **De Dulle Griet,** 50 Vrijdag Markt, tel. 091-242455; and **Het Waterhuis aan de Bierkant,** 9 Groente Markt, tel. 091-250680.

Leuven
Domus. Pioneering brewpub in the shadow of Stella Artois and one of Europe's oldest universities (with a brewing course). Beers made on the premises fewer than they once were. Students are no doubt amused to order Con Domus, which turns out to be a Pils with an excellent hop flavour and malt background. Nine draughts and 60 or 70 bottled beers. Studenty clientèle. 8 Tiense Straat. Open from 9.00 am every day. Tel. 016-201449.

Louvain-la-Neuve (separate community, with brewing university for French-speakers)
Le Brasse-Temps. 1A Place des Brabançons. Open from 10.00 am weekdays. Closed Saturdays, 6.00 pm till midnight Sundays. Tel. 010-45-70-27

Mechelen
Den Stillen Genieter. Comprehensive choice of gueuze. 9 Nauwstr.
Open daily from 7.30 pm. Tel. 015 21 95 04

Mons
L'Alambic, 25 Place du Marché aux Herbes. About 80 beers. Snacks. Tel. 065-346007.
La Podo, 43 Rue de la Coupe. Traditional "brown" café. More than 100 beers. Snooker, billiards. Tel. 065-347077.

Namur (City and province)
Les Artisans Brasseurs. Brewpub in the city centre. Run by a brewing family, and popular with local home-brewers. Beers include a crisp, fruity, Blonde; and a refreshing, bittersweet, lemony, Blanche; both under the name Marlagne. Two stronger (6.0w; 7.5v) brews are Aldegonde Ambrée, cookie-like and caramel-ish; and Speciale Blonde, creamy and banana-like, with a good balancing dryness. A Christmas beer is sweet and spicy. 2 Place de la Station. Open Monday - Thursday 10.00 am - 7.00 pm, Friday and Saturday till 11.00 pm. Closed Sundays. Tel. 081 23 16 94
Le Chapitre. 4 Rue du Séminare. Open weekdays, 12.00 pm - 2.00 pm, Sat from 5.00 pm. Closed Sundays. Tel. 081 26 04 90
Shop: **La Table de Wallonie,.** About 300 beers, and spirits. 6 Rue de la Halle. Closed Sunday and Monday. Tel. 081-22.06.83.

Elsewhere in the province, the village of Mariembourg, near Couvin, has the brewpub **Des Fagnes** (see chapter of White Beers). Despite being family-oriented, this pub does not sell Coca-Cola. There is lemonade or fruit juice if you insist, but a sweet, dark, beer called Cuvée Junior is recommended. Seasonal brews range from a March beer (with a fruity malt character) to a pepper Christmas brew (actually flavoured wth basil).
Museums: The province of Namur also has the **Musée des Bières** (concentrating on glasses) at 19 Rue de la Gare (tel 081-41-11-02; fax 081-41-25-81) , in the village of Lustin. This is between the city of Namur and Dinant. and the Gambrinus Museum (beer trucks) at 2a Fontaine St Pierre, Romedenne. This is between Dinant and Philippeville.

Ostend
Hotel Taverne Botteltje, 19 Louisastraat. Beer-café (more than 200 brews), restaurant (sometimes with beer dishes) and small hotel. Ostend is a main port for ferries from Britain. Taverne Botteltje's hotel is a good place to begin a visit. Tel. 059-700928; fax 502856.
't Ostens Bierhuis, 14 Louisastraat. British owner. Opens at 2.00. Closed Mon, Tues. Tel. 059-70.67.01.

Poperinge
Café de la Paix. Extensive list. Also beer cuisine. 20 Grote Markt. Tel 057-33-95-78. Further addresses in Hops chapter.
Shop: **Noel's Beerstore,** on the N38 highway, 2km S of Poperinge. Opens 9.30am-8.30pm, closes for lunch 1.00-2.00. Closed Mon.

Ypres (Ieper).
Ter Posterie, 57 Rijselstr. Tel 057-20-05-80. Closed Wed.

OUTSIDE BELGIUM

FRANCE

Northern France
Bars, **Le Pub McEwans**, 143 Rue Gustave Delory, Lesquin (near Lille airport). A Belgian-accented bar, with branches in other French towns. Tel. 20-96 06 30
Restaurants: **L'Gaïette,** 30 rue Massena, Lille. Tel. 03 20 54 81 88, **L'Rijsel Estaminet,** 25 rue du Gand, Lille. Tel 03 20 15 01 59, **Le Hochepot,** 6 rue Nouveau Siècle, Lille. Tel. 03 20 54 17 59
Shops: **Boisson Cash Dubus,** 27 Place de la République, Villeneuve d'Ascq. Tel. 03 32 05 41 23, **A les Chopes,** 69 Place Nouvelle Aventure, Lille Wazemme, Tel. 03 20 13 95 25,
Cave Rohart, Rue Faidherbe, Lille.

Paris
Bouillon Racine. Specialises in Belgian beers, with emphasis on small breweries, notably Cantillon. Spectacular interior in Art Nouveau style. Open from 8.0 breakfast, featuring the outstanding beer cuisine of Olivier Simon himself from the Belgian town of Bouillon. 3 rue Racine (near Boulevard St-Michel).Tel. 01-44 32 15 60
Au Général La Fayette. About 40 Belgian beers. 52 Rue La Fayette. Tel. 01-47 70 59 08
Taverne St Germain, 155 Boulevard St Germain. Tel. 01-42 22 88 98
La Gueuze. More than 80 Belgian beers.19 Rue Soufflot, near Boulevard St-Michel. Tel. 01-43 54 63 00
Taverne des Halles, 12 rue de La Cossonnerie. Tel.01 42 36 26 44
Hall's Beer Tavern. More than 50 Belgian beers. 68 rue St-Denis. Tel. 01-42 36 92 72
Au Père Tranquille, 75 avenue Daumesnil. Tel. 01 43 43 64 58
La Taverne de Rubens, 12 Rue St-Denis. Tel. 01-45 08 14 59
Au Trappiste. Abut 150 Belgian beers. 4 Rue St-Denis. Tel. 01-42 33 08 50
Le Sous-Bock, 45 rue St-Honoré. Tel. 01-40 26 46 61

Amsterdam
Belgique. Belgian beers and jenever gins in a tiny bar. 2 Gravenstraat. Just off Dam square. Open from 11.00 am. Closed Tues. Tel. 020-625-19 74.
In de Wildeman. World-class beer café. In former gin distillery. A delightful place in which to drink, with a separate room for non-smokers. Off Nieuwendijk shopping street. (3 Kolk Steeg. Opens at noon. Closed Sun. Tel. 020-63-82-34-8.
Zotte. Near Leidseplein. Specializes in Belgian beers. Noisy and smoky. 29 Raam Str Opens 4.00 pm daily. Tel. 020-62-68-694.
Shop: **De Bierkoning**, 125 Paleisstr (just behind the Royal Palace), central and friendly, tel. 020-625-23-36

Breda
De Beyerd. A pioneering establishment, very highly regarded, run by the family De Jong, who have played an important part in the beer café movement. No connection with the similar-sounding cafés De Beiaard, in Amsterdam and other cities. 26 Boschstraat. Opens at 10.00 am, closed Wed. Tel. 076-21 42 65

Oosterhout (near Breda)
Café de Beurs, 4 Klappeijstr. Open daily. Tel. 01 62 45 34 77

Delft
Trappistenlokaal Het Klooster. 2 Vlamingstr. Tel. 015 21 21 01 3

Eindhoven
Shop : **Bieren en Pintelieren**, 2 Pasqualiniestr. Open from 9.00 am Tuesday - Saturday. Tel 040-24 35 42 2.

Enschede
De Geus. A taste of Belgium in Grolsch country 2 Oude Markt .
Open daily from 10.30 am Tel. 053-43 10 56 4.

Haarlem
Bruxelles. Good selection, and sometimes cuisine à la bière.
16 Lange Wijngaardstr Opens at 5.00 pm Tel 023-53 14 50 9.

The Hague
Speciaalbier Café den Paas. Cosy café in the old town. 16a Dunne Bierkade.
Open daily from 3.30 Tel. 070-36 00 019.

's Hertogenbosch ("Den Bosch")
Café de Deugniet. Trappist and artisanal beers in Heineken country. 55-57
Verwersstr Closed on Mondays. Tel. 073 61 40 30 8

Maastricht
Biercafé Take One. Rechtstraat 28. Open daily from 4.00 pm but closed Wednesdays. Tel. 043 32 1 64 23
Café 't Pothuiske. Het Bat 1. Open daily from 10.00 am. Tel. 043 32 16 00 2

Purmerend
Biercafé de Bonte Koe. Over 100 artisanal beers. Near the tourist towns of Volendam and Edam Opens Monday - Thursday 7.30 pm from 4.00 pm Friday and Saturday (also 4.00 am - 7.00 am Tuesdays for cattle market). Tel. 02-99 42 11 24

Rotterdam
Bierlokaal Locus Publicus.. Student café. By tram or metro to Oostplein ("East Square"). 364 Oostzeedijk. Open daily from 4.30 pm. Tel. 010-43 31 76 1.

Sneek
Kafé de Draai. In Frisian lake country. 13 Wijde Noorderhorne. Opens Tuesday-Saturday from 10.00 am, Sunday and Monday from 5.00 pm. Tel. 05 15 42 28 66

Utrecht
Jan Primus. Pioneering beer café through two decades. Friendly clientèle' knowledgeable staff. 27-31 Jan van Scorelstraat. Opens at 3.00 pm. Tel. 030-25 14 572.
Café Ledig *Erf. 3 Tolsteegbrug. Open daily from 11.00 am. Tel. 030 23 17 57 7*

Wageningen
De Vlaamsche Reus. Fourteen beers on tap, 120 bottled. Knowledgeable staff. 21 Hoogstraat. Opens Monday-Thursday 3.30. Friday - Sunday from 2.00 pm. Tel. 03 17 41 28 34

GERMANY

Berlin
Mommsen Eck am Brunnen. Bar at 45 Mommsen Strasse, Tel. 030 324 2580
Shop: **Ambrosetti at Schiller** Str. 103, Tel: 030 312 47 26 www.ambrosetti.de e-mail info@ambrosetti.de

Darmstadt
Shop: **Bruno Maruhn.** Very extensive selection of world beers at 174 - 176 Pfungstädter Strasse. Tel. 061 515 7279

Hamburg
Shop: **Haus der 131 Biere.** Very extensive selection of world beers, mail order available, Karlshöhe
27. Tel. 040 640 7299. E-mail 131biere@bier.de Internet: www.biershop.de

Heidelberg, Karlsruhe, Stuttgart
Loewen Thor. One of the most unusual beer pubs in Germany. This restored baroque inn, decorated
with religeous artefacts and antiques, specialises in the beers and dishes of Belgium. 4 Bruchsaler
Str., in the village of Gondelsheim. Tel 07252-66 76 Equidistant from the three cities above. Shop:
Bierothek. Extensive selection of Belgian and other international beers at Leopoldstr. 6, Karlsruhe.
Tel. 0721-203 666 0

ITALY

Milan
Shop: **A Tutta Birra,** 15 Via L.Palazzi. Tel and Fax 02-20 11 65.

DENMARK

Copenhagen
Barley Wine. Belgian-oriented beer shop on Laederstraede, parallel to the main
pedestrian shopping street.
Brasserie Degas, Jernbanegade. Excellent French food served with Belgian
beers in a city-centre bistro.
Café Amsterdam, 2 Corte Adelers Gade, also in the centre. Informal restaurant
rather than café in the Belgian sense.

Odense
Carlsens Kvarter. 35 to 40 Belgian specialities, including rarities such as Drie Fontainen Oude
Geuze and is the only Danish stockist of all three Westvleteren beers. Hunderupvej. Open
Monday- Saturday from 11:00 am, Sundays from 1.00 pm. 19 Tel. 063 11 01 10
Internet: www.carlsens.dk

Kolding
You'll Never Walk Alone. Long list of Belgian specialities, including a range of abbey and Trappist
beers, and draft Hoegaarden Wit, Westmalle Dubbel. Klostergade 7A. Open Monday - Thursday
from 12.00 noon, Friday and Saturday from 11.00 am and Sunday from 2.00 pm (closed Sundays
during summer) Tel. 075 50 80 44
Internet: www.denengelskepub.dk

FINLAND

Helsinki
Punavuoren Ahven. Approximately forty bottled Belgian beers and two on tap 12
Punavuoren Katu Tel. 09 47 80 33 50 12
One Pint Pub. Canal-side pub that privately imports beers from small and already closed Belgian
breweries. The pub has a Belgian week early each year when it offers more tan 70 beers (call for
details) 2B Santa Katu Tel. 09 56 2610 1

SWEDEN

Stockholm
Akkurat. Bar and Restaurant with a very extensive range of Belgian beers. Also cask ales from
Britain, and single malts. 18 Hornsgatan. Tel 08-64 40 01 5
Duvel Café. Belgian beers (approximately 20 on tap and 60 bottled) with lots of different mussel
dishes. 50 Vasa Gatan, Tel. 02 34 8 20
Järntorgspumpen. Half a dozen Belgian specialities on draught. 83 Jarn Torget. Tel 08-20 05 10

Pubs
Apart from Stella, Hoegaarden and the Leffe range, few Belgian beers find their way into pubs in the United Kingdom. A pub that does carry a range of Belgian beers is therefore noteworthy.

South of England
The Rising Sun. Extensive selection of Belgian and other imported beers. Beers used as an ingredient in the kitchen. Beer-friendly food 14 Heathcote Road, Epsom, Surrey. Tel. 01372 740809

London
The White Horse. Essential visit. Well chosen selection of imported and British beers. One of the first British establishments to offer cuisine à la bière. 1 Parson's Green. Tel. 020 7736 2115. Internet: www.whitehorsesw6.com. e-mail. inn@whitehorse.com

North of England
The Mason's Arms, Strawberry Bank, Cartmel Fell, Windermere. Tel. 015395-68436).

Scotland
Café-bar Negociants, Lothian Street, near Edinburgh University. Tel. 0131-225.63.13.

Restaurants

Leek (Staffordshire)
Den Engel. Long established restaurant serving cuisine à la bière to compliment over 120 Belgian beers. Tel 01538 37 37 51

London
Abbaye, The Belgian Brasserie, 55 Charterhouse Street.
(Branches in Bromley, and South Kensington) Tel. 020 7813 2233

Belgo Restaurants

Young, loud, style-conscious but somewhat eccentric restaurants offer basic Belgian dishes with an extensive range of Belgian beers. Wait staff wear monastic "habits". Branches:

Belgo Noord. Original Belgo with interior by designer Ron Arad. 72 Chalk Farm Road.
Tel 020 7267 0718
Belgo Centraal. Close to the Royal Opera in the tourist centre of Covent Garden.
50 Earlham Street. Tel. 202 7813 2233
Belgo Zuid. Not in the south but in the fashionable western district of Notting Hill. 124 Ladbroke Grove. Tel 202 8982 8401

Offshoot from Belgo

Bierodromes. these slightly surreal bars offer light Belgian snacks and a large selection of appropriate beers: 173 - 174 Upper Street, Islington. Tel 020 7226 5835; 44-48 Clapham High Street, Clapham. Tel. 020 7720 1118; 71 St. John Street, Clerkenwell. Tel. 020 7608 0033; 680 Fulham Road. Tel. 020 7751 0789; 67 Kingsway, (Bloomsbury/Covent Garden area) Tel. 020 7272 7469. Branchees planned outside London.

The Porterhouse. Sister establishment of it's Dublin namesake (see below). Serves Porterhouse beers brewed in Dublin together with an extensive selection of international brews. Belgiumis well represented. 21-22 Maiden Lane. Tel. 020 7836 9931

Manchester
The Market Restaurant has British and Belgian brews. 104 High Street at Edge Street, M4 1HQ. Evening only. Tel. 0161-834 37 43.

Tunbridge Wells
Sankeys. Bar with wide selection of Belgian beers. 39 Mount Ephraim. Tel 01892 511422

Nr Wells, Somerset.
Wookey Hole Inn. Good selection of Belgian beers on draught. Wookey Hole, nr Cheddar. Opens 12.00 pm - 3.00 pm, 6.00 pm - 11.00 pm. Tel. 01749 676677

Shops

Edinburgh
Peckham's, 155-9 Bruntsfield Place. Tel 0131 229 7054 www.peckhams.com. Also in Glasgow.

Lincoln
Small Beer, 91 Newland Street West Tel. 01522-52 86 28

London
The Beer Shop, 8 Pitfield Street, near Old Street Tel. 020-77 39 37 01

Preston
The Real Ale Shop, 47 Lovat Road Tel. 01772 20 15 91

Sheffield
Small Beer, 57 Archer Road Tel. 01522-52 86 28

Surrey
Hog's Back Brewery, Tongham, between Farnham and Aldershot Tel. 01252-78 30 00

York
The York Beer and Wine Shop, 28 Sandringham Street, off Fishergate Tel. 01904-64 71 36

IRELAND

Dublin.
The Porterhouse. Brewpub with its own exceptional beers and a large selection of international specialities including many from Belgium. 16/18 Parliament Street. Tel. 01-672 80 87
Belgo Dublin. 17-19 Sycamore Street, Temple Bar. Tel 01-672 7550

CANADA

Francophone Canada has taken Belgian beers more strongly to its heart than the English-speaking provinces. Some of the better-known brews are becoming more widely available, though the selection is limited. In Canada, liquor stores are run by the state (ie the provincial government).

Montreal
L'Actuel, 1194 Peel Street. Tel. 514-866-1537.
Bieres et Cie; 4350 St-Denis, 844-0394
Le Bistro des Bieres Belges, 2088 rue Montcalm, St Hubert. Tel. 514-465-0669.
Le Boudoir; 850 Mont-Royal Est, 323-0673
Le Futenbulle; 273 Bernard Ouest, 276-0473
Le Petit Moulinsart, 139 St Paul. Tel. 514-843-7432.
Witloof, 3619 rue St Denis. Tel. 514-288-0100.
Le Zinc, 1148 Mont-Royal Est, 523-5432
La Maison des Bieres Importees, 1418 Cartier. Tel. 514-522-0506.

Quebec City
Thomas Dunn pub, 369 St Paul. Tel. 418-692-4693.
Restaurant **Mon Manege a Trois,** 102 Boulevard Rene Levesque. Tel. 418-649-0478.

Quebec Province
Auberges des Douceurs Belges, 121 des Falaises, Pointe-au-Pic (four to five hours North of Montreal, beyond Quebec city). Tel. 418-66574.80. **Restaurant Le Bruxelles,** 150 Boulevard St Madelaine, Trois Rivieres (between Montreal and Quebec City). Tel. 819-376-8536.

Toronto
C'est What, 67 Front Street East. Belgians and Canadian microbreweries. Tel. 416-867-9499.
Allen's, 143 Danforth Avenue. Belgian beers at a New York Saloon in a Greek neighbourhood of a Canadian city. Tel. 416-463-3086.

Calgary
Buzzard's, 140 10th Avenue SW. Bar-restaurant, with some Belgian beers among an international selection. Tel. 403-264-6959.

Vancouver
The small chain Fog'n'Suds has some Belgian beers among its international selection.

Alaska
Cafe Amsterdam, 530 East Benson Street, Anchorage. Tel. 907-274-0074
Humpy's Hookline & Sinker, 610 West 6th Avenue, Anchorage. Tel. 907-276-2337
stores: **Brown Jug**, all locations. **Carrs Safeway**, all locations, **Fred Meyer**, all locations

Arizona
Camelback, 2002 West Camelback Road, Phoenix. Tel. 602-246-2961

California
Le Petit Cafe. Bistro/bar. 2164 Larkin, San Francisco. Tel. 415-776-5356.
Mrs. Gooch, 15315 Magnolia Boulevard, Sherman Oaks. Tel. 818-501-8484
The Slanted Door, 584 Valencia Street, San Francisco. Tel. 415-861-8032.
Toronado. Pioneered Belgian beers in the Bay area. Eclectic rock music. 547 Haight Street, San Francisco. Tel. 415-863-2276.
Stores: **Beverages and More.** State-wide chain, Cannery Wine Cellars, 2801 Leavenworth, San Francisco. Tel. 415-673-0400. **Holiday Wine Cellers,** 302 W. Mission, Escondido, CA. Tel 760-745-1200
Whole Foods, there are over 30 stores and supermarkets throughout California.

Colorado
Tattered Cover. The bookshop that pioneered the idea of coffee and drinks among the shelves. 1536 Wynkoop Street, Denver. Tel. 303-629-1704.
Stores: **Applejack,** 3320 Youngfield, Wheatridge. Tel. 303-233-3331. **The Wine Company,** 5910 South University Boulevard, Littleton. Tel. 303-759-1313

Connecticut
Ancona's, 720 Branchville Road, Ridgefield. Tel. 203-544-8958.
Coastal Wine & Spirits, 103 North Main Street, Branford. Tel. 203-481-9400.
Fresh Fields, 90 East Putnam, Greenwich. Tel. 203-661-0631.
Glenro, 487 Monroe Turnpike, Monroe. Tel 203-261-6166

Washington DC
Brickskeller. Pioneering beer bar. Huge selection in bottles. Regular tutored tastings. 2523 22nd Street, N.W. Tel. 202-293-1885.
Stores: **Cairo Liquor,** 1618 17th Street N.W. Tel. 202-387-1500, **Chevy Chase,** 5544 Connecticut Avenue, Tel. 202-363-4000. **Whole Foods & Fresh Fields,** all locations throughout the capital district.

Illinois
Goose Island. Chicago' best-known brewpub also has Belgian beers. 3535 North Clark Street, Chicago. Tel. 773-832-9040.
Hopleaf Bar, 5148 North Clark, Chicago. Tel. 773-334-9851.
The Map Room, 1949 North Hoyne, Chicago. Tel. 773-252-7636.
Stores: **Armanetti's Liquor,** 385 West Lake Street, Emhurst. Tel. 708-833-9800. **Binny's,** 124 Old McHenry Road, Buffalo Grove. Tel. 847-459-2200. **Sam's.** One of the world's great liquor stores. Huge selection. Astonishing miscellany. 1000 West North Street, Chicago. Tel. 312-664-4394.
Whole Foods, All locations throughout Illinois

Indiana
Big Red, 418 North College, Bloomington. Tel. 812-339-7345.
Union Jack, 924 Broad Ripple Avenue, Indianapolis. Tel. 317-257-4343.

Kentucky
Party Source, 95 Riviera Drive, Bellevue. Tel. 606-291-4007.

Louisiana
DBA, 618 Frenchmen Street, New Orleans, 504-942-3731.
Whole Foods, 3135 Esplande, New Orleans. Tel. 504-943-1626.

Maine
Tully Bottleshop, Aubuchon Plaza, Route 1, Wells. Tel. 207-641-8622.

Massachusetts
Bukowski's Tavern, 50 Dalton Street, Boston. Tel. 617-437-9999.

Colonnade Hotel, 120 Huntington Avenue, Boston. Tel. 617-424-7000.
Redbones BBQ, 55 Chester Street, Somerville. Tel. 617-628-2200.
Spirit Haus, PO Box 506, Amherst. Tel. 413-253-5384.
Sunset & Big City, 130 Brighton Avenue, Allston. Tel. 617-254-3331.
Stores: **Big Y,** 150 North King Street, Northampton. Tel. 413-584-7775. **Blanchard's,** all locations.
Boston Post Road, Wayland. Tel. 508-358-7700. **Bread & Circus,** Mountain Farms Mall, Route 9,
Hadley. Tel 413-586-9932; 115 Prospect Street, Cambridge. Tel. 617-491-0040; 317
Bullard's Market, on North and Greene Streets in Medfield, Ma. Tel. 508-359-4462. **Cambridge
Mall Liquors,** 202 Alewife Brook Parkway, Cambridge. Tel. 617-864-7171. **Harvard Provisions,** 94 Mt.
Auburn Street, Cambridge. Tel. 617-547-6684. **Kappy's,** all locations. **Marty's Nejaime's,** 193
Harvard Avenue, Allston. Tel. 617-782-3250. **Town & Country Liquors,** 1119 Riverdale Street, West
Springfield, Tel. 413-736-4694. **Yankee Spirits,** 628 Washington Street, Attleboro. Tel. 508-399-5860;
PO Box 191, Sturbridge. Tel. 800-339-2231.

Michigan
Cadieux Cafe, 4300 Cadieux Road, Detroit. Tel. 313-882-8560.
Store: **Zingerman's,** 422 Detroit Street, Ann Arbor. Tel. 313-663-3354.

Minnesota
New French Cafe, 124 North 4th Street, Minneapolis. Tel. 612-338-3790.
Stores: **Edina,** all locations, **Lucia's,** 1432 West 31st Street, Minneapolis. Tel. 612-823-7125. **Surdyk's,**
303 East Hennepin Avenue, Minneapolis. Tel. 612-379-3232.

New Jersey
Carlo Russo Wine & Spirit World. 102 Linwood Plaza, Fort Lee, NJ. Tel. 201-592-1655
Fresh Fields, 701 Bloomfield Ave, Montclair. Tel. 973-746-5110.
Ramsey Liquors, 47 W. Main St., Ramsey NJ. Tel. 201-327-0353
Rutherford Wine House, 207 Park Ave., Rutherford, NJ. Tel 201-964-9463
Shopper's Paradise, 551 North Broad St., Elizabeth. 908-352-3259.
Sparrow Wine & Liquor, 126 Washington Street, Hoboken. Tel. 201-659-1500.
Wegman's, 240 Nassau Park Blvd., Princeton. Tel. 609-919-9300.

New Mexico
Kokomon Circus, US Highway 285, Pojoaque. Tel 505-455-2219.

New York City
The Blind Tiger Ale House. Well-reagrded muti tap pub in Greenwich Village. 518 Hudson Street
(on the corner of West 10th St.), Manhattan. Tel. 212-675-3848
Burp Castle. Specialises in Belgian beers. Waiters dressed as monks. Service variable. 41 East 7th
Street, Tel. 212-982-4576.
Cafe Centro. Smart bar-restaurant in the former Pan-Am (now MetLife) building. 200 Park Avenue
F11, Tel. 212-818-1222.
Cafe de Bruxelles. Bistro. 118 Greenwich Avenue, Tel. 212-206-1830.
DBA. Beer-lovers' favorite. 41 First Avenue, Tel. 212-475-5097.
The Ginger Man. Very popular, well-run, Midtown pub, with a good selection. 11 East 36th Street
(between 5th and Madison), Manhattan. Tel. 212-532-3740
Markt. Belgian restaurant. Interbrew products and others. 401 West 14th Street, Tel. 212-727-3314.
Mugs Ale House, 125 Bedford Avenue, Brooklyn. Tel. 718-384-8494.
Waterfront Ale House. 155 Atlantic Avenue (at Henry Street), Brooklyn. Tel. 718-522-3794
Waterfront Ale House. 540 2nd Avenue (at 30th Street), Manhattan. Tel. 212-696-4104
Stores: **B&E Quality Beverage,** 511 West 23nd street (between 10th and 11th Avenues), Manhattan.
Tel. 212-243-6812.

Dean & Deluca, 560 Broadway, Manhattan and other locations. Tel. 212-226-6800. **Fairway,** all
locations. **Le Monde,** 2885 Broadway. Tel. 212-531-3939. **Lucky Beverage.** 29-10 21st St, Astoria,
Queens. Tel 718-278-1500. **Pioneer,** 289 Columbus avenue (at 74th St.), Manhattan Tel. 212-874-9506
Teddy's, 96 Berry Street, Brooklyn. Tel. 718-384-9787. **Thrifty American Beverage.** 256 Court at Kane,
Brooklyn. Tel. 718-875-0226, **Vol de Nuit,** 148 W. 4th St., Manhattan. Tel. 212-979-2616

New York (suburbs and state)
Blue Tusk, 165 Walton Street, Syracuse. Tel. 518-472-1934
Country Inn. 1380 County Rd. 2, Krumville (upstate NY). Tel. 914-657-8956.
The Gingerman, 234 Western Avenue, Albany. Tel. 518-427-5963.
Mahar's Public Bar. 1110 Madison Ave. , Albany, NY. Tel. 518-459-7868.
Man of Kent, Route 7, Hoosick Falls. Tel. 518-686-9917.
Waterzooi Belgian Bistro. 850 Franklin Avenue, Garden City, NY. Tel. 516-877-2177
Stores: **Alex & Ika,** 11 Main Street, Cherry Valley. Tel. 607-264-9315. **Consumer's Buffalo,** 3230 South
Park Avenue, Buffalo. Tel. 716-826-9200. **D'Agostino,** all locations. **Dean and Deluca,** all locations.
Fishkill Beer & Soda, 159 Main Street, Fishkill. Tel. 845-897-5412. **Frontier Beverage Buffalo,** 137
Grant Street, Buffalo, Tel. 716-863-6280. **Katonah Beverage,** 24 Woodsbridge Road, Katonah. Tel.

914-232-7842.**Party Source,** 2410 Erie Boulevard, Syracuse. Tel. 315-446-8281.**Pizza Plant,** 5110 Main Street, Williamsville. Tel. 716-626-5566.**Premier Gourmet,** 3465 Delaware Avenue, Kenmore. Tel 716-877-3574.**Sam the Beer Man,** 1164 Front Street, Binghamton. Tel. 607-724-5225. **Wegmans** (some 50 locations in Central and Western NY) **Whole Foods,** all locations.

Ohio
Jungle Jim's, 5440 Dixie Highway, Fairfield. Tel. 513-829-1919.

Oregon
The Heathman (Hotel bar), SW Broadway at Salmon, Portland. Tel. 503-241-4100.
Ashland, 38 Lithia Way, Ashland. Tel. 541-488-2111.
Burlingame Grocery, 8502 SW Terwilliger Bvd. Portland. Tel. 503-246-0711

Pennsylvania
Brigid's. Belgian-accented restaurant. 726 North 24th Street, Philadelphia. Tel. 215-232.32.32.
Cuvée Notredame, Belgian restaurant. 1701 Green St, Philadelphia. Tel. 215-765-2777
Monk's. Renowned for beer dinners, with rare brews and well-researched Belgian dishes. 264 **South Sixteenth Street,** Philadelphia. Tel. 215-545-7005.
Stores: The Foodery, 324 South 10th Street, Philadelphia. Tel. 215-928-1111. **Kunda Beverage,** 349 South Henderson Road, King of Prussia. Tel. 610-265-3113. **Shangy's,** 601 State Avenue, Emmaus. Tel. 610-967-1701. **Terry's Deli,** Darby Road, Havertown. Tel. 610-446-0117. **Sharp Edge,** 288 West Stuben Street, Pittsburgh. Tel. 412-922-8118.

Texas
The Gingerman, 5607-1/2 Morningside, Houston. Tel. 713-526-2770. Branches in Dallas and Austin. Stores: **Central Market,** all locations. **Whole Foods,** all locations.

Virginia
Belgique Gourmande. Bistro within reach of Washington, D.C. 302 Poplar Alley, Occoquam. Tel. 703-494-1180.
Vintage Cellars, 1313 S. Main St., Blacksburg. Tel. 800-672-9463.

For information on sourcing Belgian beers in the United States contact, Vanberg & DeWulf, 52 Pioneer Street Cooperstown, NY 13326, 800-656-1212 fax 607-547-8374, e-mail info@belgianex-perts.com.

JAPAN

Tohoku and Hokkaido
The Beer Inn, Onda bldg. B1F, Minami 9-jo, Nishi 5,
Chuo-ku, Sapporo-shi, Hokkaido. Tel. 011-512-4774.
Hokusaikan Biiru-tei, 26-1 Dotemachi, Hirosaki-shi, Aomori. Tel. 0172-37-7741.
Crepuscule Cafe, Sendai-Mediatake 1F, 2-1 Kasugacho,
Aoba-ku, Sendai-shi, Miyagi. Tel. 022-716-0120.
Dabos, 1-6-19 Ichibancho, Aoba-ku, Sendai-shi, Miyagi. Tel. 022-211-6816.

Tokyo metropolotan area
Cafe Hoegaarden , 2-20-16 Yoyogi, Shibuya-ku, Tokyo. Tel. 03-5388-5523.
Brussels Kanda, 3-16-1 Kanda-Ogawamachi, Chiyoda-ku, Tokyo. Tel. 03-3233-4247.
Brussels Harajuku, 1-10-23 Jingumae, Shibuya-ku, Tokyo. Tel. 03-3403-3972.
Brussels Kagurazaka, 75 Yaraicho, Shinjuku-ku, Tokyo. Tel. 03-3235-1890.
Brussels Nishiazabu, 3-21-14 Nishiazabu, Minato-ku, Tokyo. Tel. 03-5413-5333.
Champ de Soleil, 1-10-6 Uchikanda Chiyoda-ku, Tokyo. Tel. 03-5281-0333.
Cerveza, Coco-Roppongi bldg. B1F, 3-11-10 Roppongi, Minato-ku, Tokyo. Tel. 03-3478-0077.
Bois Cereste, Kiyokawa bldg. B1F , 2-13-21 Akasaka, Minato-ku, Tokyo. Tel. 03-3588-6392.
BELGO, B1F, 3-18-7 Shibuya, Shibuya-ku, Tokyo. Tel. 03-3409-4442.
FRIGO, B1F, 2-11-20 Yoyogi, Shibuya-ku, Tokyo. Tel. 03-5371-0666.
M's B, Otani bldg. 2F, 3-9-10 Shinjuku, Shinjuku-ku, Tokyo. Tel. 03-3356-0733.
Billy Barew's Beer Bar Ebisu-Minami, AM bldg. 2F, 2-1-11 Ebisu-Minami,
Shibuya-ku,Tokyo. Tel. 03-5721-8480.
AGLIO, 3-42-1 Matsubara, Setagaya-ku, Tokyo. Tel.03-5300-1955.
Popeye, 2-18-7 Ryogoku, Sumida-ku, Tokyo, Tel. 03-3633-2120.
Le Temps Perdu, 2-78-10 Nogecho, Naka-ku, Yokohama-shi, Kanagawa. Tel. 045-242-9777.
COPA, Ando bldg. 2F, 1-9 Shiratoridai, Aoba-ku, Yokohama-shi, Kanagawa. Tel. 045-985-0037.
Milwaukee's Club, Shirayuri bldg.2-3F, 3-13-4 Sakaecho, Kawaguchi-shi, Saitama. Tel. 048-253-8875.

Central Japan
Barley, Washington Hotel-No.2 B1F, 3-12-22 Nishiki, Naka-ku, Nagoya-shi, Aichi. Tel. 052-953-0087.

Shirayuki Brewery Village GRAND-PLACE Restaurant, 1701 Takayanagicho, Meito-ku, Nagoya-shi, Aichi. Tel. 052-772-0147.

Kinki region
The Flying Keg, 6 Tanakasato-no-mae machi, Sakyo-ku, Kyoto. Tel. 075-701-0245.
NIPPO, 1-8-19 Sawanomachi, Sumiyoshi-ku, Osaka. Tel. 06-6605-8600.
Dolphins Tenmabashi, Diapalace Otemachi 1F, 1-2-6 Hirano-cho, Chuo-ku, Osaka. Tel. 06-6942-8890.
Dolphins Sakaisujihonmachi, 1-7-1 Honmachi, Chuo-ku, Osaka. Tel. 06-4705-0012.
KEN-West, 3-3-16 Kitahama, Chuo-ku, Osaka. Tel. 06-6227-0207.
Pomme Galette, 5-20-2 Toyoshin, Higashiyodogawa-ku, Osaka. Tel. 06-6320-7228.
Shin Hankyu Hotel - Ajour, Hankyu terminal bldg. 17F, 1-1-4 Shibata, Kita-ku, Osaka. Tel. 06-6372-5101.
Rakkudanushi, 2-2-13-101 Yamamotodori, Chuo-ku, Kobe-shi, Hyogo. Tel. 078-242-3031.
Bonne Biere, 1-22-5 Nakayamatedori, Chuo-ku, Kobe-shi, Hyogo. Tel. 078-261-8818.
Busy Bee Cafe, 9-12 Minamishowamachi, Nishinomiya-shi, Hyogo. Tel. 0798-68-1933.

Kyusyu
Beer Restaurant Odin, Ginza bldg. Shimo-dori, Kumamoto. Tel. 096-325-9230.
Hotel Marix Lagoon, 15-8 Chikusacho, Miyazaki. Tel. 0985-28-6161.

Shops

Tohoku and Hokkaido
Ebisu-ya, 6-5-19 Sakaedori, Shiroishi-ku, Sapporo-shi, Hokkaido. Tel. 011-851-2727.
Juji-ya, 5-18 Suehirocho, Hakodate-shi, Hokkaido. Tel. 0138-22-1777.
Meiji-ya Sendai Ichibancho Store, 1-2-25 Ichibancho, Aoba-ku, Sendai-shi, Miyagi. Tel. 022-222-8111.

Tokyo metropolotan area
Tobu Department Store, 1-1-25 Nishi-Ikebukuro, Toshima-ku, Tokyo. Tel. 03-3981-2211.
Takashimaya Tokyo Store, 2-4-1 Nihonbashi, Chuo-ku, Tokyo. Tel. 03-3211-4111.
Takashimaya Shinjuku Store, 5-24-2 Sendagaya, Shibuya-ku, Tokyo. Tel. 03-5361-1370.
Tokyu Department Store Toyoko Store, 2-24-1 Shibuya, Shibuya-ku, Tokyo. Tel. 03-3477-4308.
Beer House KEN, 2-23-7 Fuchu-cho, Fuchu-shi, Tokyo. Tel. 042-369-7710.

Central Japan
Kiya, 3-6-7 Marunouchi, Naka-ku, Nagoya-shi, Aichi. Tel. 052-962-1471.
Beer Spot, 3-50 Sakurayama-cho, Showa-ku, Nagoya-shi, Aichi. Tel. 052-841-1150.
Shirayuki Brewery Village GRAND-PLACE, 1701 Takayanagicho, Meito-ku, Nagoya-shi, Aichi. Tel. 052-772-0146.

Kinki region
FERTA Sanbangai Store, Hankyu Sanbangai B2F, 1-1-3 Shibata, Kita-ku, Osaka. Tel. 06-6292-2222.
Shiragikuya, 2-3-2 Yanagawa-cho, Takatsuki-shi, Osaka. Tel. 0726-96-0739.
Kioka, 9-288-3 Ootorinakamachi, Sakai-shi, Osaka. Tel. 0722-62-1341.
Sogo Kobe Store, 8-1-8 Onogaradori, Chuo-ku, Kobe-shi, Hyogo. Tel. 078-222-8120.
Shirayuki Brewery Village Chojugura, 3-4-15 Chuo, Itami-shi, Hyogo. Tel. 0727-73-0524.

Kyusyu
Iwataya Z Side, 2-5-35 Tenjin, Chuo-ku, Fukuoka. Tel. 092-726-1111.
Huis Ten Bosch World Liquor Shop, 1-1 Huis Ten Bosch-cho, Sasebo-shi, Nagasaki. Tel. 0956-27-0212.

Index

C

LIEFMANS KRIEK *CHIMAY* *PAX PILS*

SEZOENS *LIMBURGSE WITTE* *DE TROCH CHAPEAU FRAMBOISE*

STELLA ARTOIS *LEFFE BLOND* *GOUDEN CAROLUS*

BELLE-VUE KRIEK *HOEGAARDEN WITBIER* *MALHEUR*